To Andy,
   So good to work together for the Alabama Crimson Tide! You have been a real blessing to me.

Roll Tide + God Bless,
Wayne Atcheson
Num. 6:24-26

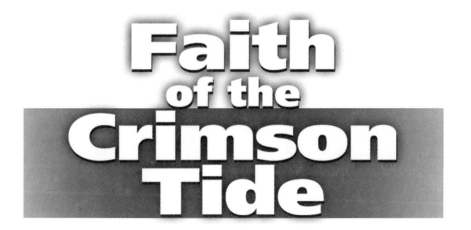

WAYNE ATCHESON

FAITH OF THE CRIMSON TIDE

Wayne Atcheson, Faith of the Crimson Tide

ISBN 1-929478-22-4

Cross Training Publishing
P.O. Box 1541
Grand Island, NE 68802
(800) 430-8588

Copyright © 2000 by Cross Training Publishing

Library of Congress Cataloging in Publication Data in Progress.

Cross Training Publishing
P.O. Box 1541
Grand Island, NE 68802
1-800-430-8588

Photo Credit:
Larry Fields (cover); Calvin Hannah, Tuscaloosa News; Kent Gidley, University of Alabama; Gary Warner, Fellowship of Christian Athletes; Russ Busby, The Billy Graham Evangelistic Association; Family photos by families and Daniel H. Vaughn, Vaughn Photography. Cover Design: Britton Advertising, Montgomery, AL

TABLE OF CONTENTS

BY JOHN CROYLE

How do you and I determine or measure the success of our favorite team or sport? It is a won/loss record or competing for yet another National Championship that drives us into a state of undying devotion to our particular coach, team or sport. Obviously, the answer is determined by our level of personal commitment. How many times have we gotten through a season and, whether our team won or lost, there was that same nagging question, "Is that all there is?"

In this book, Wayne Atcheson has skillfully put together the true life stories of men and women who found the answer to this question. There is more to life than a won/loss record or believe-it-or-not even a National Championship. When facing cancer, a National Championship doesn't mean much. The joy of a win pales in comparison to the joy of holding your adopted son for the first time. Courage is not only for the athletic field, but is exemplified when you confess to the world that you have made a mistake. The disappointment of losing a game means nothing when your childhood dream is snatched away from you. Finally, having faithful friends who surround, comfort and keep you from feeling alone when a life crisis comes, outweighs the applause of man.

Before every football game that Coach Bryant coached, he would call his team together and give these words before the battle would start. "Remember in every game there are four or five plays that are pivotal to the outcome of the game. You never know when they will come or if you will be the hero or the goat. The key is to be ready and to do your best on every play."

Life is like a ball game because you never know when these inescapable life events or "plays" are going to come before you. In the following pages we get to witness how people like you and me experience the true depth of their faith. Let us stand in awe, respect, and rejoicing as they open their hearts and souls to share their joy of the journey through the trials and testing of faith.

Here are real people in real life experiences from the University of Alabama family who exemplify the wisdom of the passage, "Tis better to be in the sea of life's storms with Jesus in your boat, than to be on shore without Him."

John Croyle
Founder and Executive Director
Big Oak Boys' and Girls' Ranches

AUTHOR'S NOTE

BY WAYNE ATCHESON

The idea for this book came while sitting on the back of a bus. The caravan of Crimson Tide staff buses was returning from Atlanta after Alabama stunned Florida 34-7 to win the Southeastern Conference Championship on December 4, 1999. The revelation was a gift from God. Another book idea hadn't worked out. It was between 1:00 and 2:00 a.m. when everyone seemed asleep that I heard the Lord say, "Why don't you write a book about all those people in the athletic department who have great stories of faith to tell?" For an hour, people and ideas came to mind and I became so excited that I never fell off to sleep the entire trip back to Tuscaloosa. The Lord even gave me the title of the book, *Faith of the Crimson Tide*.

I knew that night that this was my next book. Never in my life had I received such a knowing word from God. It was so clear and I was thrilled about the project. Over the past several months, I had the opportunity of sitting down with every personality in this book. I listened intently to their stories. As I wrote their moving accounts, I must confess that tears were shed. Many have suffered great pain, but through their faith, they have triumphed. You will need a Kleenex box handy for certain parts I must warn you.

There are also thrilling stories of role models that all young people should read. Adults will benefit also because youth in this book display incredible faith and courage rarely found today. There is a wide range of human experiences that encourage the heart in patience, love, decision-making, adversity, hardship, forgiveness and even death.

These personalities also share laughter and humorous circumstances that will tickle your soul. The sideline and locker room inside

7

stories are the kind that every fan and reader loves. You will find it inside these pages. You will be amazed as you probe inside the lives of all these people who live in the arena of big time college athletics.

A very special word of gratitude to my daughter Elizabeth for her invaluable suggestions and editing skills. A published writer herself, her efficient work was a blessing to her dad. Also, special thanks to daughter Amy who closely reviewed the final manuscript. My deepest appreciation most especially to everyone who allowed me to share his/her story. Thank you for walking us through your journey of faith.

Every story turned out to be my favorite. Enjoy, be encouraged, moved and inspired as you read about the *Faith of the Crimson Tide*.

Wayne Atcheson
August, 2000

A portion of the proceeds goes to the following organizations:

Fellowship of Christian Athletes
The Shaun Alexander Family Foundation
The Robert Scott Foundation
Big Oak Boys' and Girls' Ranches

CHAPTER ONE

SHAUN ALEXANDER

He was an All-American running the football on Saturday afternoons, but on Wednesday nights he became a cheerleader.

"How do you feel?" were Shaun's first words as he shouted in the microphone to 250-300 student/athletes gathered at Fellowship of Christian Athletes Wednesday night meetings at 9 o'clock.

"I feel great," came smiling and enthusiastic faces in response to the school's most popular student and best athlete.

Then he would ask again seeking a louder response. "How do you feel?" The audience would give a louder, "I feel great," as the tempo began to build with a rousing answer.

Then Shaun, the cheerleader, would break into a cheer.

"Give me a J," and the crowd would respond in a cheerleader chant, "You've got your J, you've got your J, you've got your J." The student/athletes became a cheering section as they broke into a clapping rhythm as if they were at a pep rally or game itself.

Shaun would yell, "Give me an E," and the crowd would chant, "You've got your E, you've got your E, you've got your E."

"Give me an S," Shaun would shout with a big broad smile enjoying their response, "You've got your S, you've got your S, you've got your S."

"Give me a U," and the crowd would follow with "You've got your U, you've got your U, you've got your U."

Then he would say, "Give me an S," and the students would get louder, "You've got your S, you've got your S, you've got your S."

Then Shaun would holler, "What do ya got?" The crowd would scream back, "JESUS!"

"Who's the King?" said Shaun and the response was "JESUS!"

"Who's the Lord?" and the reply was "JESUS!"

"Who's the Man?"................"JESUS!"

"Who's the King of Everything?"..............."JESUS!"

Then at the conclusion, everyone would break into loud applause

9

after a fun cheer led by the popular young man they loved and cheered for on Saturday afternoons in the stadium.

Shaun seemed to enjoy the moment as much as scoring a touchdown for the Crimson Tide. His smile said it all. It was a thrilling moment, a memory for everyone present each night.

When God made Shaun, he included a complete package of leadership qualities. Shaun's capacity for being out front started early in his life.

"When I was in the fifth grade and about 11 years old, one day a group of us were riding our bicycles around in our neighborhood. One of my friends passed me up and I turned on purpose and everybody turned and followed me. I still remember thinking even then, 'There must be something about me that makes people want to follow me.'

"I began to also notice as a young boy that the things I said and the things I did, others my age kind of came to." Shaun explains. "It could be something simple like, 'Hey y'all, let's go play basketball.' Everybody could be swimming and they would get up out of the pool and go play basketball. I'd think to myself, 'Ah.' So I began to think that I was blessed with leadership.

"I was ten years old when I came to Christ. It was a real experience for me. I loved church. I loved to see people get excited about the Lord even at that age. In my church at St. Stephen's Missionary Baptist Church they did.

"So as I began to recognize that people followed me and listened to what I had to say, I also knew they would listen to me about Jesus Christ. At least, they would have an interest in the things of Christ just because my faith meant so much to me."

From that time on, Shaun undertook a leadership role in the classroom at school, in athletics, in church and socially. Leadership proof came for Shaun when he was elected class president in the ninth, tenth, eleventh and twelfth grades at Boone County High School in Florence, KY.

God had tapped Shaun on the shoulder and he didn't shirk the charge. Too, Shaun claimed Christ early and his relationship with Christ became as natural as running the football.

Carol and Curtis Alexander had another son two years before Shaun named Durran. Like Shaun, Durran had the same leadership quality and winsome personality. He, too, went through high school playing football and other sports while serving as class president.

Durran chose Notre Dame but not for football or even baseball or any other sport. Durran played quint drums in the Irish's marching band. What gifts God gave Carol and Curtis! Having two young men with talent, intelligence, leadership ability and faith attending Notre Dame and Alabama is quite a rarity and a proud achievement.

Shaun could have played football for Notre Dame. He could have played at Michigan, Ohio State, other Big Ten schools and most any place he wanted. Florence, even though it is in Kentucky, is less than ten miles from Cincinnati. So Shaun lived on the border of northern and southern colleges from which to chose.

How did Shaun choose Alabama? Was it the rich football tradition? Was it the Southeastern Conference? Did he have family down there? Was it the weather?

It was none of the above. "It was the Southern hospitality," says Shaun with a big smile knowing that his answer was a big surprise. "The atmosphere of being around the people caused me to believe that, without a doubt, there was something special about the place.

"I found the people were so nice when I came to visit," says Shaun. "People were always getting extra napkins for you or getting ice for you. They were so friendly and enjoyed waiting on you and being hospitable. I really liked that and it made quite an impression on me.

"Also, I could tell right away that the people loved football. At my high school, everyone loved football. You could say something about football and people would say, 'Oh yeah, we are the best.' That was definitely the attitude of the Alabama people. Some people don't like that, but I do. I like the fact that people at Alabama walked around and said, 'Oh yeah, we're one of the best you know.' Every time."

So making sure Shaun had plenty of napkins and ice, with charm and a smile, got Alabama a prize recruit. That might not work for every recruit, but it worked for Shaun. In the next four and a half years, Shaun Alexander's worth to the University would be difficult to measure in dollars and cents, and a dozen other intangible ways.

Upon his arrival in 1995, Alabama had a stable full of running backs. Shaun came in as a *Parade* and *USA TODAY* All-American and as the Kentucky Player of the Year. He had led Boone County to two state titles. Even as a junior, he had 2,401 yards rushing and scored 42 touchdowns. His 6,657 career yards rushing was 9th all-time best nationally and his 110 touchdowns were 5th all-time best for prep football players.

Shaun also brought a 3.5 GPA with him to Tuscaloosa. He was an honor student.

Shaun agreed to be redshirted. That's not an easy decision for a young talent with his credentials, but he was mature enough to accept the role. He was one of the best scout team running backs in Alabama history that year.

The following spring, Shaun spoke at an FCA Coaches Breakfast at the Sheraton Four Points Hotel on Paul Bryant Drive across from the athletic complex. "My goals at Alabama are to be All-American, to be Academic All-American and to be Alabama's first Heisman Trophy winner," said young Shaun to the 85 high school coaches gathered. It was quite a statement for one who had not run the first play for the Tide.

Shaun was there to give a five-minute testimonial of his faith. He told the coaches how much he loved God and that his talent came from Him as well.

The words came out as if this young man believed in his ability and his heart was in tune with his lofty goals. His words of personal faith in Christ tacked on to his aspirations as a player caused the coaches to leave thinking they had heard from an unusual young man. At least, they departed with thoughts of keeping an eye on this Alexander kid.

All spring and summer, Shaun was always mentioned as a future phenom at Alabama. But with seasoned and experienced men like Curtis Alexander and Dennis Riddle ahead of him, even future All-Americans have to wait their turn.

Shaun and Curtis were of no relation, but it was ironic that Curtis was the same name as Shaun's father back in Florence.

Shaun's first season finally rolled around. With the 1996 team, it would be Coach Gene Stallings last as head coach. Shaun started the season as the third team running back behind Alexander and Riddle. He got his first carry against Bowling Green in Birmingham in the season opener. He rushed six times for 19 yards as Alabama won 21-7.

As fate would have it, Shaun scored his first touchdown against Kentucky, his home state's team. It was a ten-yard run for the game's first score as Alabama trounced the Wildcats 35-7 in Bryant-Denny Stadium. The first TD came in the homecoming game which was the fifth game of the season.

Shaun's first eight games were ho-hum type of stuff for a third stringer. He did move up to second team after Curtis fractured his left wrist in the fourth game against Arkansas. Still, Shaun had no carries in that game.

In fact, in the first eight contests, Shaun had 28 carries for 144 yards. Alabama was cruising, however, with a 7-1 record. The lone loss was a tough one to Tennessee in Knoxville 20-13 after going into the game undefeated with a 7-0 record. Shaun had two carries for eight yards.

The next game was in Baton Rouge against the LSU Tigers. No one on earth could have predicted what Shaun was going to do that night on ESPN before a national TV audience. He was about to make history in an Alabama football uniform.

All week the media kept reporting that Curtis Alexander would be returning for the first time in five games. That meant that Shaun would slip back to third team for the LSU battle.

On Friday, Alabama flew into Baton Rouge and ran through their usual Friday afternoon light workout in majestic Tiger Stadium. It was to be Shaun's first trip to the place where Billy Cannon had his famous 89-yard punt return for a 7-3 victory over Ole Miss in 1959. Besides, Alabama had not lost in Tiger Stadium since 1969, an amazing feat in itself. Alabama fans love the trip to Baton Rouge. A football game is electric there and the seafood is worth the journey down there alone.

Video games were catching on fast in 1996. Players were known to take their games with them and hook them up to their motel TV sets. Shaun and his roommate, Montoya Madden, who was the fourth running back, had brought along a video favorite called "Coach K." It was of all things, a basketball video named after the famous Duke coach Mike Krzyzewski.

At the 11 o'clock curfew, Shaun and Montoya decided to play a few minutes of "Coach K" before they dropped off to sleep. They were still playing at midnight. At 1 a.m., the video action had them more awake than sleepy. At 2 a.m., they decided that since Curtis was back this week, they wouldn't get but four or five plays between them. So they played "Coach K" until 3 a.m.

Even though he needed to get his rest, Shaun has a reputation for needing only four or five hours of sleep a night.

Both teams were ranked in the top 15. Both had only one loss. The game kicked off and the first quarter was a defensive affair. On Alabama's first offensive possession in the second quarter, a pass interference call against LSU moved the ball forward to the 36-yard line. Four plays later, Shaun sprinted around one end for a 17-yard touchdown for a 7-0 lead.

Curtis Alexander couldn't go after all. So Shaun got the call much earlier than expected. The score of 7-0 stood at halftime.

A failed fake field goal on LSU's second possession of the third quarter set up Alabama's second touchdown. On the first play from the 27, Shaun took the ball, headed to the left side and exploded 73 yards to paydirt, seemingly untouched. It was a thing of beauty. It was unbelievable for the redshirt freshman. It was a big league run. It was what Alabama fans had been waiting for all season long. The extra point was blocked, so it was now 13-0.

Alabama's defense stopped LSU cold on three consecutive posses-sions. With 2:08 left in the third quarter, Shaun was off to the races again. This time he sprinted 72 unbelievable yards for yet a third touch-down to capture a 19-0 lead. The extra point failed again. The media and fans looked through their field glasses to see if Shaun had an "S" on the front of his uniform.

Shaun got a fourth touchdown late in the game on a 12-yard scam-per to make the final score: Shaun Alexander 26, LSU 0. Shaun had scored all four touchdowns. He had run the ball only 20 times but for an Alabama school record 291 yards. Incredible!

Shaun had broken Bobby Humphrey's record of 284 yards in a sin-gle game against Mississippi State in 1986 as a redshirt freshman. He had given notice that he was for real. Many newspaper headlines the next day read, "Alexander The Great." Shaun received every SEC and national accolade given the following week for his historic game.

The rushing record still stands and the game ball is encased in the Paul Bryant Museum. Maybe they should have put the "Coach K" video in the case with the ball.

The story of that incredible night did not end until the next morn-ing. The team arrived back in Tuscaloosa at Bryant Hall at 1 a.m. The next morning at 9:30, Shaun walked into his Sunday School class taught by his good friend Jeff Reitz at the Calvary Baptist Church, just as he always did each Sunday morning. Jeff, a graduate assistant in strength and conditioning, had a large class and he and Shaun were close friends.

"I believe 100 percent that God gave me everything I have and that's why it is not hard for me to get up on Sunday mornings after game days to attend Sunday School and church," Shaun said in an inter-view a couple of weeks after the game.

"It is one way I can thank the Lord and praise Him for blessing my life. I love Bible study and worship. My relationship with the Lord is everything to me."

The next week at Mississippi State, Shaun didn't start but got 106 tough yards to Dennis Riddle's 103. Alabama lost a heartbreaker, 17-16. Shaun had a touchdown run of 11 yards. He didn't see much action against Auburn and Florida in the SEC championship game. The Tide edged Auburn 24-23 in Birmingham and lost to Florida 45-30.

The season had a sweet ending for Shaun, however. It was Alabama vs. Michigan in the Outback Bowl in Tampa. Much was said about Shaun passing up Michigan for Alabama two years earlier. It was Coach Stallings' last game and a win would give him 70 in seven years as the Alabama head coach. A victory would send the popular coach into retirement with a remarkable record.

Michigan led 6-3 at the half. Then All-American linebacker Dwayne Rudd intercepted a Brian Griese pass and returned it 88 yards for a touchdown with 12:13 left in the fourth quarter. With five minutes to play, Alabama led 10-6 and forced Michigan to punt. Alabama had the momentum. Alabama took possession on its own 23-yard line with hopes of making first downs and running the clock out or scoring.

At this crucial point in the game, Shaun got the call to go in at running back. He ran the ball four consecutive times including one gain of 16 yards. He had moved the ball to Michigan's 46 yard line.

As Shaun was moving the ball, Michigan called a time out. A brief interlude followed on the Alabama sideline.

Running back coach Ivy Williams asked Shaun in a challenging tone, "Do you want to score?" A little startled by the comment, Shaun replied, "Sure, I want to score." It looked like a setup. Shaun was fresh. He was moving the ball and things were working perfect for Alabama as the clock kept moving as well. Then it was like he played a trick on the Michigan defense. Shaun hit left tackle, juked the linebacker and burst into the clear for a 46-yard touchdown romp against the Wolverines. It happened in an instant and it was pure joy for Shaun.

Shaun had rushed for all 77 yards in that scoring drive on five plays.

The big run made the score 17-6. A late charge by Michigan made the final score Alabama 17, Michigan 14. It was celebration time and it gave Alabama an impressive 10-2 record in Shaun's first year on the field.

Three weeks prior to the bowl game, Coach Mike DuBose had been named to replace Coach Stallings as head coach. It would not affect Shaun's status. Shaun would have supported whomever the University selected. He respected Coach DuBose highly, whose defense was one of the nation's best in 1996.

Off the field, Shaun delighted in accepting speaking engagements in churches and to youth groups wherever he was invited. He never missed an FCA meeting on Wednesday nights. He could always be found in Sunday School and worship at Calvary Baptist on Sunday morning and again on Sunday night. He got involved in Bible studies in Bryant Hall and was already established as a role model and an inspiration to so many.

An NCAA ruling discontinued athletic dorms on college campuses after Shaun's second year. Sadly, Bryant Hall, with its class and tradition, gave way to the Hackberry Apartments down near the river, which adjoin the campus. Shaun and Reggie Grimes were roommates those first two years in Bryant Hall in room number 300.

Reflecting back on the Bryant Hall days, Shaun smiles with cherished memories. All of the Alabama greats for nearly 40 years had called Bryant Hall home. At least Shaun had two years there. Then it was the more spacious Hackberry Apartments in the fall of 1997 with roommates Sharmari Buchanan and Travis Smith.

During the all-important recruiting months of January and February following the Michigan game, Shaun was called on every weekend by recruiting coordinator Randy Ross to host recruits. Shaun was a natural recruiter. His warmth, friendship, charisma and genuine love for people were an awesome benefit in the recruiting process.

Shaun would take recruits bowling, to the malls, to his room and other players rooms for get-acquainted chats and to church. When the recruit headed home on Sunday, Shaun was his friend. He had a way of making a young high school senior feel welcome and at ease.

This particular year was the first of four consecutive recruiting years that would be ranked among the best in the nation. Shaun was a big contributing factor.

Spring Training 1997 found Shaun once again as third team behind Dennis Riddle and Curtis Alexander. No one ever forgot his big game against LSU and what he was capable of doing. His seven touchdowns in 1996 averaged an amazing 33 yards per score. That fall, he would be a sophomore and eager to prove himself again. It would be Coach DuBose's first season as head coach.

It was absolutely crazy for anyone to predict the 4-7 season that loomed ahead, absent a bowl game. Alabama jumped out to a 3-1 record losing to Arkansas by one point (17-16) in Tuscaloosa.

In the opener against Houston in Birmingham, Shaun saw most of his action in the fourth quarter. He carried the bulk of a 71-yard drive that culminated with a 22-yard touchdown as Bama looked good 42-17.

In the fourth game, Shaun led all rushers with 66 yards on 16 carries as Alabama beat Southern Mississippi 27-13. The next week, Alabama lost a heartbreaking overtime game at Kentucky 40-34. Shaun ran 14 times for another 66 yards. After losing to Tennessee, Alabama performed well at Mississippi in a 29-20 win and Shaun had 51 yards on five tries.

Then the season ended with four consecutive losses to Louisiana Tech (26-20), LSU (27-0), Mississippi State (32-20) and Auburn (18-17). Due to a sprained left foot, Shaun missed all but the Auburn game. After his banner game against LSU the year before, he didn't see any action against the Bengal Tigers, a big disappointment to Shaun and all the Alabama fans.

However, Shaun was back for the Auburn game and played impressively. Auburn entered the game with an 8-2 record and Alabama was 4-6. All indications pointed to a Tiger rout in Auburn's Tiger Stadium. Lance Tucker got his only career start at quarterback replacing Freddie Kitchens. However, in the third quarter, Freddie and Shaun took over and put together a 61-yard drive that ended with Shaun racing in with the final 12 yards for a touchdown and a 17-6 lead. Alabama was playing like a different football team. Auburn faithful were in a state of shock.

Shaun played most of the second half when the game was on the line. Alabama had the ball with two minutes remaining and a 17-15 lead. Except for any kind of a mistake, it looked like a sure Alabama victory. Shaun was called on with four consecutive carries. An 11-yard run got a crucial first down. There was movement and Alabama tasted victory as the clock was closing down. What a win it would be to overcome underdog odds going into the game in front of the Auburn crowd.

It was third down and eight. One more Shaun run up the middle even without a first down and a punt safely booted away would seemingly seal the victory. However, most all Alabama and Auburn fans remember what happened next. A screen pass from Kitchens to Ed Scissum resulted in a jarring tackle just as he received the ball and Auburn recovered the loose football. Shock waves rang throughout the stadium. After four plays to position the ball in front of the goal post, Auburn's Jaret Holmes kicked a 39-yard field goal through the uprights with :15 seconds left to win by an 18-17 margin.

For Shaun, the second half was some of his best play of the season, no doubt his best in a key matchup. There was no bowl game his sophomore year, but in 1998 he would inherit the running back position. Dennis Riddle and Curtis Alexander had completed their years with the Tide.

Shaun's next game would produce a major mark in the history of Alabama football.

First, there was recruiting again in January and February. Shaun was right in the middle of it once again with new recruiting coordinator Ronnie Cottrell. Tyler Watts, Freddie Milons, Kindal Moorehead,

Admaad Gallaway, Reggie Myles and Aires Monroe were among the top players recruited. Fifteen of 29 signees were from out of state.

FCA involvement increased for Shaun as he became a part of the leadership team. A group of six to eight athletes met each Monday morning at 7 a.m. at Jack's restaurant next to the practice field to discuss meetings, plans and progress of the FCA group. Shaun was right there for an exciting time of talking about the weekend, the game and FCA ministry while eating sausage and ham biscuits, pancakes and grits.

Sunday School and worship at Calvary Baptist remained as regular as football practice for Shaun. Speaking engagements picked up and he enjoyed those opportunities to stand before audiences and share his life and faith in Christ.

Spring Training went well as Shaun was now first team. He lived with high expectations from the media and the fans, but this was what Shaun wanted. He gloried in the opportunity. He was ready to run the football as many times as his number was called.

A summer highlight included a Fellowship of Christian Athletes camp one week in June at Black Mountain, NC. Shaun served as one of 60 huddle leaders. FCA huddles consist of ten high school athletes and one leader. Shaun led every one of the athletes in his huddle to Christ who were not Christians when they arrived. He had a jubilant time and the 600 athletes from every southeastern state were powerfully influenced by Shaun's vibrant and enthusiastic stand for Christ.

Shaun, already known by the conferees as a star player for Alabama, had gained hundreds of new friends and admirers. They would feel a close kinship in Christ as they would now follow Shaun throughout his football career. Though young, Shaun recognized his influence and impact upon younger athletes. He indeed was fulfilling some of the happiest days of his life in Christ.

The addition of 10,000 upperdeck seats and 81 skyboxes on the east side of Bryant-Denny Stadium was perfect timing for the 1998 season. The newly installed Jumbotron was the largest on any college campus stadium in America. Capacity was now up to 83,818.

The first game was a first ever meeting with Brigham Young University in Tuscaloosa on September 5, 1998. It was a hot, sultry day. The kickoff was at 6 p.m. and an ESPN national audience awaited. Alabama fans filed into the grand ole stadium that had taken on a beautiful, handsome and flattering new look.

It was like a Grand Opening. Fans felt good just to have a seat, just to be at this special game in the renovated stadium. The Jumbotron with instant replays on the large screen was highly entertaining itself. The noise level was considerably higher and now Alabama had a genuine home field that could intimidate opponents.

So everything was perfect for the kickoff. It would be Shaun's first start in an Alabama uniform. You could have cut the atmosphere with a knife. The adrenaline had every Alabama player pumped to the maximum, but none more than Shaun apparently.

Alabama came out smoking and Shaun scored two touchdowns in the first quarter on runs of five and 37 yards for a 14-0 lead. In the next quarter, he got most of the calls on a 65-yard drive and scored from one yard out. It was Alabama 24-14 at the half with Shaun's three touchdowns.

BYU made it 24-24 going into the fourth quarter as the night skies fell. Half of the game was in the daytime but Alabama fans love a rare nighttime game in Bryant-Denny on campus. Shaun delivered in the fourth quarter scoring two more touchdowns from 28 and two yards out.

For the game, Shaun had FIVE touchdowns for an Alabama school record in one game. All five were rushing TDs. He chose a good time to do it. It was one of the most electrifying game settings in Alabama football history and before a record crowd in Bryant-Denny Stadium. *The Birmingham News* headline read, "High Five for Shaun."

Six other former players had scored four touchdowns in a game including Bobby Marlow, Johnny Musso, David Casteal, Siran Stacy and Dennis Riddle. Shaun, himself, had four against LSU as a freshman. Plus, no one else had ever scored 30 points in a game for Alabama.

Shaun had another football that would be displayed in the Bryant Museum for his superlative night. Alabama won an exciting ball game 38-31. Shaun and his FCA buddy Ryan Pflugner, the kicker, scored all 38 points. The following week, Player of the Week honors came from the SEC and nationally. No player in the nation had a better performance on opening weekend of the season.

Shaun stayed healthy all season and started every game.

The next week against Vanderbilt in Birmingham, Shaun only scored three touchdowns of 36, 8 and 35 yards. It was his second 200-plus rushing game. He ran only 20 times for 206 yards and was again SEC Player of the Week. Not bad for your first two starts.

Two losses in a row followed at Arkansas 42-6 and against Florida 16-10 in Tuscaloosa. The disastrous Arkansas game saw the Crimson Tide net only 152 yards total offense and a tough Florida defense zeroed in on Shaun, holding him to 57 yards rushing.

Alabama regrouped for Mississippi and determined Shaun was back to his magic. Behind 17-10 going into the fourth quarter, Shaun took a pass from Andrew Zow that covered 33 yards and a touchdown to knot the score at 17-17. In the Tide's second ever overtime game, Shaun got 19 yards from where the ball was spotted on the 25. From there, Ryan Pflugner kicked a game winning 22-yard field goal for a 20-17 win. Shaun had 125 yards rushing and caught three passes for 72 yards.

The next week against East Carolina, Alabama jumped to a 21-0 halftime lead only to win 23-22. The deciding points came when Kenny Smith blocked a PAT attempt and lateralled it off to Kecalf Bailey who ran the distance for two points.

Alabama then faced Tennessee in Knoxville. The Vols were on their way to the national championship. With 5:11 left in the third quarter, Shaun had a brilliant 44-yard sprint to the goal line to make the score 14-11, Tennessee. Shaun popped through the middle of the line and ran down the center of the field alone and in a flash. Alabama faithful felt an upset coming but had not yet taken a seat when Peerless Price returned the ensuing kickoff 100 yards and the Vols went on to win 35-18. Shaun had a good day with 132 yards on 26 carries.

Shaun had a career high 36 carries for 141 yards the next week in a 30-20 victory over Southern Mississippi. Then, Shaun made his second and final trip to LSU and what a game it turned out to be. LSU led 16-7 late in the fourth quarter. All hope, almost, was lost for Alabama. It looked like the first defeat in Baton Rouge since 1969 was inevitable.

Alabama drove 62 yards in five plays in 0:52 seconds with Shaun catching a 21-yard TD pass from Zow. The clock showed 2:24 left in the game and LSU was up 16-14. Daniel Pope kicked a perfect onside kick that was recovered by Jason McAddley at the LSU 40.

On the first play, Shaun got 14 yards to the 26 yard line. On third and nine from the 25, Zow took to the air and an LSU defender tipped it but only into the hands of Quincy Jackson for a touchdown with 0:38 seconds left. A two-point pass from Zow to Michael Vaughn gave Alabama an exhilarating 22-16 victory. It was one of those 'never say die' situations that sure enough came out victorious.

Shaun had 109 yards rushing to give him exactly 400 yards rushing in his two games in Tiger Stadium, a remarkable feat. He also caught four passes for 60 yards.

Mississippi State was ready for Alabama the following week. Under overcast skies and a steady drizzle, State's James Johnson ran for a school-record 237 yards to gain a 26-14 victory. Shaun led Alabama in rushing (20 for 60) as usual and also led in receiving. He had 110 yards on five receptions, one for a 40-yard TD from Zow.

Still smarting after the one-point defeat to Auburn the previous year, Alabama fans almost demanded a victory over the War Eagles in Birmingham. Always determined in the big games, Shaun delivered, but not before Auburn jumped to a surprising 17-0 lead.

Shaun scored a 13-yard touchdown to get Bama on the scoreboard midway in the second stanza. In the third quarter, he had a 43-yard TD reception from Zow and added an 8-yard TD run in the fourth quarter. His three touchdowns brought Alabama back for a 31-17 victory. Shaun played 60 of the 64 offensive plays.

On December 19, Derick Moss of *The Montgomery Advertiser* wrote a sports column on the state's five most intriguing and influential sports figures of the year. Shaun was his No. 1 selection. "Alexander embodies all that is right with college athletics," Moss wrote. "He's a good student, polite, a team player, and articulate spokesman for the team. He is one of the truly good guys in sports." It was a most complimentary gesture for Shaun and it echoed what thousands thought of him.

Alabama took a 7-4 record to Nashville to meet Virginia Tech in the inaugural Music City Bowl. Bama fans purchased every ticket available and were happy to be bowling again. It was a late afternoon ESPN game in Vanderbilt Stadium, which seated 41,600.

The game for Alabama surprisingly was as bad as the weather. At kickoff, freezing rain and sleet fell from the skies as the temperatures hovered around the freezing mark. It wasn't the kind of weather bowl game fans dream about. It was miserably cold.

Alabama ran into a buzz saw in Virginia Tech. Who would have thought this team would be playing for the national championship one year later against Florida State in the Sugar Bowl? The Hokies whipped Alabama 38-7. Their halftime lead was only 10-7.

Offensively, both teams had 15 first downs each for the game. Tech had 278 total yards to Alabama's 274. Alabama turned to the passing game and Shaun caught eight for 87 yards. However, Tech blocked two punts, intercepted three passes and converted scores on almost every turnover. Alabama would recover from such an embarrassing defeat and play in fine fashion the next season.

On the year, Shaun scored 17 touchdowns and compiled 1,563 all-purpose yards. Honors included first-team All-SEC *Birmingham News* and second-team All-SEC Coaches and Associated Press.

During the 11 regular season games, Shaun was in on 615 plays, an average of 56 plays a game. That made Shaun a happy camper.

He had one season left to play for Alabama. But would he take it or leave early for the National Football League?

CHAPTER TWO

SHAUN ALEXANDER
1999-2000

"THE QUOTABLE SHAUN ALEXANDER"

"When I'm running behind Chris (Samuels) and I get to the line of scrimmage, there's usually one dead body or two badly injured guys or three guys wounded on the ground. It just depends on what kind of mood Chris is in"... *Shaun on All-American tackle Chris Samuels and the NFL Draft's third selection.*

"I think it's just like the quarterback who replaced (Louisiana Tech quarterback) Tim Rattay. That kid comes in there and throws the ball into triple coverage and gets a touchdown out of it. And I think if the kid would have thought about it, he wouldn't have thrown the ball into triple coverage and they probably wouldn't have won the game. I sort of feel like that. I really do not know how rowdy it's going to be, how crazy it is going to be until I get down there and just react to it. The less I know, the better"... *Shaun's reaction to playing Florida in The Swamp for the first time in 1999.*

"The cows moo at you differently and the dogs bark at you a little louder. Even the birds don't like us in Auburn"... *Shaun prior to the Auburn game at Auburn his senior year.*

"Does he (Coach DuBose) deserve to be Coach of the Year? Yes. You lead your team to do spectacular things through so many hard times in a place where football is everything. You keep them focused enough to win a conference championship. Coach DuBose became a great man. And his changing into a great man is what helped us change into a great team"... *Shaun's statement to The Miami Herald two days before the Orange Bowl.*

"What's wrong is that Coach will get this contract extension, and it looks like a reward for winning the SEC. I don't like it. He should be rewarded for turning his life around and for going to the right person, Jesus Christ, for the answers—not for winning football games"... *Shaun to The Washington Post during Orange Bowl week.*

"God wants to shine in your life. Let Him in. You'll find real love, real peace and real joy. He made this earth for His children. Don't just be apart of it. Be the heir. Own it. God wants us to have it. He'll give you more than anything the world will. Take it"... *An inscription Shaun gave a 12-year-old boy who wrote and requested an autograph near the end of Shaun's senior season.*

"I don't drink, smoke or swear. I don't have any tattoos, priors or posses. I don't wear much jewelry. I go to church every Sunday and, as old-fashioned as it might sound, I don't believe in premarital sex. I can cook ... a little. Mostly I'm into fruits, vegetables and Doritos. I'm at 215 pounds and I want to stay there. But I won't give up the Doritos"... *ESPN magazine story Shaun granted a month before the NFL Draft in April, 2000.*

To stay or declare for the NFL by January 8, 1999 was frequently on Shaun's mind in December.

Shaun put the media off by saying he would make a decision after the Music City Bowl, which was played on December 29th. He didn't want the matter to interfere with his bowl game performance.

"I don't want pressure on me that I have to perform well because it's my last game," said Shaun days before the game. "I want to be super-relaxed and have fun." It was the usual maturity of Shaun coming forth. It was the right attitude to take.

On Wednesday, January 6, Shaun requested a press conference in the media room of the Alabama football complex. The room was jammed with media from throughout the state. Coaches, teammates, friends and some fans found a place to stand around the media as Shaun approached the desk where the head coach has his press conferences.

In a fresh haircut, wearing a dark jacket and with a cross around his neck, Shaun took his seat as everyone awaited his decision. He had only told a handful what his decision was. Many felt he would forgo his senior season for the NFL.

"This has been a tough and challenging decision. I have decided that next year I will wear the crimson and white for the University of Alabama," Shaun announced to the relief and applause and cheers of everyone but the media, who were doing their job of getting the story.

"What it boiled down to is being a kid again. If I go to the NFL, I've got to be a grownup. I want to have fun with the guys. That weighed more than where I would be picked in the draft. I made my decision on Monday when I flew back to Tuscaloosa. I wanted to see if I would really miss this place and I thought I would. I want to get the team to the SEC championship game and try to win a national championship."

Coach Mike DuBose acknowledged, "I was nervous about his decision. We could be returning the best football player in the nation and that is big for our team."

For Shaun, it was back to the classroom because in May he would be graduating with a degree in marketing. The high school honor student would graduate in four years. It spoke volumes about his role model status. Education was always a priority with Shaun.

Then January and early February always meant assisting with the all-important recruiting process. Shaun helped reel in another nation's best recruiting class for the Crimson Tide when the recruits visited on weekends. Shaun had a big influence on Brandon Miree from Cincinnati, a running back much like Shaun on and off the field. Others included Antonio Carter, Santonio Beard, Dante Ellington, Jarret Johnson, Kenny King and Saleem Rasheed.

As Shaun accepted numerous speaking engagements during the spring, he would always talk about his decision on returning for his senior year. "I fully realize the impact I can have with my platform to serve Jesus Christ and let others know how much my faith means to me," Shaun would say. "That is one of the main reasons I returned. I want to share God's love with as many people, especially young people, as I can while I am in the spotlight."

One of Shaun's finest opportunities to share his faith came during the West Alabama Festival with Franklin Graham on April 30-May 2 in Coleman Coliseum. At the Saturday night service before an overflow crowd of 20,000 people, Shaun shared for five minutes how much his faith in Jesus Christ meant to his life.

"My faith means everything to me," Shaun said with a gleam in his eye. "I discovered Jesus as a 10-year-old boy and he has never let me down. If you have not accepted God's gift of eternal life and placed your faith and trust in Jesus Christ, I urge you tonight to make that all-important decision. When Franklin finishes his message, he will give an invitation for you to receive Jesus Christ into your heart. I hope you will accept this free gift of eternal life tonight."

A month prior to the Festival, Shaun attended four consecutive Christian Life and Witness Classes held at FCA meetings for training as a counselor. When hundreds came forward to make decisions for Christ at the three Festival services, Shaun served as a counselor. Russ Busby, photographer of the Billy Graham Association, caught Shaun counseling a 16-year-old boy, explaining to him how he could become a Christian. The picture appeared in the West Alabama Festival wrap-up story in Billy Graham's monthly magazine, *Decision*.

On May 15, Shaun was back in Coleman Coliseum. This time he was wearing a cap and gown. He marched and received his diploma after four years at the Capstone. Naturally, the media delighted in catching Shaun in a cap and gown rather than a football helmet and uniform.

Shaun had an enjoyable summer since he didn't have to take any classes. He worked out rigorously. Two of his summer weeks were spent at Fellowship of Christian Athletes camps in Black Mountain, NC again and he also attended a leadership camp at King College in Bristol, TN. A top college athlete like Shaun attending two weeks of FCA camp is most admirable. Shaun couldn't have been happier attending them.

"FCA camp is just amazing. I think it is because you come real close to God. You come closer than you ever thought you could," explains Shaun. "You come to understand some things about life and how great God is. He can truly bless you. You learn that God can touch you at any time and any place, and pull you through any situation.

"You learn a lot of that in life itself, but at FCA camp, you can feel it. You feel it so much; it is just hard to understand unless you've been there. So that's why I want everybody to try it. In life, you sometimes hear a song or a sermon and you feel God's presence.

"It is like a camp fire and you pour a little gasoline on it and you see it flame up and see it go real, real high. That's how everyday life is. But when you go to an FCA camp, it is like somebody at camp taking that same fire and throwing a whole gasoline tank on it. Then it explodes. I mean it is huge. You feel it all around you. That's what an FCA camp is like. God is mightily felt. I mean he jumps through your body and explodes. It is just amazing.

"That's the biggest reason I tell other athletes to go to an FCA camp. I can't imagine people living their entire lives without having that feeling at FCA or some other great camp. Then for the people who have gone, I can't imagine them turning around and away from Christ after they have been through a camp experience."

The inspiration Shaun received at the camps had much to do with FCA record crowds on campus the following fall semester. Some crowds exceeded 300 and the average attendance was 240 each Wednesday night with Shaun presiding. Meetings were held in the spacious College Annex across the street from Calvary Baptist Church and one block from Bryant-Denny Stadium.

During the months of June, July and August, Shaun was showcased on the covers of every football magazine in the southeast and every newspaper tabloid in Alabama. He was heralded as a Heisman Trophy candidate and a pre-season All-American. His presence gave Alabama a bonafied star recognized nationally as the Crimson Tide sought to regain top ten status after a 7-5 season and a 4-7 season the year before.

Two weeks before the first game, Shaun was elected a captain along with Chris Samuels, Cornelius Griffin, Miguel Merrit, and Ryan Pflugner. It was a proud honor for Shaun and no one in Alabama history deserved it more as a leader.

Since 1964, the Calvary Baptist Church has held Squad Sunday to honor the football team and coaches. Today, all other sports are included. The attendance is like Easter at Calvary. Both services are attended by 1,800 people. The special guest speaker was Dr. Ross Rhoads, who is chaplain for the Billy Graham Evangelistic Association and works closely with Franklin in his Festivals.

Each year, the football team votes on the Charlie Compton Award given to one player for outstanding Christian leadership. It is a treasured honor for the recipient. When Shaun Alexander was announced by Pastor Bruce Chesser, the congregation burst into applause. Everyone knew of Shaun's devout faith and his joy in sharing it through his life as a student and athlete.

If Shaun had any doubt or regrets about staying at Alabama for one more year, they had been erased long ago. It had been a fabulous eight months and the football season hadn't even started yet.

SENIOR SEASON 1999: For Shaun, the 1999 football season was not what could have been, but what truly was a thrill of a lifetime. Every week was full of great expectation and a personal challenge. Alabama and Shaun were in for a magical journey which started at the very same place the last game had been played, Vanderbilt Stadium in Nashville.

VANDERBILT: It was unbearably cold at the Music City Bowl against Virginia Tech. It was miserably hot and humid with temperatures over the 100 mark in the same stadium eight months later. With 12 and a half minutes remaining to play, 17-point underdog Vandy was ahead 17-14 and was playing well against twentieth ranked Alabama.

In a span of two minutes and 55 seconds, Shaun scored two touchdowns to pull out a 28-17 victory. The second was a 55-yard TD pass from Andrew Zow. His first of three touchdowns came with 0:38 seconds left in the first half from two yards away to tie the score at 7-7 at halftime. Six carries and one catch covered 45 yards of the 51-yard drive. His big-play timing was exceptional. Shaun had 109 yards rushing and 85 yards in pass receptions. "Shaun shines over Vandy," was *The Birmingham News* headline the next day.

"I thought Shaun Alexander was the difference in the game," said Coach DuBose. Cecil Hurt of *The Tuscaloosa News* wrote, "The difference in the game was the press conference back in January where Shaun Alexander said he was coming back for his senior year."

HOUSTON: Before the game, Shaun told his teammates to "get ready for one of the best offensive days in Alabama history." His premonition was right as the Tide rolled up 505 yards of offense, 275 on the ground and 230 in the air in Birmingham. Shaun scored three more touchdowns to give him 32 for his career. He surpassed the great Bobby Marlow who had 30 in 1950-52. Shaun was now third on the all-time touchdown list.

"I like scoring touchdowns more than I worry about yards. It's probably because I can count them during the game," Shaun quipped. "I know that if I can step it up I can get more touchdowns for our team to win. That's always been a big thing for me, to make sure we score some points. I've just been blessed with the opportunity to do it."

For the second consecutive week, Shaun was selected the Southeastern Conference "Player of the Week." Against Houston, he had 167 yards rushing and one 25-yard pass reception that was the game's first touchdown.

LOUISIANA TECH: Two years earlier, Louisiana Tech had stunned Alabama 26-20. It was revenge time against a team that had Tim Rattay, one of the best quarterbacks in the nation. With three minutes gone in the third quarter, he had his team ahead of Alabama 15-3.

After a 42-yard Tech field goal, Coach DuBose slipped Shaun in on the kickoff. The short kick went straight to Shaun and he zig-zagged 76 yards for a touchdown. It was unbelievable. It was also his first of two returns for the season. It also was followed by a 30-yard Shaun TD run nine minutes later and Alabama captured the lead 18-15. Shaun got another 14-yard TD in the fourth quarter and Chris Kemp added a 32-yard field goal with 2:36 remaining to give the Tide what appeared to be a safe 28-22 lead.

Rittay, who was 27 of 50 passes for 368 yards, was knocked out of the game. Sean Cangelosi came in and performed a miracle. Starting at his own 23, Cangelosi moved his team to Alabama's 28-yard line. It was fourth and 22 with two seconds left in the game. Cangelosi threw a Hail Mary in the end zone, and Brian Stallworth leaped high and came down with the ball surrounded by defenders. The extra point was good and the game ended right there with Tech the winner, 29-28. Bama fans walked to their cars in a daze.

However, Shaun had another good day with 173 yards rushing on 30 carries, plus the kickoff return. His three touchdowns gave him nine in three games, a feat perhaps never done before in Alabama history.

ARKANSAS: With their backs to the wall, Alabama faced fourteenth ranked Arkansas in Bryant-Denny Stadium. The Razorbacks had flat out embarrassed the Crimson Tide at Fayetteville the previous year. Before the long day was over, Alabama had survived an unusually played game 35-28.

Shaun lost two fumbles, Zow had three interceptions and one other turnover amounted to six for the day. Still Alabama scored 35 points. "We could have scored 50 without the turnovers," said Coach Charlie Stubbs, the Tide's play-caller. Alabama got 494 yards of total offense, 301 in the air with Freddie Milons and Jason McAddley having over a 100 yards each in receptions.

Shaun got key yardage on scoring drives as he accumulated 165 yards on 34 carries. He climbed the career rushing ladder moving into second place behind Bobby Humphrey. He moved past Tide great Johnny Musso on his 12-yard touchdown run, the only TD for him on the day.

A pressure cooker type of game, it ended as the Louisiana Tech game did the previous week on a Hail Mary pass from 31 yards away by Clint Stoerner. Tony Dixon batted this one down, however, to seal the deal.

FLORIDA: "One of my two greatest memories at Alabama among many occurred in the locker room before the Florida game in the Swamp," Shaun reflected on his career. "Coach DuBose said, 'You guys know we are going to beat Florida today. The only problem is the only people in the whole wide world who believe it or know are us here in this locker room.' I thought that was real cool. Ah, good speech Coach. Good speech.

"I really had a gut feeling that we were going to play great. I always think we are going to win and people who know me know I think that way. But this was different. Man, I thought that was a great speech."

No. 3 Florida had a nation's best 30-game home winning streak in The Swamp. Florida had won four straight games over Alabama since the 1992 SEC championship game. The Crimson Tide entered the game No. 21 in the nation knowing they were facing a tough game in The Swamp.

"We were up at halftime (13-7). We are going into the locker room and I'm like, all we have to do is finish," Shaun remembers with great delight. He had scored Bama's only first half touchdown. Midway in the third quarter, Florida had a 42-yard pass interception for a touchdown. Not to be denied, Shaun took a pass from Zow for a 42-yard touchdown two minutes later.

Less than three and a half minutes remained in the game when Florida misplayed a punt and Alabama recovered on the Gator 22. On fourth and one from the 13 and behind 33-26, Shaun got the call on the right side and not only got the one yard but bolted into the end zone for a touchdown with 1:25 left. Chris Kemp kicked the PAT sending the game into overtime with a 33-33 tie score.

Shaun won the coin toss call just as he did to start the game. Florida had the first offensive possession and scored in six plays. Harrow struck the Gators when the PAT sailed wide to the right side of the goal post. The pressure was now on Alabama but an extra point could win with a touchdown.

"We get out there and it's in overtime and I'm thinking, 'Man, this is about to happen.' When they scored and missed the extra point, I'm thinking to myself, 'Score on the first play Shaun. Score on the first play.' I ran up to Coach (Ivy) Williams and I said, 'Hey, I like this play right here. It was a counter to the left side off of Chris Samuels that we hadn't used all day. Coach Williams gets on the phone and suggests upstairs that we run the play. So they said, 'You've got your play.' If you get your play, it doesn't matter if there are 20 folks out there, you've got to run through all 20 of them.

"I just thought, 'Don't go down and we've got the game won.' I think there was one guy and I just had to pick my feet up and use what God gave me, a little toughness. It was just great. I knew when I got in the end zone it was over with." Tight end Shawn Draper also delivered a crushing block that allowed Shaun to cover the final 10 yards. Shaun had indeed bolted for 25 yards on the first play as pandemonium erupted among the Alabama faithful as a nationwide TV audience looked on.

Even though Kemp missed the extra point with the scored tied at 39-39, Florida was offsides. Bradley Ledbetter snapped it again and Patrick Morgan held it as this one was booted true for an incredible 40-39 upset of the Gators in The Swamp. "Tide Floods The Swamp," was an appropriate headline by *The Tuscaloosa News.*

Shaun came out of the game battered and bruised. "They were just a physical team. I got punched a couple of times. They knocked my helmet off on one play and I bit my lip. It's a physical game. That's why football is so awesome. Not a lot of people can play it," Shaun said in interviews after the game.

Shaun also came out of the game with four touchdowns, 106 yards rushing on 28 carries and 94 pass receiving yards on four catches for a total of 200 yards.

Coach Steve Spurrier complimented Shaun's play by saying, "I don't usually comment on opposing players. We stopped him a lot and a lot of times we didn't stop him. And he ran through us a bunch."

Shaun also recalled two things that happened during the week that helped in preparation. "Coach Jeff Rouzie came in on Tuesday and told us that Alabama was 6-1 against the Gators in The Swamp. He just left it like that and we thought, 'Ah, we are supposed to beat them down there. It kind of changed the mode of everything. After that, we went from hoping to believing we were supposed to win.

"Then on Wednesday night at FCA, Jeremiah Castille (former Tide all-century defensive back) was our speaker. He spoke to us and reminded us of David and Goliath. We were the underdogs. We took that to heart. God's been good to us through it all. And today, He even showed He had a good sense of humor."

The SEC made Shaun "Player of the Week" for the third time in five games. The upcoming off week came at a good time to heal some wounds.

HEISMAN TALK BEGINS: "Alabama's Alexander makes strong case to Heisman Watch," was the headline on the CBS SportsLine written by Dennis Dodd on Monday, October 4 after the Florida game.

"There are plays during a season that transcend numbers," Dodd wrote. "They are plays that make a difference in the entire season, that define the character of a player and a team. Shaun Alexander made one of those plays Saturday. Playing in the fabled Swamp, Alabama's senior tailback burst off a tackle and scored the game-tying touchdown in overtime against Florida.

"The 25-yard run tied the game at 39. The 40-39 Bama victory was the defining point of the season. Arguably, there has been no bigger upset this year. The run was clutch. It shocked both sidelines. It changed the course of the season."

Later in the story, Dodd summarized, "OK, so this is the second week in a row this space has featured Alexander. We have no agenda here except picking the right guy for the Heisman. Right now, it's Alexander. Good guy. Good player. Most of all, unless you're busy paying off a costly civil suit, a good story."

Dodd listed his Heisman Watch Top 5: 1. Shaun Alexander; 2. Joe Hamilton (Ga. Tech); 3. Peter Warrick (Florida State); 4. Ron Dayne (Wisconsin); 5. Drew Brees (Purdue).

In other Heisman polls, CNN/SI and ESPN had Shaun No. 2 and USA Today had him No. 3. Overall consensus had Shaun No. 2 behind Hamilton.

MISSISSIPPI: CBS cameras were on Alabama and Shaun for the third consecutive week at Oxford. The Rebels sported the nation's second best rushing defense, giving up only 45 yards per game and only four rushing touchdowns in six games. How would Shaun handle such a problem? He gained 57 yards with 6:30 left in the first quarter!

Coach Ronnie Cottrell said at FCA the previous Wednesday night that Shaun was going to get 200 yards rushing Saturday. Shaun shredded the Rebels defense, sure enough, with 214 yards on the ground and scored three touchdowns. Alabama, ranked eleventh, won a dramatic 30-24 victory over 21-ranked Ole Miss.

It was Shaun's sixth consecutive 100-yard rushing performance and he became only the 17th player in SEC history to pass the 3,000-yard rushing mark. Only Bobby Humphrey had done it before for Alabama.

"He's a coach's dream," said Ole Miss coach David Cutcliffe after the game. Shaun told the press, "I played alright. That wasn't the best game I ever played, but I played alright." The SEC made Shaun their "Player of the Week" to tie Auburn's Bo Jackson (1984) and Brent Fullwood (1985) for four such honors in one season.

HEISMAN UPDATE: On Monday, October 18, Dennis Dodd of CBS Sportsline had Shaun No. 1 in the Heisman Trophy race ahead of Joe Hamilton, Drew Brees, Chris Weinke and Corey Moore.

"Right here, right now, Alexander is the most complete back in the country," wrote Dodd on his Internet page. He backed his statement up by posting Shaun's stats: 155.8 rushing yards per game/third in the country; 206.33 all-purpose yards per game/first in the country; 17.0 points per game/first in the country.

So if the vote had been taken seven weeks into the season, Shaun Alexander would have likely been your Heisman Trophy winner. No one in the country had fared better. Add to that the tough competition in the Southeastern Conference and Alabama's schedule had been ranked No. 1 toughest all season.

The following Wednesday, Shaun was featured on the front page of *The Tuscaloosa News* in an article entitled, "Alexander makes kids top priority." At 8 a.m. on Tuesday, Shaun was interviewed on four national radio shows, followed by questions from *The Cincinnati Post*, ESPN.com and *Sports Illustrated*.

"There are just some things I've got to do, to take time out to make sure that little kids get to see other people who are living their lives for Christ and let people know that they can be a success at whatever they want to do," said Shaun while visiting Westlawn Middle School.

On Thursday, the student newspaper, *The Crimson White* ran a two-page spread with a red background that said in white letters, "HEISMAN" and below it "37." Dorm, sorority and fraternity windows were covered with the paper sign for weeks. Also, the Alabama Media Relations department made weekly updates on Shaun's Heisman website.

Shaun didn't mind the attention and the interviews. He would always put the team first and say the Heisman will take care of itself.

ESPN MID-SEASON TOP MOMENTS: On October 18, John Crowley of ESPN.com ran a feature listing the TEN TOP MOMENTS of the first half of the 1999 season.

No. 1 was "Alexander Shreds Florida in OT." Crowley described Shaun's unforgettable and breathtaking performance against Florida. He also added, "The 40-39 win established him as a bonafide Heisman candidate. It also put a serious dent in Florida's air of invincibility at home, while stirring up memories of Alabama's 1992 national championship."

It was quite a high and glorified honor for Shaun to be so recognized when there had been so many heroic individual moments and top games played.

TENNESSEE: For the first time since 1930, Tennessee would come to Tuscaloosa instead of Birmingham to face Alabama. The Vols were defending national champs and No. 5 in the nation and Alabama was No. 10. It was a long awaited day for Tide fans to have the game on campus. Both teams were good and also ready to play. So were 86,869 fans, the largest crowd ever to see a football game in the state.

On a day when they wanted to play well, it turned out to be a frustrating day for Alabama. The one bright spot for the offense was a 99 and a half yard drive on its second possession of the game. It ended with a 26-yard TD pass from Zow to Shaun for Alabama's only score of the game.

Zow injured his ankle moments later and was ineffective the remaining game. Tennessee's defense allowed Bama's high-powered offense just 267 yards. Shaun had 98 yards rushing on 20 carries and caught six passes for 50 yards.

To catch the attention of CBS TV cameras, students made signs that read, "Can't Beat Shaun for Heisman."

Tee Martin led Tennessee to a 21-7 victory in a game of high expectations that ended with a rare disappointing note in a big game for Bama. "What hurts me more than anything is that we lost to a team that could have made us look like national champions if we had won," said Shaun who always looks for the ultimate prize.

Late in the game, Shaun suffered an ankle injury. "They rolled up my ankle with a minute-30 left, but I'm fine," he said. This time Shaun was wrong. It was worse than he thought.

MONDAY NIGHT PARTIES AT SHAUN'S PLACE: During Tennessee week, Mike Griffith of *The Knoxville News-Sentinel* came to Tuscaloosa early. He did a feature on Shaun and attended the Wednesday night FCA meeting.

Wrote Mike, "It's Monday night, and the party is at Shaun Alexander's apartment. Well, OK, it's not exactly the type of party you might expect on a college campus." Then he quoted Shaun, 'We have our Bible study on Monday nights. Usually about 12 to 15 guys come over. It's fun. We memorize a scripture verse and talk about God and life.'"

Mike had heard of Shaun's commitment to Christ and he came away even more impressed with his faith than expected. Shaun also said, "I'm not going to push religion down anyone's throat. I've noticed in some places in the South it's kind of like that. I'm more laid back with it. I mean, every day we all struggle with sin and trying to live our lives right. I'm not perfect, but it's my goal to try and live like God would want me to."

"Take sex before marriage," Mike wrote. "Alexander said he plans to remain celibate until he's wed, which is not to say he doesn't think about things." Shaun followed his commitment up by saying, "You know that's hard at a school like Alabama with all the pretty girls. I mean, I'm human like anyone else. You just try to look down or away, you know?"

SOUTHERN MISS: As much as they rehabilitated to be ready for the homecoming game with Southern Miss, Shaun and Andrew's ankles were not ready for Saturday's game. Representing 92 percent of Bama's offense, both would dress out and wear white baseball caps all afternoon on the sidelines.

Undergoing intense treatment to be ready, Shaun explained, "We've had whirlpool, icing, worn an air boot, gel, ice cups, anti-inflammatory cream and a partridge and a pear tree." Their ankles were too tender for play.

Alabama rebounded from a disappointing defeat to Tennessee and won convincingly 35-14. Shaun Bohanon subbed for Shaun and Tyler Watts for Andrew. Both played exceptionally well for their first starts and against the nation's No. 20 team. The defense was awesome with eight sacks and held Southern Miss to minus-13 yards rushing.

Shaun's Heisman hopes took a slight hit. He could have had another big game. Hopefully, he could go against LSU in another game.

LSU: Hoping to play one last time against a team with which he had great success, Shaun's ankle was still not ready. He did attempt a cameo appearance. Not at full speed, Shaun got 18 yards on 14 carries, which spoke to the condition of his ankle. He did score Alabama's first touchdown in the second quarter from one yard out. Shaun played only three snaps in the second half.

The Tide had a nice 23-7 lead with 3:07 remaining in the third period. LSU scored ten unanswered points to make it 23-17. However, the game ended with LSU on the one yard line and 0:10 seconds remaining. Quarterback Josh Booty ran a pass-option play to the right, put his head down to score, but collided at the goal line with Reggie Myles and Marvin Constant as time expired. Alabama escaped with a victory and a 7-2 record.

Shaun's one consolation was that his touchdown gave him Alabama's single season record for points (114) and touchdowns (19).

Shaun's opportunity for the Heisman Trophy had diminished due to a badly sprained ankle. Still, two big games were left and the team had much to play for, a chance to be in the SEC championship game.

MISSISSIPPI STATE: It would be Shaun's last game in Bryant-Denny Stadium. On Wednesday, it was announced that Shaun would start with swelling and be heavily taped. Shaun was still leading the SEC in rushing and was on the verge of breaking records.

Miss. State was 8-0, No. 8 in the nation and sported the nation's top-ranked defense. Alabama was 7-2 and No. 11. It was quite a match-up for CBS cameras nationally. Alabama had lost to the Bulldogs three straight years. It was billed as the ultimate "physical matchup."

This time, Alabama showed its muscle and emotion and thumped the Bulldogs 19-7. Shaun's Heisman hopes dashed away but he was still productive as he hobbled for 54 yards on 24 carries and caught two passes for 54 yards. He had a 6-yard TD run in the second quarter. "The ankle was better than last week," said Shaun. "But I still can't do all the things I want to do. When they rolled on it, I didn't feel as much pain. That's improvement."

Coach Jackie Sherrill gave Shaun high praise. "It's evident he wasn't 100 percent. Even at 80 to 90 percent, he's better than 99 percent of the (tailback) people in the country. He can run right through you or has the ability to set you up and then move away from you."

Alabama's defense held State to 24 yards rushing. Shaun's roommate Shamari Buchanon had a beautiful 37-yard TD reception for the last TD. Zow and Freddie Milons had good days for the offense.

Amid the rousing celebration of a great victory and the seniors' final game, Shaun suggested a curtain call. Players streamed back on the field to thank the students and fans. Shaun stood in front of the student section waving his hands like an orchestra conductor with cheers, chants and celebration. It was indeed a special moment for Shaun.

AUBURN: Shaun's superhuman heroics in the fourth quarter at Auburn would go down as perhaps the finest quarter of individual play in Alabama's history.

Auburn (5-5) and playing in their backyard before 85,214 fans had controlled the football game for three quarters and was leading 14-8. Up to this point, Alabama had managed two field goals and a safety. Shaun had just 44 yards at the half on 11 carries. Alabama (8-2) and No. 8 in the polls was fighting desperately for a spot in the SEC championship game.

"I told Shaun at the start of the fourth quarter that he had been blessed by God with a lot of ability and that he was capable of taking the game over," Coach DuBose told the media after the game. "He did."

Apparently, it was all Shaun needed to hear to spark a fourth

SHAUN ALEXANDER 1999-2000

quarter that saw him run for 101 yards on 11 carries and score three touchdowns to lift the Tide from the debts of despair to frenzied delirium. Shaun woke the Tide up in time for a sensational 28-17 comeback victory, Alabama's first in five tries in Jordan-Hare Stadium.

"I was going to play harder because I felt like I hurt the team by staying in there and not making the plays. Everybody's got a job to do and mine is to score touchdowns. And I didn't do my job. That made me turn it up a bit," said Shaun who was still not a 100 percent.

Coach DuBose said of Shaun, "I don't know where he is in the Heisman race, but there can't be a better football player in this country than Shaun Alexander." Auburn's coach Tommy Turberville had high praise for Shaun also. "One-man show. The difference in that game was one guy: Shaun Alexander. We couldn't tackle him."

At 8:58 p.m. on this night game played on November 21, Shaun scored on a 5-yard sweep with seven minutes to play to become Alabama's all-time rusher. His 182 yards gave him 3,468 yards, surpassing Bobby Humphrey's 3,420 yards in 1985-88.

His three touchdowns of 8, 5 and 5 yards gave him 23 for the SEC season record previously held by Georgia great Garrison Hearst who had 21. Of the hundreds of running backs to play in the SEC, it was truly a special accomplishment for Shaun.

"The SEC Championship has been our goal from the beginning," said a happy Shaun to the media. "I think winning it would beat the Heisman. I'm just so excited about our team and the way we've been playing. I'm proud of them. It's just amazing. I'm still a little speechless."

FLORIDA – SEC CHAMPIONSHIP: "You can't beat the same team twice in one season," was the talk for two weeks leading up to the SEC championship game with Florida in Atlanta's Georgia Dome. On Oct. 2, Alabama upset the Gators 40-39. Two months later on Dec. 4, *The Atlanta Journal-Constitution* headline read, "Grudge Match."

"We want an SEC championship to prove that Alabama football is back to where it is supposed to be," said Shaun in the story. "But the problem is, Florida wants it, too. When you have two groups of guys who want the same thing, it can get pretty intense. But when it comes right down to it, we've got to make more plays than they do. But, they've got guys who can make those plays, too. That's why a game like this is so much fun."

Coach DuBose remarked, "Everybody knows how tough it is to beat Florida once because Steve (Spurrier) hasn't lost too many games (20) since he's been there. Obviously, it's even harder to beat them twice. At the same time, we know we can beat them." *The Journal-Constitution* ran a graph that said Coach Spurrier was 12-3-1 in 'revenge games' at Florida.

Alabama and Florida entered the battle with identical records (9-2 overall, 7-1 SEC). Florida was ranked No. 5 and Alabama No. 7. The Gators were a 7-point favorite. ABC was set for a nationwide prime time 8 p.m. kickoff. In the last three previous SEC title games against the Tide, Florida had won all three by a total of 31 points.

No one in his wildest dreams could have imagined that Alabama was about to go out and embarrass Florida to the tune of 34-7. Impossible? For sure, except when you have a defense that held Florida to 114 yards, a career low for Coach Spurrier in Gainesville. Add to that Florida's total possession time of 19:49 to Alabama's 40:11 and it can and did happen.

In the October game, Shaun had scored touchdowns on his last pass reception and final two runs. So the Gators with the second best defense in the nation were ready for Shaun. Still, he rushed for 98 yards on 30 carries including a seven yard TD. However, Bama had other weapons. The night belonged to speedster Freddie Milons who had a spectacular 77-yard touchdown run after taking a direct snap from center in the shotgun formation early in the fourth quarter. Milons was the game's MVP.

Florida quarterback Jesse Palmer said it best, "Alabama played better than us and Alabama played harder than us. They beat us good, on defense and on offense. There wasn't anything we could do."

The Tuscaloosa News had some appropriate story headlines that read, "Twice As Nice," "Second To None," "Sweet Dome Atlanta," and "Return To Glory."

For Shaun, the game gave him three wishes that came true. First, an SEC championship (Bama's twenty-first), Alabama was back to national respectability, and an SEC championship ring for his finger.

Earlier, Shaun cited that there were two special moments in his career that stood out. The first was Coach DuBose's "great speech" in the locker room before the first Florida game. Now for the second top moment.

"When we came back out of the locker room after beating Florida the second time, we were shaking hands, wearing our SEC championship hats and celebrating in the Georgia Dome. I just thought, 'Man, we have finally got a championship.' It was so neat taking pictures in the locker room with the trophy. I felt that now I am a part of the elite guys and elite teams that came to Alabama and got a championship. It was neat."

POST-SEASON AWARDS RUSH IN: Perhaps Shaun received more honors than any other player in Alabama history. His 15 school records is a record in itself. His 24 touchdowns and 144 points were SEC records and he tied for most touchdowns (19) rushing.

SEC "Player of the Year" awards came from the SEC Coaches in a unanimous vote. He received the same award from the Associated Press, *The Birmingham News, The Mobile Press,* and *The Football News.* Also, being named Academic All-SEC was so important to Shaun.

Shaun led the SEC in rushing with 1,399 yards and reached 1,000 yards in the seventh game against Tennessee, faster than any back in Alabama history. He missed one game and hobbled with an injured ankle in two others or the stats would have been greater.

Almost overlooked, Shaun joined the great Herschel Walker as the only other SEC player to record back-to-back 100-point seasons.

First team All-American honors came from CNNSI.com and The Dick Butkus All-American team. Shaun was teamed with Wisconsin's Ron Dayne on both selections.

Second team All-American awards came from the Associated Press, *The Sporting News,* and *The Football News.*

Late in the season, Dennis Dodd of CBS SportsLine gave his choices for individual national awards. On the Doak Walker Award for the nation's best running back, Dodd wrote, "This one's easy. If the award is truly for the best overall running back, then Alabama's Shaun Alexander is the winner. (Ron) Dayne can have his Heisman and rushing record. Let someone else win the prestigious Doakie."

On Thursday, Dec. 9, Shaun flew to Orlando for the College Football Awards at Disney's Wide World of Sports Complex. Shaun had a superb time with all the stars of the 1999 season, but the Doak Walker Award went to Dayne. Shaun was runner-up.

It seemed like a perfect award for Shaun in many ways. How many other great players would be up for the award who wore the same number (37) as Doak Walker?

As for the Heisman, the three games with an ankle injury in the second half cost Shaun dearly. The biggest disappointment was not being invited for the big Heisman show in New York City. Shaun, the SEC "Player of the Year," finished in seventh place behind Dayne, Joe Hamilton, Michael Vick, Drew Brees, Chad Pennington and Peter Warrick.

With class, Shaun responded, "I had goals for myself and they've been realized. My goals were to be part of this senior class and help bring this program back to championship level. We've accomplished that. I have no regrets."

ORANGE BOWL VS. MICHIGAN: Shaun's last Alabama game would include a week on Miami Beach and a stay in the beautiful Wyndham Resort Hotel. It would be the Crimson Tide's fiftieth Bowl game, the most of any college team. The mighty Michigan Wolverines, national champs two years earlier, were the opponent for the January 1, 2000 FedEX Orange Bowl. It would be played in Pro Player Stadium, site of the Super Bowl 11 months earlier and home of the Miami Dolphins.

Asked about the tempting nightlife of Miami, Shaun said, "I am not worried about the older players, but only the younger players who are in a big city for the first time under these circumstances. But I will make sure that everyone stays out of trouble." The statement typified Shaun's sense of responsibility as a leader and sincere concern for his teammates. Shaun always felt like he was everybody's big brother.

On Tuesday morning, he joined Coach DuBose and Ryan Pflugner in sharing their faith before 2,000 at the Fellowship of Christian Athletes Orange Bowl Breakfast. A few days later, the night before the game, he prayed a moving prayer at Prayer Time in Ryan's room with 15 teammates just before midnight when the year 2000 was approaching.

As soon as the gathering broke up, Shaun rushed to the beach. He found a spot alone and ushered in 2000 on his knees. "It was a special moment and I just wanted to thank God for my life and I wanted to ask His blessings upon a new direction that was about to unfold for me in the months ahead with the upcoming NFL. I also asked God to allow us to shine and glorify Him in the bowl game," said Shaun reflecting.

Alabama (10-2) was ranked No. 5 and was a one-point favorite over Michigan (9-2) and ranked No. 8. For two and a half quarters, Alabama was clearly in command of the game 28-14. Freddie Milons got the fourth TD on a sizzling 62-yard punt return, and Shaun scored the first three touchdowns.

Alabama held Michigan to 37 yards rushing. But Tom Brady threw 46 passes, completed 34 for 369 yards, all Orange Bowl records. None were intercepted. Michigan tied the game at 28 and on the last play of regulation attempted a 36-yard field goal to win. Lanky Phillip Weeks leaped high to block the kick to send the game into overtime.

Shaun won the coin toss causing Michigan to take the ball first.

Tight end Shawn Thompson caught a 25-yard touchdown on the first play. The PAT put Michigan up 35-28 in no time flat. Alabama ran onto the field confident. Shaun ran for four yards and Zow found Antonio Carter in the end zone for a 21-yard touchdown. A second overtime seemed apparent… but wait a minute. Ryan Pflugner's kick went outside the right upright by the length of a football. In a flash, the game was over. It was way past midnight and Michigan celebrated 35-34.

After a prayer on the field, Shaun put his arm around Ryan's shoulder and walked him off the field to the dressing room. "I just wanted to let him know that I loved him and I felt for him a lot. It's a game of inches. Sometimes it falls for you and sometimes it doesn't. We're still really proud of this team. Life goes on. We'll be all right," said Shaun.

Even in the loss, Shaun went out in his usual style. His three touchdowns set an Alabama bowl record. His 161 yards rushing on 25 attempts was five yards shy of Sherman Williams' record in the 1995 Citrus Bowl. His 50-yard TD run was the longest against Michigan in a bowl game, eclipsing the previous record of 46 yards Shaun scored against the Wolves in the Outback Bowl three years before.

The game was like Flag Day as Alabama was penalized by the Pacific 10 Conference crew an incredible 18 times for 132 yards. Nine came in the fourth quarter alone. The Tide also dearly missed All-American tackle and Outland Trophy winner Chris Samuels who missed the game with a knee injury.

SENIOR BOWL IN MOBILE: Even though Tennessee's Tee Martin was from Mobile, Shaun seemed to be the toast of the town for the Senior Bowl week. Over 100 NFL scouts, head coaches and assistant coaches looked the talent over each day in detailed fashion.

Among many activities, the highlight of the week for Shaun came Thursday night at the Mobile Convention Center at the Fellowship of Christian Athletes Rally. Some 2,000 local high school and junior high students and athletes jammed the huge room to hear several of the college seniors share their faith.

Tee Martin shared beautifully before Shaun wrapped things up as the featured speaker. Shaun had never been better before a group. Carey Casey, national FCA Senior Vice President, made a challenging appeal for the youth to respond and 210 decisions for Christ were made.

SHAUN ALEXANDER WAY: On March 2, the City of Florence (KY) and Boone County High School saluted Shaun by naming a street after him. It would be called, "Shaun Alexander Way."

For his magnificent high school and college football career, a cere-

41

mony was held before the high school student body. Shaun credited his parents, Carol and Curtis Alexander, and his brother, Durran, for their support and guidance through the years. It was a thrilling day for Shaun in his hometown.

NFL DRAFT: As a perspective first round draft choice, Shaun experienced the ultimate that a top player wades through before draft day. The Combine in Indianapolis in February is big with all the college seniors working out under tight security.

NFL scouts would fly into Cincinnati where Shaun moved to in January to work out and be near his agent. Teams would fly Shaun to their city for a workout and for various psychological tests. A huge crowd of scouts gathered on Pro Day at Alabama's Indoor Practice Facility on March 21st. Shuan was in tip-top shape and impressive in the drills, sprints and jumps under intense pressure.

On the day before Draft Day on Saturday, April 18, Shaun performed a long-awaited dream. He placed his hand print and cleat marks into the Walk of Fame that surrounds Denny Chimes, the campus landmark at the center of the campus. It has been a football Captain's privilege since 1947. The cheerleaders, members of the Million Dollar Band, Coach DuBose and a good crowd of fans gathered for the noon ceremony.

On Saturday morning early, he flew from Birmingham to Cincinnati to await the draft with dozens of family and friends at the Montgomery Inn Boathouse Restaurant. The New York Giants, Baltimore Ravens, Arizona Cardinals, Pittsburgh Steelers, New York Jets and Detroit Lions had indicated strong interest in Shaun. Many sources predicted Shaun as high as the tenth pick.

"Seattle called the night before the draft while I was in Tuscaloosa," Shaun remembers vividly. "My cell phone rang and the voice on the other line said, 'Hey, I'm from Seattle' and I said, 'Hey, how are you doing?' Then the phone cut off. A minute later, the phone rings again. I answered it again and said, 'Hey, how are you doing? The voice said, 'Is this Shaun?' I said, 'Yes,' and then the phone cut off again.

"I turned to my friends and said, 'Well, it looks like I won't be going to Seattle. I just hung up on them twice.' As it turned out, my batteries had run down."

"Draft Day was a nerve racking experience. It goes so slow. After about three hours, Seattle called and told me they were about to draft me. This time the phones worked and I became a Seattle Seahawk."

Shaun was picked 19th in the first round. "I am going to a good team. They were in the playoffs last year. Their running back, Ricky Watters, is in his tenth year. So I can back him up and be even a better player. They also have some strong Christians on the team and I love that. Besides, No. 37 was open and I always hoped that the team that drafted me would have it available. I got my wish."

Shaun also discovered that his running back coach will be Coach Stump Mitchell whom he had met at an FCA camp a year earlier. That was pleasing news for Shaun. His strength and conditioning coach will be Kent Johnston who was at Alabama in 1983-86.

Friends who know Shaun and his need for only four or five hours of sleep each night found it amusing that Seattle fit due to the popular movie, "Sleepless In Seattle."

A most amazing omen involved Shaun's initials…SEA…, which are the first three letters of Seattle.

THE SHAUN ALEXANDER FAMILY FOUNDATION: In the spring of 2000, Shaun established his own foundation to touch lives of people for various needs. His heart of compassion for others so early in life is a true testimony of his faith and focus on other people. On July 7, 2000, Shaun held his first Foundation Dinner at the Bryant Conference Center in Tuscaloosa. He passed out checks to the RISE Foundation, Big Oak Boys' and Girls' Ranches and the Fellowship of Christian Athletes.

NO. 37 AND PSALMS 37:4: As a tenth grader at Boone County High School, No. 44 was the most popular number since several top-flight linebackers had worn it. Shaun had the opportunity to wear it, but since he was a running back he opted for another number. The two available were No. 9 and No. 37.

"Since I couldn't think of anyone in college or pro who had made it big with No. 37, I asked for that jersey," says Shaun remembering the day so well and always looking for a challenge. "Since I came to Alabama, many have suggested what a good number it was for me. As a Christian, some have said the 3 represents the Holy Trinity and the 7 is the complete number in the Bible. So I always thought, 'That's cool.'"

Every autograph that Shaun gives, he always writes "Ps. 37:4" underneath his name. The Psalms scripture verse says, "Delight yourself also in the Lord, And He shall give you the desires of your heart."

It's the perfect verse for Shaun. He'll always be known for touchdowns, making big-time plays in big games, running for more yards and scoring more points than any other player in Alabama history.

But because he did delight himself in the Lord with his ever-present smile, uncompromising stand, and warmhearted Christian spirit, God has indeed blessed Shaun abundantly and beyond measure. He will be known just as much as a Christian role model as he was a football player.

We love you Shaun and we thank you.

CHAPTER THREE

COACH RONNIE COTTRELL

Why does a coach leave a team ranked No. 1 most every week for two years for another team that has just gone 4-7?

No, he had not lost his marbles. No, he had not grown tired of seeing such phenomenal success as a coach for the Florida State Seminoles. No, it wasn't because he had always been an Alabama fan growing up in Brewton, AL.

This man is Ronnie Cottrell, Alabama's Assistant Head Coach and Recruiting Coordinator.

Most of Ronnie's friends thought he had gone berserk and were shocked when he left FSU, the nation's top college football program the previous ten years, for even Alabama, coming off a losing season in 1997.

Explanation? When God speaks to one of His sons, he cannot resist what He tells him to do. You may not understand it yourself at the time, but when God calls, you must obey. So Ronnie heeded the call as any Christian should. He took a huge leap of faith and switched Florida State coaching togs for Alabama's.

After Coach Mike DuBose completed his first season as head coach in 1997 with a dismal 4-7 mark, he let four of his assistant coaches go. Florida State had just finished with a 10-1 season and was ready to prepare for Ohio State in the Sugar Bowl.

On the Birmingham talk shows the day the coaches were released, Ronnie Cottrell was the first coach mentioned for an Alabama position. Florida State's quarterback coach Mark Richt and different coaches from all over the place were also mentioned.

"I'm at home that night and I get a phone call from Jerry Green, a high school coach in Montgomery," Ronnie remembers distinctively. "Jerry was an assistant coach for me in earlier years at Flomaton (AL), and he is a big Georgia fan. He called and said, 'Ronnie I hear that you are coming to Alabama?'

"Then I said, 'Jerry, I am not coming to Alabama. You can forget that. They were 4-7 and didn't even win a home game this year. You can forget about that. I'm not coming to Alabama.'

"Because of it being announced, I had media people calling me and, of course, I made no comment. During the week, I went to talk with Coach (Bobby) Bowden and said, 'Coach, I am getting all of these calls. I haven't heard anything from Alabama. I just don't see myself going to Alabama. He said, 'Don't worry about it, Ronnie. If they are interested, they will go about it the right way.'

"On a Friday, we were to begin practice for the Sugar Bowl with Ohio State. Monday night of that week, Coach DuBose called me at my house after he got permission from Coach Bowden. It was pretty late at night. Jean had already gone to bed.

"He said, 'Ronnie, this is Mike DuBose. I'd like to talk with you about a position at Alabama.' That position he was talking about was Recruiting Coordinator. I told him at that time, 'Coach, I am just not interested right now at this time, but I really appreciate it.'

"But Coach was very persistent. I really admire him now for the way he handled it. He wasn't pushy, but he was persistent. He said, 'Well, Ronnie, I really would like to talk to you about it. I know you like Alabama. I know you grew up an Alabama fan. I'd just like to talk with you. The worst thing that could come out of it is that maybe you could tell me some things that would help us get this thing going back in the right direction.'

"Then he said, 'Do you think you could come after the bowl game?' I said, 'Well, Coach, if I come after the bowl game, I am not coming to Alabama. I just couldn't do that. If we go through the bowl game and get into recruiting in January, I couldn't go that deep into recruiting with this group of players and walk away.'

"He said, 'Well, when do you all start practice for the bowl game?' I said, 'Friday.' Then he said, 'How about tomorrow?' I was just amazed when I agreed to come. I was still thinking that I would come just to maybe help him if I could. The thought of leaving Florida State was still not a consideration.

"The next morning I went in and told Coach Bowden that I was going up to talk with Coach DuBose. I told him again, 'Coach, I really don't think I have an interest in this job, but I would like to go and talk to him.' Then he said, 'Ronnie, that's no problem. Go ahead.'

"So that night, they sent the school plane down for Jean and me. Coach DuBose was on the plane. He'd ask questions and they were very specific questions about how we would do certain things in recruiting.

It was a 45-minute flight. He spoke to Jean when we got on the plane, but that was all. He sat across from me on the plane very intense. I just really respected his competitiveness and his intensity and passion for Alabama.

"Still, I felt like I was going through the motions. I was telling him things we did but in an information sort of way. Coach dropped us off at the Sheraton Four Points Hotel on campus. Then the last thing he said was, 'Ronnie, I can't promise you that you are not going to be bothered here by the media. You will find that Alabama is a very special place. They take it all very seriously here.'

"I check in and, of course, there is media seemingly waiting for me. I saw TV cameras and reporters who sought to ask me questions as I tried to get to the elevator. I also had several of them call me in my room. It was obvious that this wasn't your average college football program. So the next morning, Polly (DuBose) took Jean and me to breakfast. Later that morning, Coach DuBose met with me for a couple of hours. He talked to me about different things.

"Basically, as he walked me through the football complex, I was reminded of the passion that I used to have for Alabama. More than anything else, God was softening my heart. He was breaking down the barriers that I was putting up in what I wanted to do and thought I had to do. Also, I began to think about what was right in the eyes of God. In the eyes of the world and the flesh, I was thinking of why you wouldn't do this.

"But as I sat in Coach's office (Polly had Jean with her) Coach asked me to come to Alabama. There was no question in my mind that God spoke to me and told me this is what I was supposed to do. I felt a clear sign and voice from God that I was supposed to help that man.

"Right after that moment, Coach DuBose said, 'Ronnie, what I would like for you to do is to be the Assistant Head Football Coach at Alabama. You will coach the tight ends and be the Recruiting Coordinator.' Obviously, I was flattered by his offer and plan. We finished our talk together and right then, I indicated to him that I would come. So we agreed and shook hands. I left his office and went over to the hotel to tell Jean what had transpired.

"I shared with her exactly what had happened. She, too, had similar feelings that this was something special. She also knew if I felt this was God's will, we had to do it regardless. God had prepared her heart as well for this change.

"So we went back to Tallahassee and I was up all night. The Alabama media were asking, 'Are you going to come?' The Florida media were asking, 'Are you going to leave?' Mark Richt, the offensive coordinator and a dear Christian friend of mine and Dave Van Halanger, our strength and conditioning coach and FCA advisor, both said to me, 'Ronnie, you have got to have peace about it and you have got to make sure this is God's will for your life.'

"Well, I knew and was very confident that was what was supposed to happen. So when I went to see Coach Bowden to talk to him about it. He was upset a little bit. He didn't want me to go. He said, 'Do you want me to be happy for you?' knowing he was not. But after I explained it to him believing that it was God's will and there was an opportunity there to make a difference, he understood. Since that time, he has been very encouraging.

"Coach Bowden has been like a father to me and that's what made it the most difficult. Leaving him and the players you had recruited was not easy. What I have found in college coaching, though, is that there is never a good time to leave. You can't find that date that is the right time. So I think it was God's plan to leave the way I did.

"One thing I told Coach DuBose before I took the job and Coach Bowden before I left was that I was not going to recruit anybody that we were recruiting at Florida State. I could not call a single player that they (FSU) were recruiting. That did make it a little difficult. My contribution was not as great the first year at Alabama. But it did help make a good clean separation and transfer to Alabama."

So three days after Ronnie's interview with Coach DuBose, he became Alabama's Assistant Head Football Coach and began work immediately. It was tempting to stay with Florida State through the bowl game, but Ronnie felt his place was at Alabama. He hit the recruiting trail with a passion to sell Alabama. He dealt with negative recruiting after a 4-7 Alabama season by telling prospects that he himself had chosen Alabama. "I told those guys to choose Alabama like I did. I encouraged those players to seek God's will in selecting a college and have a peace about it like I did."

Meanwhile, as Ronnie left Florida State for Alabama, the Seminoles went on to defeat Ohio State 31-14 and ended up third in the nation in the Associated Press final poll.

When Alabama's recruits signed the dotted line in February, it was hailed as "the most highly-rated class in this decade," by Forrest Davis. Another recruiting expert, Tom Lemming, had Alabama's class rated No. 4 in the nation. "This class compares with any team in the nation," said Bobby Burton, another recruiting evaluator. Alabama had signed such future standouts as Tyler Watts, Freddie Milons, Kindal Moorehead, Admaad Galloway, Marvin Constant, Reggie Myles, Terry Jones and junior college transfers Cornelius Griffin and Miguel Merritt.

In his first game in the 1998 season, Ronnie experienced an electrifying opener as Alabama dealt Brigham Young a 38-31 defeat. Alabama had just added 81 skyboxes and 10,000 new seats in Bryant-Denny Stadium to add to the drama. The season's last game, a 31-17 win over Auburn in Birmingham, was another highlight of a 7-4 year. It ended in Nashville with a 38-7 loss to Virginia Tech in the Music City Bowl.

Meanwhile, down at Tallahassee, Florida State went through the season undefeated and ranked No. 1 most every week of the season. The Seminoles carried an 11-0 record into the Fiesta Bowl to face Tennessee for the national championship. The Vols prevailed 23-16 for the national title, as injuries forced FSU to play with a third team quarterback.

By now, Ronnie had a full year to recruit for Alabama. Once again, the Crimson Tide signed one of the nation's top classes. Several Parade and SuperPrep All-Americans headed the list including Kenny King, Saleem Rasheed, Antonio Carter, Dante Ellington, Jarret Johnson, Brandon Miree, Matt Lomax and Santonio Beard. As in the previous class, other top recruits that signed did not qualify academically but would join the team after two years in junior college.

Ronnie stated to the media that, "This recruiting class compares to the best one I had at Florida State."

Things were looking good at Alabama. At Florida State, Ronnie was considered by many experts and coaches as the finest and most successful college football recruiter in America. Proof of his work was signing the *USA Today* Offensive and Defensive Players of the Year, not once but twice, at the same time. Also, Ronnie had been FSU's Recruiting Coordinator since 1990, and the team had won 10 or more games every year in the 90's.

It was Ronnie's desire to work with Coach DuBose and the staff to deliver the same caliber of athletes for Alabama as he had for Coach Bowden and FSU.

However, year 1999 would bring an unexpected spiritual challenge that would further test Ronnie's decision in joining Alabama a year earlier. It came on Thursday, August 5th, four days before the freshmen reported for fall practice. Coach DuBose admitted in a press conference of having an improper relationship and asked the team, staff, University and fans for forgiveness.

It struck the coaching staff hard because they feared that their jobs were in jeopardy. Coming off a 7-5 season was pressure enough. The season was three weeks away. Ronnie knew he had a decision to make. How was he to respond as a Christian?

"When it was first announced, it was upsetting," Ronnie sadly remembers. "I had to seek God in prayer and in the Bible because I was hurt. We were all hurt as a staff. People wanted our reaction immediately. After I read different passages in the Bible, God convicted me and said, 'What if Mike DuBose was your own brother?'

"My daddy told me when I was growing up, 'When things are the worst they can be, that's when you have got to be your best.' I felt like it could not be worse for him. So I just tried to encourage him at that time and continued to do the job that I came to do."

From the outset with Coach DuBose, Ronnie had agreed to be a spiritual leader for the team by incorporating ideas that spiritually motivated the team at FSU. In his first season in 1998, Ronnie suggested a different format for Team Chapel on game weekends. Former Tide players and other speakers spoke each week the year before, but Ronnie suggested having a Team Chaplain that would speak every week. So Dr. Bruce Chesser, pastor of the Calvary Baptist Church, was selected by Coach DuBose among several suggested. Keith Pugh, a former Tide receiver and First Baptist Church pastor at Sylacauga, would continue to speak at the Birmingham games.

Ronnie also suggested a voluntary Prayer Time before each game on Friday night before curfew in a player's room. It would include Bible reading and prayers by the players with Fellowship of Christian Athletes advisor Wayne Atcheson. Ronnie implemented other ideas to bring deeper spiritual emphasis and make available uplifting input for the players.

Personally, he always felt the need to support Coach DuBose from the first day. "From the very beginning, I met some godly people who surrounded the football program. I would always ask them to pray for Mike DuBose. I would ask them to pray that he would have wisdom to carry out his job because I thought it was the most powerful position in the state of Alabama.

"I remember that Coach Bryant could say something that could change a whole state. Eventually, his stature grew so that he could change things in the nation. I knew what a dynamic position Coach DuBose had.

"When I came, he had just made some hard decisions. He had to release some men who were outstanding coaches from his own staff. I felt like it was so important that my role would be to support him and to be available to help him when he needed me as assistant head coach. When a head coach has to make a tough decision, he no doubt feels alone. But I wanted to make sure that he knew he had a man who supported him. I wanted him to know I was his man."

So now Ronnie found himself supporting his head coach in a manner totally unexpected in his personal integrity. How was Ronnie to respond? What would he say? What would he do? There was no way he could jump ship back to FSU.

When hardly anyone spoke out for Coach DuBose and most called for his resignation, Ronnie faced the TV cameras and reporters as they emerged on Tuscaloosa. It was Sunday after Coach DuBose's Thursday press conference when the freshmen reported. The media stuck microphones in the faces of the freshmen asking their reaction to Coach DuBose. Ronnie was also there and spoke out for Coach DuBose on the 6 and 10 o'clock TV newscasts and to the state newspapers.

"I have no less confidence in Mike than I had before," Ronnie said to the media who crowded around him. "I love Mike DuBose. He is going through a very difficult time. It is a personal issue and we need to move forward from it. He needs our support.

"When you have crisis, your family needs you. Mike DuBose gave me the opportunity to come to Alabama. In fact, I chose to come here because of Mike DuBose. Somebody told me right after the announcement Thursday that this would pull us together or tear us apart. I believe it has pulled us together. Coach DuBose has clearly admitted that he made a mistake and I am not going to judge him because I care greatly for him and his family."

Ronnie felt that someone needed to step up and back Coach DuBose. He felt convicted to be that person along with supportive statements from several players for their coach. Still Coach DuBose and his staff were on shaky ground. Rumors still persisted that Coach DuBose would be asked to step down. Ronnie's name was even circulated as the person who would replace Coach DuBose if that happened.

Alabama opened the season back in Nashville, the site of the Virginia Tech disaster in its last game. The day was a scorcher as Alabama beat Vanderbilt 28-17 and Houston the next week 37-10 for added relief. The next week, Louisiana Tech scored on their last possession of the game and shocked Alabama 29-28. After the game, some felt that Coach DuBose would be terminated.

Instead, Shaun Alexander, Chris Samuels and company reeled off seven victories in the next eight games, including a stunning 34-7 victory over Florida to win the Southeastern Conference championship. Alabama was ranked 5th in the nation after playing the nation's toughest schedule. The team would play Michigan in the Orange Bowl and lose a heartbreaker in overtime, 35-34. Its final record was 10-3.

Coach DuBose and his staff had dodged machine gun bullets at the outset of the season, but had reached stardom at the end. It was an incredible turnaround. The skeptics had been run out of town and replaced with fans going ballistic over an SEC championship. Truly it was amazing.

Along the way, God gave Ronnie affirmations that his coming to Alabama was the right thing to do. Ronnie welcomed every one.

After the turbulent episode concerning Mike DuBose prior to and early on in the 1999 season, it was surprising who helped Ronnie get through a stormy time the most.

"Coach DuBose was actually the one who encouraged me through it all. He really changed. His renewed faith and his trust in God, that this was going to work out and that he was suppose to be there doing this job as football coach, encouraged me. Though most of the world thought we were going to be terminated, we weren't. We had a lot of pressure after the Louisiana Tech loss but Coach was very dynamic in his position with our team, and holding that team together."

Ronnie felt that his job was to support Coach DuBose and that he did when times were bleak at best. After the disastrous loss to Louisiana Tech, Alabama rebounded under extreme pressure and sharp criticism the next week against Arkansas with a 35-28 victory. Then came the 40-39 overtime shocker over Florida at Gainesville. Winning takes care of most any despair in athletics.

As the season rolled on, many good things occurred spiritually through FCA Wednesday night meetings, Friday night Prayer Times, game day Chapel services and countless other encounters as players and coaches came together through seemingly impossible odds. Ronnie rarely missed an FCA meeting even at 9 p.m. on Wednesday nights during the season to encourage players who attended.

"When Shaun Alexander mentioned my name at the Orange Bowl FCA Breakfast and thanked me for my contribution, that really meant so much to me that morning," says Ronnie. "God filled my heart when Shaun said he was glad I came to Alabama. Then he mentioned others and why this had been such an exceptional year.

"Then on New Year's Eve night, January 31, 1999, at our team meeting, something very special occurred. We would be playing Michigan the next night. Coach DuBose in his remarks to the team began to talk about the new millennium that was just an hour or so away. He talked about a new start for the millennium and how we needed to be in prayer for each one as they faced the months and year ahead.

"During the day, one of the players on the team suggested we have a prayer as a team that night. Coach DuBose immediately responded that having a prayer was a good suggestion. He said, 'Anyone that wants to stay for the prayer, we will come together right up here in front of the room. Then we will have a prayer.'

"Usually in a situation like that half your team will leave. But not a single player left. Not one player walked out of that room. The players walked up to the front and got in a huddle just like they would before a game. Then Coach DuBose led a prayer that was just extremely strong. It was a moving few moments the team and staff had together.

"It was a confirmation to me that the greatest thing that this team had accomplished was not just winning, but they had learned about a commitment to our Maker, who made it all happen. I can tell you, it spoke to Ronnie Cottrell. At that moment, I wasn't thinking that in four days Florida State would be playing for the national championship.

"After we lost the game by one point, I went into the locker room there was Ryan Pflugner who had missed the extra point. I hugged him and tried to encourage him. Just the way he handled that situation again was a testimony of this football team.

"Though I look back at what were probably the two toughest years of my life, again they were the most rewarding and the most educational. So many of these incidences are going to prepare me to be a better coach.

"Many times I thought about the passage of scripture (Matthew 7:24-29) that talks about the wise man who built his house upon a rock. The rain and floods came and the wind beat upon that house but it didn't fall. That is what I continued to think about through those two years when the low moments happened.

"Also, at Chapel on the day of the Orange Bowl game, Bruce Chesser spoke on Luke 9:62 which says, 'But Jesus said to him, No one, having put his hand to the plow, and looking back, is fit for the kingdom of God.' That spoke to me that day that if you are in God's will, you are not to look back. You are not to question God. That scripture and Bruce's message was another affirmation that I had made the right decision in coming to Alabama."

Ronnie's heart and mind didn't change four days later when Florida State defeated Virginia Tech 49-26 in the Sugar Bowl to win the national championship with players he had recruited. There was a purpose for Ronnie at Alabama ordained of God.

"As if I had not received enough affirmation, it all culminated for me when I attended Derrick Thomas' funeral in Miami in January. Coach DuBose was one of eight speakers. His talk was so powerful that after he finished, he received a standing ovation. I had never been as proud to work for a man as I was that day. For me, it was my greatest affirmation of leaving Florida State for Alabama. I was called to be a coach to make a difference in the lives of young men. But at Alabama, I came to help Mike DuBose also.

"I could see that by being at Alabama, that in a small way I was able to help him and make a difference. But truly the person that had made the greatest difference in Mike DuBose's life was God. He opened his remarks at Derrick's funeral by saying, 'I am a new Christian.' That really touched me."

When Coach DuBose hired Ronnie, he sought a man who would primarily be his Recruiting Coordinator. In Ronnie, he got a man who would also be a servant to him and stand by him through his lowest moments. He got a Christian brother as well.

"From the beginning with Coach DuBose, whatever job he gave me to do, I wanted to do it in a way that he wouldn't have to worry about it," says Ronnie. "Whether it be the recruiting process, the coaches' retreat, the camp, the coaches' clinic, FCA Breakfast, the Chapel or Prayer Time on Friday night, I wanted him to always know that area of his football team was taken care of.

"That became my focus on whatever he gave me to do. I felt like if I could do that, he could devote himself to other areas. There might have been something we didn't totally agree on, but after we talked about it, I did whatever he told me to do

"Since this past fall, he has wisdom and such a peace that I think has come from his study of the Bible, personal quiet times, Christian books he's read, from meeting with other Christian men, his church, and other means of personal spiritual growth. I see his power and influence as we walk through a restaurant or hotel. People scramble to see him. The thing I see is not only is he a great football coach and a great man, but here's a man who has a great Christian influence.

"Though there will be doubters and scoffers as the Scribes and Pharisees in the Bible, I think he is going to make a great difference in many lives in the most powerful position at the University of Alabama."

From where did Ronnie become such a man himself to be a servant to other people?

Ronnie's exciting journey in the Florida State and Alabama college football programs began in such places as Brewton, Kinston and Flomaton in South Alabama. As a boy of nine years, he was baptized at the Alco Baptist Church outside of Brewton. The Alabama Crimson Tide became his team. At T.R. Miller High, he played football, basketball and baseball. The latter was his best sport.

He enrolled at Jefferson Davis Junior College in Brewton and helped his high school coach Frank Cotton coach his team that year. Then Ronnie got married after one year and dropped out of school. For a year, Ronnie climbed telephone poles working with Southern Pine Electric Cooperation. Ronnie then paid a visit with Troy State head coach Charlie Bradshaw and told him of his desire to be a coach. The receiver coach had just left, so Coach Bradshaw had Ronnie coach receivers in 1981 as a student coach. The next year, Ronnie coached the linebackers, some of which were older than he was.

Ronnie got his degree in 1983 at Troy State and at age 24 became the head football coach at Kinston High School (AL), a Class 1A school. His high school coach, Frank Cotton, had inspired Ronnie to pursue coaching. "I always felt that if I could affect one boy's life in a manner that Coach Cotton had affected mine, it would be a very worthwhile life. I saw then the difference and impact a coach can have on young people. Coach Cotton was only 5-6, 160 pounds, but he was a giant of a man."

Kinston had back to back 1-9 records when Ronnie took over. "We promptly went 1-10. I always make a joke that I turned that program around," says Ronnie with a smile. The next year, Kinston was 6-4 and "it was probably one of the most satisfying years I've ever had as a coach."

Then the superintendent at Flomaton called Ronnie about coming there as head football coach. "I told him I didn't have a suit, didn't have a tie or anything. I told him I didn't think I was prepared. But he told me to come over and talk anyway." For three straight years, Flomaton went to the state playoffs and had never been previously. His last two teams went undefeated.

While at Flomaton, Ronnie took 26 players the first summer to the

Florida State football camp "to show them good competition and what it took to win," says Ronnie. "Coach Bowden was so cordial and invited us back and we continued to return because it helped our football team tremendously." After three years at Flomaton, Ronnie coached a playoff team at W.S. Neal in East Brewton for one year.

After having been previously approached, Ronnie this time accepted Coach Bowden's offer to be a graduate assistant on the FSU staff as assistant receivers coach and assistant recruiting coordinator in 1989. Ronnie moved his family to Tallahassee for his first taste of big time college football coaching. Staff changes the next year saw Coach Bowden promote Ronnie to be FSU's first full time Recruiting Coordinator.

The rest is history. Florida State finished in the Top Five in recruiting every year Ronnie was there before moving on to Alabama. In 1994, recruiting coordinators were required to coach so Ronnie coached the middle linebackers for two years and the tight ends for two years before moving on to Alabama. Ronnie always coached the kickers at FSU also.

At FSU, Ronnie gained the reputation as being the finest and most successful college football recruiter in America. God blessed Ronnie Cottrell with a gift in conversing and communicating with people. His folksy mannerisms and personality fits recruiting to a tea. His love for young men comes through. Ronnie is genuine and down to earth and always presents himself in an upbeat, friendly and classy manner. He gets close to recruits and parents quickly and they respond to his warmth and cordiality. Recruiting is in his blood. He loves it.

His deepest compassion, however, is for the souls of young men. He wants them to know Jesus Christ and to have a personal relationship with Him. He knows this is their ticket to a successful life. This is their sure way of getting the utmost from the gifts God has given them.

After Ronnie gets a recruit under his wing, he clings to him and cares deeply for his life as a student, football player and as a person.

You wouldn't be wrong in saying that Ronnie's chief aim is to recruit young men and inspire their spiritual growth through Jesus Christ. He's always asking players, "Did you go to church Sunday? Are you going to FCA tonight? We have Chapel at 10:30. Be there now."

His obedience to Christ in accepting the call at Alabama has come with no regrets. Ronnie is in coaching to serve Christ wherever he is led.

Alabama got a prize recruit when they got Ronnie Cottrell!

CHAPTER FOUR

COACH MIKE DUBOSE

Mike DuBose is living proof that only God can deliver a man from the depths of despair to peace in the midst of a storm and joy beyond belief.

Mike would be the first to tell you that he is first and foremost "a sinner saved by grace." Being the Head Football Coach of the famed Alabama Crimson Tide football team is huge. Today, there is a higher power that grabs Mike's allegiance far more than even the mighty Crimson Tide.

Since the early days of Coach Paul Bryant's tenure as head coach, many regard the Alabama head football coach as perhaps the No. 1 position in the state. Therefore when the news of Coach DuBose's involvement in an improper relationship broke, many were disturbed. Many felt the coach should resign. It came a week before the team reported for the 1999 season. It was the main conversation piece in the entire state. It was indeed a bombshell.

Still, no matter how critical, harsh and cruel the public outcry may have been, when a man turns to God with a repentant and broken heart, God takes over. That's when God best demonstrates His love, mercy and grace in a person's life. No one can mend a life better than God through His son Jesus Christ. His power is unstoppable and His love restores a broken person to a new plateau of service.

When David committed adultery with Bethsheba, he was one of God's choicest servants. When he came to God with a broken and contrite heart asking God for forgiveness, God restored him and even said that he was a man after "his own heart." God honors a person who pleads for forgiveness and comes before Him broken and repentant.

God also restored unto David the "joy of his salvation," as David prayed. God comes to the rescue of sinners who repent. That's His business. He had much rather forgive than judge.

When faced with the stark reality of losing his family and one of the best coaching jobs in athletics, Mike quietly turned to God. While many were calling for his job, Mike found solace with God. Deep inside, he knew this was the only choice. Getting close to God was a hunger Mike had in his heart.

With a godly wife like Polly DuBose, Mike found in her support and encouragement that he needed the most. His pastor, Curtis Petrey at Christ Church, was his confidant, regular accountability partner and a man of God he needed to lean on. Several other friends in the church also provided strong support and love. Shaun Alexander, Chris Samuels and Ryan Pflugner gave good words of encouragement through the storm as did other coaches and staff. At the outset of his search for a relationship with God and His son Jesus, these were the people who meant the most to the hurting coach.

Hundreds of letters of support with scripture references and prayers from everywhere had an affect on Mike. There were plenty of negative remarks and suggestions, but the encouraging ones helped Mike get through August and September. Many in the media felt that Mike would not be around to coach the first game. Some speculated that he would be fired or forced to resign. Some media were known to have res-ignation or firing stories ready when the day came. Blistering letters to editors of statewide newspapers were written ridiculing Mike. When Alabama lost to Louisiana Tech by one point in the third game, in the eyes of many, it was sure reason to let the coach go.

After the Arkansas win the next week and the incredible overtime win over Florida the following week, the media and public skeptics qui-eted down. During the bitter and controversial weeks, Mike reverently placed his life in the hands of God. Peace and calmness became his spir-it. He was learning that what God thought of him was far more impor-tant than media critics and abusive comments from fans. Mike DuBose was becoming a new man, a new coach and a new Christian.

For several weeks, Mike addressed every alumni and Red Elephant booster group with an apology before he began his remarks. He would ask for their forgiveness and would express how sorry he was that he had embarrassed them and the University of Alabama. It was a sincere statement made from a humble heart. He didn't have to do it, but he was convicted that he owed the people an apology.

Through weeks of uncertainty surrounding the Alabama football program, everyone concerned had their opinion of Mike's fate. But God had His opinion as well. His child Mike would weather the storm, develop a deep personal relationship with His son Jesus and remain as Head Football Coach of the Alabama Crimson Tide. That was God's plan for Mike DuBose regardless of what anyone else thought.

Mike found that God does not turn his back on anyone who publicly acknowledges his sin and privately spends time on his knees crying out to God for forgiveness and mercy. When you are a public figure and appear before 83,000 plus crowds, national television audiences, and a weekly statewide television show, it takes devotion and dependence upon Christ to withstand the pressure and the response from the scrutinizing public. Mike was developing that kind of patience and peace in a miraculous change that was taking place in his life.

Friends who had known Mike for years recognized a genuine and repentant spirit. His office was more accessible. Humility was evident in his voice and approach. It all occurred at the very busiest and most critical time for a head coach, the beginning of fall practice and the football season. Yet Mike turned to God and made precious time for Him.

The television program *Biography* has as its motto, "Every Life has a Story'" When Mike DuBose was raised in a housing project called Yawkey Apartments in Opp, AL, being the head football coach at Alabama must have been the furthest thing from his mind. Opp is a small southern Alabama town of 7,000 people on Highway 331. People go through Opp to get to the Florida beaches. It is 25 miles north of the Florida state line.

"If you described the town of Opp when I was growing up, there was so much love among everybody," says Mike with fond memories of his hometown. "Everybody knew everybody. Just about everybody you saw, you called them by their first name. Our family didn't have very much. We even moved around within the community."

When Mike was seven years old, a very important event occurred in his life.

"When we lived in government housing, as I walked out the front door, there lived a Pentecostal pastor about ten feet to our right. I went to his church occasionally. Our family didn't go to church much. I will never forget on one Saturday afternoon they were going to have a peanut boil and cold Dr. Peppers. I love boiled peanuts. So I agreed to go.

"They showed a film. The film was about hell. I don't remember anything else but it was about fire, continuous rolling fire. I don't remember one thing about Jesus. I don't remember one thing about God in that service. But I knew I didn't want to go to hell. I didn't know anything about heaven. But I knew I didn't want to go to hell."

Mike, who learned the value of hard work as a child, had a typical childhood for a southern Alabama boy.

"I learned how to work at an early age. I cut grass with an old push lawn mower. It wasn't gas operated, just old rotary blades. I cut yards, sold *Grit* newspapers and did so many jobs boys do to make money. There was always baseball, basketball and football games going on. I learned how to play and compete there.

"My father Ray worked for Dr. Pepper and later for Pepsi Cola in nearby Luverne. My mother Euna worked in the textile factories in Opp and took care of the family. I had an older brother, Jimmy, and two younger sisters, Janet and Renee."

In the ninth and tenth grades, Mike got a lifeguarding job at the Opp City Pool. Like most small towns, almost everyone at that age congregated at the pool in the summer months. It was there that Mike met Polly and a relationship began to kindle.

Mike teases Polly and says, "She grew up on the rich side of town." Polly was one of three children of Roy and Jane Martin who owned a furniture store in Opp.

"The week we met, they had a youth revival at Polly's church, the First Methodist Church. I asked Jesus to come into my life and He did. But I never got into the Word. I never developed a personal relationship with Jesus. I accepted Him but then I went about the world.

"I had a plan. I had a good plan I thought. I remembered that film about hell and I knew I didn't want to go there, but I never got into the Word. I was in the flesh. I was of the world and I was enjoying that life. I said, 'I'm going to live this life. I am going to live of the world and right before I die, I'm going to ask Jesus to come back and save me. Then I won't have to worry about going to hell. I'll go to heaven.' That was my plan but God had a different plan."

At Opp High, Mike was a standout athlete in football and in baseball. He hit .606 as a catcher. He received a football scholarship at Alabama and became a star linebacker during the 1972-74 seasons. Coach Bryant's teams were SEC Champions all three years and National Champions in 1973. They compiled a 30-8-3 record and Mike played in the Cotton, Sugar and Orange Bowls. It was a special honor for Mike to earn jersey Number 54. It was popularized by his hero, Lee Roy Jordan, who grew up in Excel, just 40 miles from Mike's hometown.

Polly also came with Mike to Alabama. It was not just because Mike came, but, "I don't think Polly's dad would have let me continue dating her had I not gone to Alabama," says Mike with a big laugh.

Following his graduation, Mike stayed on at Alabama as a graduate assistant and got his Master's degree. Polly, one year younger, completed her degree in Home Economics. It was during this time that Mike and Polly were married on August 8, 1975 in the Opp First Methodist Church.

"When we left Alabama, we vowed that we would not come back until Mike was on the sidelines as a coach," Polly recalls in a serious tone. "We loved Alabama and it was just a dream and a goal we had and we stuck to it."

The road back to Alabama began as an assistant coach at Fairhope High School. Then Mike became the head coach at Prattville High School. Coach Bill Oliver gave Mike his first collegiate job as defensive line coach at Chattanooga. Then Mike went to Southern Miss for one year and was hired at Alabama by Coach Ray Perkins, who succeeded Coach Bryant in 1983.

Mike and Polly had indeed kept their promise. In only eight years their dream to join the coaching staff at Alabama had become a reality. Coach Perkins took the Tampa Bay Buccaneers head job after four years and Mike followed him for the next three years with the Bucs. When Coach Gene Stallings got the Alabama job in 1990, Mike and Polly were happy to be back in Tuscaloosa. Great days lay ahead. Three years later, the Tide won the national championship with the nation's best defense. Mike coached the defensive line comprised of No. 1 NFL draft picks, John Copeland and Eric Curry.

In January, 1994, Mike was wooed by Sam Wyche and the Tampa Bay Bucs to return as a coach. It was tempting. The money was much better. He could finish out being vested for the NFL pension. Mike flew to Tampa and had the job if he wanted it. It was a tough decision. Juli, their oldest of two children, was a junior in high school. All factors were weighed against the nice monetary offer.

Meanwhile, Polly was consistent in prayer for God's will and intervention. "I was praying all day long one day and searching God's word about it," remembers Polly. "I was driving home and really was just having a pity party for myself. I didn't want to move back to Tampa. I didn't want to leave Tuscaloosa. I just cried out loud in the car, 'Lord, please don't send us back to Tampa.' Then the Lord just said to me, 'Polly, you won't ever have to leave Tuscaloosa. Your husband is going to be the head football coach at Alabama someday.'

"I said, 'Lord, how can that be?' The Lord showed me what He was going to do in our lives. I understood from Him that we would have a ministry of telling the story of what God has done and can do. I had never experienced anything like that before. I started giving God every reason why that would not happen. Then I began to think that I was going crazy and I just put it in the back of my mind. I never even mentioned it to Mike."

Tampa Bay almost had Mike but he placed a phone call to Coach Stallings and was back in the fold at Alabama. Coach Stallings felt he had lost Mike and was on the verge of hiring a replacement.

That fall when the coaches had their annual physical, a spot on Mike's lung was detected. He came home, sat Polly down and told her what they had found. There was a possibility that it was cancerous and Mike insisted that he would wait until after the season was over to face it. He felt like he owed it to his players.

"Mike went on to bed and I stayed up crying and praying," says Polly. "I began to ask God to speak to me and give me a word that could help me get through the season. I picked up my Bible and opened it up. There was one sentence underlined in red on that page. It simply said, 'For the Lord will not forget His promises.'

"When I read that, my soul was just blessed. I thought back to what God had told me in the car. Then I began to pray and search the scriptures where God had promised people things and how they believed and responded to Him. It gave me great comfort at the time."

Mike found out later that his lung was okay. There was no concern for his health. Polly kept a journal and God continued to confirm His promise to her, even though it seemed to be an impossibility.

"In the Spring of 1996, I told Mike about what God had been telling me. He said, 'Polly, I just don't see any way that will happen, but we will pray about it.'"

Says Mike, "At that time, I felt like we would have to leave and I'd be a head coach somewhere else. We would have to have success at another place and maybe the opportunity would come so that we could come back. I shudder to think what we almost did by going to Tampa. As my friend Jimmy Dill says, 'God sees the end of the parade and we don't.' Often times, we try to do things our way. We would never know where we would be today had we gone to Tampa."

Going into the 1996 season, Mike had become Defensive Coordinator replacing Bill Oliver who had gone to Auburn. Being a woman of prayer and of the Bible, Polly continued to seek God for faith and guidance.

"Before the first game, I was praying and asking God for a scripture," says Polly. "He led me to Isaiah, chapter 41, verses 10-13. It says,

'Fear not, for I am with you. Do not be dismayed. I am your God. I will strengthen you; I will help you; I will uphold you with my victorious right hand. See, all your angry enemies lie confused and shattered. Anyone opposing you will die. You can look for them in vain—they will all be gone. I am holding you by your right hand—I am the Lord your God—and I say to you, don't be afraid; I am here to help you.'

"I wrote that verse on a card, one for me and one for Mike. We just carried that scripture all season long. I would take it out and read it before just about every game. The night before the Auburn game in Birmingham, Juli, Michael and I were at home and had just finished having a devotion and prayer together. The phone rang and it was my mother. She said she had been praying for us and God had given her a scripture especially for Mike...Isaiah, chapter 41, verses 10-13. I told her that those had been the Bible verses that God had given us all season.

"Shortly after that, Mike called to tell me that Coach Stallings would be resigning the next day."

Indeed the following day after Alabama had edged Auburn 24-23, Coach Stallings made his surprise resignation announcement in the post-game press conference underneath the north stands of Legion Field.

The announcement came without a warning. It was unexpected by the Alabama family. The Alabama head football coach position is held sacred in Alabama. Speculation about the new head coach even over-shadowed the Crimson Tide's upcoming SEC championship game two weeks later with Florida. So Athletic Director Bob Bockrath began his search for a new football coach at Alabama.

On December 7, Florida prevailed 45-30 over Alabama in Atlanta to capture the SEC championship. The next day, Alabama was select-ed to play Michigan in the Outback Bowl in Tampa on January 1, 1997.

During the two week span after Coach Stallings' resignation, Mike was the overwhelming choice of most Alabama followers for the high position. It was such a thrill for Mike and Polly to see demonstrated just how much fans had felt about his coaching ability. Mike was indeed one of the finest assistant coaches in America. He had developed five first round NFL draft choices. He had coached some of the finest defenses in Alabama history. He was selected "SEC Working Coach of the Year" in 1991 and 1994. Any coach in America would have cherished having Mike on his staff, college or pro. He was held with high regard in his profession. He was one of the best in the business.

On Monday, December 9, a press conference was called and Mike

DuBose became the twenty-second head football coach at Alabama. He became the first Alabama assistant coach to move up to the head job in decades. He was the first since Coach Bryant to have been an Alabama player, assistant coach and then head coach.

What was also unique was the fact that Mike became the first head coach at Alabama to be born in the state. In spiritual terms, it did appear that God had ordained the steps of Mike DuBose to be the head coach at Alabama. Some would say from the government housing project in Opp, it was a miracle of God.

At the press conference, Mike was quick to point out, "My standing here today is proof of two things. One, that dreams do come true. Second, and most importantly, it proves that prayer does work. I am convinced that I am standing here today because of prayer."

Looking back on that emotional time, Mike recalls, "It was amazing that God had spoken to Polly over the past three years and now God had worked His plan out for us. With Brother (Oliver) leaving, my getting the Defensive Coordinator job and Coach Stallings resigning, it was amazing. If we had waited a few more weeks, we may not have been here. No one knew it, but I had been contacted by a couple of other schools about head coaching jobs. But God's plan prevailed."

Mike went through bowl game preparations and the game itself as the heir apparent for the job. The day after the bowl game, he would be the head football coach. Alabama won the game over Michigan 17-14.

God had one more strong affirmation about Mike's position as head coach for Polly and Mike.

"We came back to Tuscaloosa and when we walked into the big office of the head football coach, it was completely empty," recalls Polly in wonderment. "I felt so overwhelmed. But there were two men from Birmingham who came to help me. The walls were bare and they were decorators and commercial artists. We visited for just a few minutes about some ideas for the office.

"Then a few days later, they returned and one of the men, Ovid Ricketson, asked if he could visit with me for a few minutes. I could tell he was nervous, but he said God would not let him rest because he had something to share with me. He said he knew that God had placed us here and God had given him some Bible verses for us. He gave me a book of scriptures entitled *God's Answers For Your Life.* It was about various Biblical topics and he turned the pages and showed me the scripture he had been given by God for us...Isaiah 41:10-13.

"You can imagine how surprised I felt and at the same time

confirmation again that we were meant to be here in this office as head football coach. He also went on to say that God had shown him that the storms would come. He said we would face the storms like an eagle. The storms will come and the eagle will fly to the higher tree. You are to anticipate the storm and when the storm begins to surround the tree, the eagle will lock his wings and fly. The winds of the storm will lift the eagle up." How prophetic Ovid's statements were.

Ovid also wrote in the book, "Dear Polly, May God richly bless you and your family. He has placed you in the arena and will guide and protect each of you during the difficult and trying times ahead. Remember that He gives us victory in battle, not victory from battle. What a wonderful plan He has for you to be such a bright light. He will bring immense peace and show you many times His great love for you. He has burdened my heart to bring the verses especially to *you*. In particular, He stressed verse 13. God indicated that you would know this was a confirmation to His answer to your prayers…something only you and He would know. Please know that you and Mike and family are in the hearts and prayers of many thousands that are with you in spirit. With love in Christ, Ovid."

The message God gave to Ovid, an "angel unaware," was to be a source of divine strength and assurance for Polly and Mike. It continues to be to this day.

Mike's first year as head coach got off to a good start, winning three of the first four games. His opener was a 42-17 dubbing of Houston in Birmingham. The finale at Auburn was a disappointing 18-17 loss when it seemed that Alabama had the game won until the last minute of play. The game typified a final 4-7 record that could just as easily been 7-4 with a good bounce here and there.

Alabama got on track the next season and posted a 7-4 record with an impressive 31-17 win over Auburn. The Magic City Bowl in Nashville invited Alabama to play Virginia Tech, a team no one expected to play for the national championship against Florida State the next bowl season. Too many mistakes gave Tech a 38-7 win, but next season, Mike's third year, would be a great one.

Crimson Tide fans were primed for a banner season with All-American seniors Shaun Alexander and Chris Samuels. Alabama was to play Tennessee in Tuscaloosa for the first time since 1930. Good recruiting years gave Alabama added hope.

Then in August, just before the freshmen reported, Mike publicly apologized for an improper relationship. It was during these days and weeks of turmoil that Mike turned to God. It was indeed the greatest storm he would face in his life. He began to build a renewed relationship with Jesus Christ in the most sincere manner he knew how, by going to his knees in prayer and seeking God face to face in His word, the Bible.

Mike explains his thoughts at that crucial time in his life. "I had to stop and look at my life, who I was, where I was and where I was going. When I did, I didn't like the answer to any of it. I certainly didn't like the direction I was going because I was about to lose everything that was important to me. That included my family and the job I had dreamed about and worked hard to get. I was at the end of that rope. I could continue down that road and lose it all or I could turn to Jesus and ask for forgiveness and his grace. Thankfully, I was forgiven for it. That peace started also at that particular time."

A rush of support lifted Mike immeasurably during the crisis. "It is hard to explain how much I was helped by so many letters written to me and so many phone calls of encouragement and edification. Bible verses were sent and all of this was so affirming and so reassuring. We felt we were in God's will at that particular time and if we stayed here, then God's promise to us would be true. Because of the edification and intercessory prayers for me, I could feel inner peace and real comfort.

"I learned to stand on Jeremiah 29:11 that says, ' For I know the plans I have for you,' says the Lord. 'They are plans for good and not for evil, to give you a future and a hope.' It said to me that the Lord had a plan for us, to prosper us and give us a future. I still felt it was right here at Alabama for us."

As the season began, Mike had already established himself with complete faith and trust in Christ regardless of the pressure and harsh statements made against him. How did he manage to face such criticism and fingers pointed at him with unflattering words and judgment upon his life?

Polly remembers that critical time and Mike's response. "Mike came to the place really before the season when he just said, 'I'm living for Jesus no matter what happens. I'm living for Jesus. I'm putting everything on the altar."

Mike adds, "At the same time, I believe with all my heart that God put us here. There were a lot of other coaches more qualified to be the head football coach than I was. God put us here and God would keep us here if we did the things He told us to do.

"I was never concerned about those who wanted me out. There

was never any fear in my heart that we would have to pick up and move. If that was God's will, I would be more than happy to do it. I had peace and it was not just me. There was peace on our football team, too. Because of the spiritual leadership that Shaun Alexander and Ryan Pflugner were giving us, there was a peace on our football team.

"After the Louisiana Tech loss (third game), Monday's meeting was the best meeting we had. We had peace about going down to Gainesville to play Florida (fifth game). Nobody else in the world thought that we had a chance to win but this football team. The players and coaches felt like we would go and win the game. (Alabama won in overtime 40-39).

"I might be naive, but I never sensed any concern from the team. Early on before the season, I sensed some concern from the staff. Other than that, once we got into the season, we were together and peace prevailed among everybody."

Surprisingly, Polly expresses that peace for her came after Mike had gained peace for himself. "I wasn't quite at the place where Mike was with this until after the Louisiana Tech game. Mike just walked in peace everyday. At home when he could have been ringing his hands, and I've seen him ring his hands in other years of coaching football, he was calm and peaceful about it all. It was the best football season I've ever been through. It was the best and the hardest year of my life.

"I was not at the same place that Mike was. I was not ready to put everything on the altar. I began to study about Abraham and Sarah and how they waited for this child. God promised them a son. In Genesis 22:1, it says that God tested Abraham. He had to place Isaac on the altar. I felt that this was our goal since we left college. We had a vow never to come back to an Alabama game and sit in the stands. It would only be for Mike coaching on the sidelines. When God told me all of that, I knew God has put his stamp of approval on this and He's going to do it all. Mike and I both had to come to the place where we were willing to put our Isaac on the altar.

"Mike reached that point before I did. When we played that first game against Vanderbilt, I had never been as nervous and as scared in my entire life. Then when we lost to Louisiana Tech, Mike got up the next morning, got dressed and walked calmly out the door to do his television show. So I started to try to make a deal with God. I told Mike, 'This is going to be my prayer this week. I'm going to pray that if we win that Arkansas game, God wants us to stay here. If we lose it, then we'll pack up and go wherever.'

"I'll never forget Mike turning and looking around at me and saying, 'I'm not making any deals with God.'

"But I did," Polly exclaims. "I did come to the place, though, where I told the Lord, 'Your will be done. Your will be done.' During this time, everytime there was such tremendous pressure, a particular letter or a call or a word from God would come reminding me He was sovereign and that He was in control. He was watching over us."

Mike and Polly prayed together the Saturday morning of the Arkansas game as the pressure had mounted. It was a crucial game in Tuscaloosa after Alabama had lost to Louisiana Tech the week before. "We just prayed and let God know that we were in His will regardless of the outcome and would go wherever he wanted us to go."

In spite of six turnovers, which is enough to lose any football game, Alabama outscored a fine Arkansas team 35-28. The pressure lessened and then the great win over Florida the next week (the Gators first loss in The Swamp in 30 games) set sail for an awesome season. It ended with a first ever victory at Auburn 28-17 and then the Tide stunned Florida 34-7 to win the Southeastern Conference championship in Atlanta.

Alabama was ranked No. 5 in the nation as they faced Michigan in the elite Orange Bowl in Miami. The Crimson Tide had taken a 10-2 record into the game against what was rated the toughest schedule of any college team in America. It was a thrilling game for a nationwide television audience played on the night of January 1, 2000. Michigan won 35-34 in overtime.

It was an incredible turnaround from the turmoil in August to the jubilation in December. Mike was named SEC "Coach of the Year" by the other head coaches in the conference. He was one of five finalists for the Paul Bryant Award as national "Coach of the Year." In every interview, Mike would give the praise and glory to Jesus Christ. University President Dr. Andrew Sorensen and Athletic Director Mal Moore also gave Mike a contract extension the week of the bowl game that lasts through January 31, 2004.

By coming forward and confessing his sin before the media throng, the state of Alabama and nation, Mike found that God's grace and mercy never fails. As a bonafide public figure, he demonstrated the route a broken man should take. Fall on your knees, ask God and your fellow man for forgiveness and God will do miraculous things with a life yielded to Him.

During the Spring and Summer of 2000, Mike was asked to give his testimony in several churches. As he did, those congregations came to realize that Mike's newfound faith in Jesus Christ was the real thing. The following are excerpts from his testimony and message that God placed on his heart to say:

"I want you to look at me today not as a football coach but as a sinner saved by grace through faith. I am not worthy to stand here. There is absolutely nothing I can ever do to make me worthy to stand here. If I say anything that is of man, if man is glorified by what I say and not God the Father, may God render it useless.

"This is not about me. This is not about a football coach. This is about a cross. It is about an empty tomb. It is about Jesus at the right hand of the Father Almighty.

"It has been said that, 'To have a testimony, you have got to have a test.' I'm in the process of passing the test. I learned a lot of things through this whole process. One of the things I have learned, through this process that happened to me several months ago is that the problems, the adversities, the trials…didn't go away.

"I was never good at taking tests. The only test I ever felt comfortable taking was an open book test. I'm here to tell you today that life is a test. And it's an open book test and here's all the answers (holding up his Bible). There is never a problem that the answer is not found right there.

"In Matthew 6:25-34…in there we are told not to worry about life. Not to worry about food, what we are to eat and drink, not to worry about clothes, what we are to wear. God tells us that He will give all those things to us if we seek first His Kingdom and His righteousness.

"Then He goes on to say, 'Don't worry about tomorrow for tomorrow will worry about itself. Each day has enough troubles of its own.' In Job 14:1 it says, 'Man, who is born of woman, that is us, is a few days and full of trouble.' I want you to think about those few days for a moment also. You may live to be 100, 105 or 110, but when you compare that to eternity, that is a few days. We are going to be on this earth a few days and full of trouble.

"You and I are going to go through adversity. We are going to have problems. We are going to walk in trouble times. We are going to face trials of many kinds. It is not a question of if, it is a matter of when. What do you do? How do you handle it? Again, the answers are right there in the Bible.

"In James 1:2-4, James is the brother of Jesus, it says this: 'Consider it pure joy my brothers whenever you face trials of many kinds, for you know the testing of your faith develops perseverance, and perseverance must finish its work so that we can be made mature and complete, not lacking in anything.'

"When you go through troubles, when you face adversity, when you are going through trials of many kinds, think about it. This is a step closer to God looking at me and saying, 'That I am mature, I am complete and not lacking in anything. This makes it easier to get through those trials, those troubles and tribulations.

"Paul in I Thessalonians 5:16-18 sort of gives us a blueprint for living. He says, 'Be joyful always. Pray continually and give thanks in all circumstances. For this is God's will for you in Christ Jesus.' Guys, I struggled with that. I struggled hard with that.

"I had asked Jesus to come into my life and to forgive me of my sins. Then I read where I am to give thanks. I was going through what I thought was hell. I saw people that I respected, people that I thought were my friends saying things I didn't think I would ever hear them say.

"I saw things written that I never thought certain people would write. And I was struggling to give thanks. Then I went back and I read it again. Then it jumped out at me.

"God wasn't asking me to give thanks for what I was going through. There is absolutely nothing that is bad out there that is of God. Those bad things are from Satan. God was asking me to give thanks in all circumstances. God can take and use circumstances in all things for good.

"There is a story also in Matthew about Jesus and his disciples. They are in a boat out on the Sea of Galilee and Jesus is asleep…just peaceful, peaceful sleep. A storm comes up suddenly, the winds are blowing, the waves are coming up over the bow of the boat and the disciples are scared. Then they began to fear for their lives.

"They woke Jesus and said, 'Jesus save us. We are about to drown!' Jesus looks at them and says, 'Ye of little faith! Why are you afraid?' Then he rebukes the wind and the waves and everything becomes calm.

"Jesus will not save us from the storms of life, but He will save us in the storms of life. Just like he saved the disciples. In a life threatening situation they turned to Jesus and He does what? He saves them.

"I was at a point in my life here several months ago. I had to stop, look at myself, and I had to answer these questions? Did I like where I was? Did I like where I was going? Did I like who I was? The answer to all three questions was No. I didn't like who Mike DuBose was. I didn't like where he was going. I was going down a one way street to hell and destruction.

"I was about to lose everything that was important to me…my family and a job that I had worked my entire life to get. Jesus came in and He changed all of that. Jesus promises to save us in those life threatening situations.

"I want you to think about something else in that story. I read it several times and God sort of put this on my heart. If you look at the disciples, by trade most of them were what? Fishermen. It wasn't the first time they had ever been on the Sea of Galilee. It wasn't the first storm they had ever been in.

"If you have ever been deep sea fishing, and I have, if you have ever been in a storm you always have an eye out when you go out the next time. You look for conditions that will alert you that the storms are coming. There is a part of me that has to believe that the disciples saw the storm coming. But they didn't worry about it because they thought they could handle it.

"They didn't do or say anything until it became a life threatening situation. And then they cried out to Jesus. I have to believe that as soon as they saw the storm coming, if they had said something to Jesus then, He would have stopped it right there.

"My wife Polly, and I love her and am blessed to have her, told me several years ago that I was in trouble. She asked me to pray with her and she asked me to go to Bible study with her. I said, 'No, I don't need that. I can handle it. I'm okay. I'll make it alright.'

"The more Mike DuBose tried to handle it, the worse it became. I could have gone to Jesus six or seven years ago, and he would have done what? It didn't have to get to a desperate situation. Jesus would have said, 'I forgive you. I'll save you now.'

"All the people that were hurt, all the people that were embarrassed wouldn't have had to have gone through that. Thank God when we do get to the bottom of the pit, when we get to the end of the rope, He will save us.

"There may be some of you out there that are not in that desperate situation yet, but you know if you continue to do the things that you are doing, you will get there. Jesus will change that NOW.

Again, God does not promise to save us from the storms and fires of life. Really, it is up to us just how tense that storm is and how hot that fire becomes.

"In my cry to God, I knew I had been changed. I knew that my name was written in the Lamb's Book of Life. But I still didn't have that peace that I should have had. The final step was me realizing who the enemy really was. I thought people were the enemy. People who were writing all the articles, saying all the things...I thought they were the enemy. I couldn't get any peace from it.

"Then I read Ephesians 6:10-12. It says, 'Be strong in the Lord in His mighty power. Put on the full armor of God so that we can take our stand against the devil's schemes. For our struggle is not against flesh and blood, but against the powers, against the authorities, against the rulers of this dark world...the spiritual forces of evil in the heavenly realms.'

"People are not the enemy. People were allowing Satan to use them. Satan is the enemy. He is the one that comes to steal, kill and destroy. Once I realized that, I got peace. Because greater is He that is in me than he who is in the world. You take Jesus and you take Satan and Jesus wins every time.

"Satan tries to instill fear into us. Satan understands that you and I are saved by grace through faith. Faith and fear can't exist together. If we have fear, we lack faith. If we have faith, there is no fear.

"In Ezekiel, God tells him three times to fear not. Do not be afraid. In the Bible, we find 365 times that God says, 'Fear not.' That is one for each day of the year. In Joshua 1:6-9, God tells Joshua as he is getting ready to take over leadership of the Israelites, 'Be strong and courageous.' He wants us to have courage. What is courage? It is simply grace under pressure. What is grace? It is unmerited favor. It is a gift from God above. There is nothing you and I can do to earn it. There is nothing you and I can do to make us worthy of it. It is simply a gift out there. It is up to us whether we take it or not. It is freely given and has to be freely received.

"In 1 Corinthians 15:26, Paul tells us that the last enemy to be defeated is death. When Adam and Eve took of the fruit of the tree of knowledge of good and evil, they sinned. Sin entered the world. From that first bite to the crucifixion of Jesus, death reigned. The Word tells us that the wages of sin is death. Death took Abraham. Why? Because it had a right to. Death took Moses because it had a right to. All have sinned and come short of the glory of God.

"One day on Calvary, death messed up bad. Sin made a big mistake. Death made a big mistake. Death took Jesus. And Jesus was without sin. And God said, 'Enough. Death you shall reign no more.' And God condemned Death to death through the Resurrection. It is not only an empty tomb. It is an empty grave.

"Paul in talking to the Thessalonians said, 'Brothers, we do not want you to be ignorant about those who have fallen asleep or to grieve like the rest of men who have no hope. We believe that Jesus died and rose again. We also believe that God will bring with Jesus those who have fallen asleep in him.'

"Satan is about death. Jesus is about life and life eternal.

"I love to talk about the team concept. I never speak that I don't mention it. In every thing you and I do, we play various roles within the team concept. This church is a team. Members of this church have to play a role. This is also a team within a team within Christ's church. We are one body, one people serving one Father and serving one risen Lord. We play so many roles.

"Ultimately when you shake it all down, you and I are on one of two teams. We are on God's team or we are on Satan's team. There is no neutrality.

"You can come into this state and you can be for Alabama, you can be for Auburn, you can be for somebody else, or you can be neutral. But when it comes to Satan or when it comes to God, you are either on one side or the other. You are on God's team or you are on Satan's team.

"The longest hour that I spend is that hour when we first get to the stadium. The players are dressing. The coaches are milling about outside. I'm sitting back in the locker room by myself and I'm reflecting on the week's preparation. Have we run this defense enough times? Have we run this offensive play enough times against this defense or this coverage, or against this blitz or this stunt? Have we worked them hard enough? Have we worked them too hard? Are they focused? Are they concentrating? Are they ready?

"See, there is that doubt. There is that concern that you have got your team ready to win, knowing if you don't win, every single thing you did that day is going to be scrutinized. I'm going to have to answer for every single bit of it. It is a miserable feeling not knowing whether you are going to win or not.

"But then I always reflect back to this (the Bible). It tells you in the last chapter without question that God's team wins. You have a choice. To play on the losing team or to play on the winning team. It is a no brainer isn't it? The Word is true. God's team wins.

"My prayer for you today is that you are on God's team. All the troubles won't go away. I told you earlier, I'm a sinner saved by grace. I still sin. I still make mistakes. I still have to come before Jesus everyday and ask for His forgiveness. I'm not perfect. That didn't change. But I am trying. I am trying.

"I do know that my name is written in the Lamb's Book of Life. One day that grave of mine is going to be empty. I'm going to sit with the Father and have life eternal in heaven. Be on God's team guys. Be on God's team."

Today in Mike's personal growth, he turns to the Bible for his greatest source of strength. When he arrives at his office early in the morning, he has a devotion time alone and uninterrupted for 30-45 minutes. "I have read a number of books and devotion books, but peace for me is staying in the Bible. I read at least one chapter every day. It's Bible time, devotion time and prayer at that time for me." Before Mike leaves home, he and Polly have communion together also.

On the night before the Orange Bowl game and the last day of the twentieth century, Mike and Polly invited family and close friends up to their suite in the Wyndham Miami Beach Hotel and had communion. It was their way of entering into the new millennium.

On game days last season as the team boarded four buses and headed for the stadium, Mike would escort Polly to the last bus for the staff and coaches wives. Then he would take his place on the front seat of the first bus.

"The last thing I say to Polly before she gets on the bus," says Mike is, "God is good." Then Polly responds, "All the time."

In Mike's profession, the bottom line is wins and victories. Mike has already won the ultimate victory of a home in heaven and eternal life with God the Father. He has gained that by confessing his sins before God, asking forgiveness of sin and living for Christ each day.

Sometimes it may take storms in life to fully understand the awesome goodness of God. One thing for sure, Mike and Polly know that only God can give them what they have together today. Polly says, "I would go through it all over again to be where Mike and I are today in Christ. It has been the best year of my life." Such love, peace, happiness only comes through God and his son Jesus.

"There are a lot of people who are like I was," says Mike thinking back to his life before he came to know Jesus in an intimate way. "They feel like the fast lane is the good life. Being a Christian and being on God's team is punishment.

"I had the plan that right before I died, I was going to get right with Jesus and I was going to heaven. I knew I didn't want to go to hell. I think a lot of people have that idea. What they are missing is what I almost missed.

"Life with Jesus is a good life. It is the only life now for me."

CHAPTER FIVE

TOMMY AND ROBIN FORD

Most couples wait for a baby for nine months. In the case of Tommy and Robin Ford, they waited for ten years and when their baby finally came, they were given a 36-hour notice.

It may sound like a complicated puzzle, but it is sometimes normal procedure when God blesses a couple with an adopted child that becomes the joy of their lives.

Tommy's and Robin's story is one of patience through years of tears that brought the ultimate reward and the desire of their hearts – in God's own plan and not theirs.

As Director of Alabama's TIDE PRIDE football and basketball donor program, Tommy oversees the main revenue generating part of the Athletic Department. Robin is a pharmacist.

When Tommy and Robin married in 1984, they looked ahead with pure delight to having a family. They looked forward to the pleasure of parenthood and precious children to raise. They decided to wait three years before having their first child. Little did they know that it would be 1997, in their thirteenth year of marriage, before their enduring wish for a child came true.

Tommy and Robin both grew up in Gadsden, Alabama, in Christian homes. Since they were five grades apart in school, they didn't meet until they were out of high school, although Tommy's mother had taught Robin in the fifth grade.

"To borrow words from Ruth Bell Graham, I cannot remember a time when I didn't love God," says Robin, who accepted Christ as her Savior when she was eight years old.

Tommy also grew up in the church, but it was a Billy Graham film entitled, "For Pete's Sake," that led him to ask Jesus Christ into his life at the age of 13. He still has the ticket stub from the movie that was shown in a downtown Gadsden theater.

After finishing at Gadsden High School in 1974, Tommy followed his dream and enrolled at the University of Alabama. As a senior, he was Sports Editor of the *Crimson White* campus newspaper and cherished the opportunity to write about Coach Paul "Bear" Bryant and the great championship teams of the late 70's.

Robin attended Westminster Christian High School, a school that is now Westbrook Christian and is operated by John Croyle and the Big Oak Ranch. She chose to study Pharmacy at Auburn University because it would be an ideal part time profession for when she would one day have a family.

It was December 1981, on Christmas break when Brandon Barnes, Robin's first cousin who was also a high school friend of Tommy's, introduced the pair at the Gadsden Mall in a coincidental meeting. Three weeks prior to their meeting, Robin, a junior at Auburn, had prayed, "Lord, I really don't want to do this dating thing anymore. I will be perfectly happy with you as my only love until you just let Mr. Right come along."

At the Gadsden Mall, Brandon seized the moment and a setup took place. "Robin, have you been dating anybody lately?" he said throwing the hint out right in front of Tommy. Robin replied, "No, no, not really."

Then Tommy blurted out, "Well, you can date me!"

"How suave and debonair was that?" says Tommy about his Romeo line when they had never previously met. A few nights later, Robin was attending a Sunday School party when her father called and said, "Robin, please come home. There is a boy named Tommy Ford that has called you three times."

Robin went home and the phone rang, but it was her best friend Cynthia Cantrell calling. "I said, 'Cynthia, get off the phone. Tommy Ford is going to be calling me.' Then Cynthia said, 'Tommy Ford! I know him. Y'all are going to get married!'"

Tommy's call came, a date was made for the day after Christmas and both agree wholeheartedly that it was "love at first sight." For two and a half years, it would be a long-distance courtship. Tommy had just resigned from his job at the Gadsden Chamber of Commerce and in January would move back to Tuscaloosa to be field representative for the University of Alabama National Alumni Association. Robin would finish her Pharmacy degree at Auburn.

This Alabama/Auburn mix was fun for Tommy and Robin but the growing love they had for each other far overshadowed the rivalry school aspect.

On July 14, 1984, Tommy and Robin were married at East Gadsden Baptist Church by Dr. Levan Parker, the Headmaster and Head

Basketball Coach at Westminster. Dr. Parker was a man who had an indelible spiritual influence upon Robin. Tommy grew to love his saintly spirit as well.

Tommy and Robin rented an apartment in Tuscaloosa. Robin began working as a pharmacist at Druid City Hospital, and they joined First Baptist Church downtown. Things couldn't have been better for the young newlyweds.

"The thing about young married couples is they have everything planned out regarding children," says Tommy. "Before they get married, they will usually decide on how long they want to wait until they have children. Our magic number was about three years. Everything was going fine. We both had good jobs. Robin had moved on to Harco Drugs and we had bought our first home."

Then that magic third year rolled around and the Fords were settled and ready to begin the family they had envisioned and anticipated all along.

"Having a child was something we just thought would happen right away," says Robin in reflection. "We never had any other indication otherwise. But it didn't happen.

"My mind was filled with anxiety as I questioned God. All I desired was to have a Christian home and raise children up to love the Lord. Why wouldn't God allow me to do the very thing I felt called by Him to do? After about six months or so, my doctor said, 'Well, you know, sometimes it just takes awhile.'"

In the fall of 1989, after two more years of waiting, a laparoscopy procedure by Robin's doctor in Tuscaloosa revealed an endometrial cyst, which was successfully removed by a UAB Hospital infertility specialist. Four months after that procedure, in March 1990, Robin became pregnant.

"We thought our problems had been solved," Robin recalls, "and that the Lord had answered our prayers. Technology is such that after eight weeks you can see the heartbeat on a sonogram and that's what I saw. But then I miscarried, which was devastating in its own right.

"Again, in despair, my broken heart filled with unanswered questions and this time I was angry. I took my cue from the psalmist and many, many times vented my anger, my doubts and my inexpressible frustration to God. How could he tease me? Was I being punished? Why couldn't I just receive some sort of answer? Only deafening silence seemed to be God's response."

Robin continued to seek a solution. It was difficult for a young wife to understand why two healthy people could not bear children. "The only way I can really explain infertility is that it's an invisible physical handicap. Your body won't do what everybody else's takes for granted. It is one of those things that statistics say will affect 15 to 20 percent of couples at one time or the other."

Still with a miscarriage, there was a ray of hope. At least she had become pregnant if only for a short while.

"With mixed emotions," Robin says, "we thought the problem had been solved. We felt that at least now we could get pregnant if we just tried again. But it was not to be."

In the fall of 1990, Robin's doctor referred her back to the specialists in Birmingham for a GIFT procedure (Gamete Intrafallopian Transfer), a form of In Vitro Fertilization (IVF).

"I took drugs and shots and it was a nightmare," Robin recalls. "Even with all you go through, the chances of getting pregnant are still small. It was an intense time. There is a lot of anticipation built up. You think about it every minute of every day. Then all of a sudden, nothing happens. Emotionally and physically, it is a roller coaster. After no success, we chose to take a break for awhile."

In 1993, Robin and Tommy returned to Birmingham to see another specialist, Dr. Kay Honea, at Brookwood Hospital. Dr. Honea found and removed another cyst, after which time she recommended that Robin and Tommy undergo the In Vitro Fertilization procedure. But with this procedure came many questions for the struggling couple.

"For us, certain aspects of reproductive technology raised several ethical questions," Robin said. "How far down the technological road should you travel? It almost puts you in a position of playing God. As Christians, do we have moral and ethical limitations? We took advantage of a good portion of what reproductive technology has to offer, but we were not comfortable with certain aspects."

After almost a year of testing and preparation, the IVF procedure was performed in the fall of 1994, but it was not successful.

Tommy explains from his side what he and Robin were experiencing as the years passed with such a heavy burden. "I don't want to sound selfish on our part, but we had friends who would seemingly just *think* about getting pregnant and they got pregnant. We loved our friends and we loved their children. Their children were our children. Those children are now nine, ten and eleven years old. But in our core of friends, we were the only ones that were struggling with this particular challenge.

"The fact was that no doctor could give us a definitive reason. None of our doctors ever said we could not have children."

Tommy and Robin knew their next step, but it was not the one for which they had hoped. "We had already decided that IVF would be our last attempt at any type of infertility procedure," Robin said. "Another issue was the expense. Our insurance did not pay for the expensive fertility medicine. All in all, we spent some $10-$15,000 with nothing to show for it. Dr. Honea was very sweet about it and finally said one day, 'Well you know, maybe you just need to stop (the fertility procedures).'

"Emotionally, it was hard on me. I knew God was a God of miracles and if He wanted to perform a miracle on me, He could. I came to that point. I finally said, 'Lord, what is it that you are trying to teach us?' Infertility is a challenge on your marriage. It's the kind of thing that will make a bad marriage split apart and a good marriage stronger.

"I remember reading Phillip Yancey's book, *Disappointment With God*. In reading that book I began to feel that if God never answered my prayers the way I wanted, it was okay. I knew that God could do it but He wasn't doing it. That was the bottom line and I didn't know why."

Tommy offers a good perspective from their viewpoint. "We were on our own calendar and not on God's calendar. We had that fast food mentality that we wanted a child now. We were getting older and we were impatient. We didn't want to wait around. Beginning in November of 1994, after the IVF procedure didn't work, we went for two full years without even talking about it."

Simultaneous with their IVF procedure in 1994, Tommy and Robin were building their dream home in Hinton Place, just south of Tuscaloosa. The building process had therapeutic value and it was a way to alter their total concentration on getting pregnant after so many procedures and so many tearful nights of wondering why. Their Golden Retriever dogs, Ellie and Opie, were a pleasure, but their home lacked children, creating a huge void.

Throughout the Fords' eight-year ordeal, several close friends had asked them if they had considered the adoption route. "Adoption did not appeal to me and I did not want to do it," Robin recalls. "Cynthia Cantrell Walker, my best friend growing up and now a pediatrician in Tuscaloosa, would see babies that needed homes. She would kindly ask me every once in awhile, 'Have you thought about adoption?' But I was not ready for that. Tommy and I talked around it but we never mentioned the word adoption. I guess we were still stubborn because no one had ever told us we couldn't have children of our own."

Tommy offers another interesting thought. "We would have much preferred a doctor to tell us in the early 90s, 'Guys, forget it. You cannot biologically have children.' We could have taken it much better then because we went through eight years of wondering why.

"At the same time, we still had our hand out. God had given us each other, a great marriage, good friends, a good church, good jobs and everything we needed. We were not content with what we had. That is the fallacy that even Christians have today."

Says Robin, "It was one of those crisis times in your life when you have to say, 'Thank you Lord,' even though you don't feel it. You are not thankful but you know He is in control. We were not asking for a bad thing. It was just our next step in life and it seemed like we were stuck in a time warp. Our friends were progressing along with their lives becoming parents. Mother's Day and baby dedications at the church were the worst days for me. Those days were sad reminders. Here we were sort of feeling left behind."

All the while, God was working to prepare Robin's heart for adoption, as she followed His call to teach the four-year old children's choir at First Baptist. Being around the children was another therapeutic experience and Tommy also joined Robin in helping with the choir. "We both felt that there was not a child among all those four-year olds that we couldn't take home and love as our own," says Tommy as their hearts continued to yearn for a family.

Tommy and Robin began to ask God for a sign that would bring some hope and comfort. While listening to Christian radio, Robin heard a woman tell a story of trial and God spoke to her and said, "Can you love me even if I *never* tell you why?" To Robin that was profound. "Do I love Him even though I may never have children? Would I continue to serve Him?" Robin pondered. "My answer was, 'Yes, I would.' I prayed that if not having children was God's desire, that he would take that desire away. I even came to the point where I quit praying about it. God answers prayers by saying, 'Yes, No and wait awhile.' At that time, we didn't realize it was the latter."

Then Robin had an idea that they had not yet tried. "I said, 'You know, Tommy, people go to their pastor when they are having crises like divorce and sickness.' So we went in to see our pastor, Rick Lance. He was sitting behind his desk and I could tell he was nervous. He didn't know what was coming. So we shared with him all that we had been through to have a child. Finally he said, 'Well, have you ever thought about adoption?'"

"I'm thinking in my mind, 'This is NOT why we came here!' We went there to get a word that everything would be all right and for him to pray a nice prayer that the Lord would bless us with children. Instead, he proceeded to tell us about a friend of his who had adopted. It wasn't what we wanted to hear at the time, but God used that visit to plant a seed that helped us later on."

Then God, in His own special way, provided an "angel unaware" to come as a guest in the Fords' home. Gerry Sisk from the First Baptist Church of Snellville, Georgia, came to lead a women's seminar at First Baptist, and the Fords were asked at the last minute to host her at their home.

Robin remembers well the occasion. "Gerry was a woman of God, no doubt about it. I was so impressed with her. She knew her scripture and was so down to earth. During the seminar on Saturday morning, she told us that her first child was adopted. She told the story so eloquently of the day when her little boy came up to her and asked, 'Momma, why did my birth mother give me away?' She said, 'Well, let's go see what God has to say about it. Go get your Bible.'

"She told him to look up Psalms 139 and they read it. He read the verses that said, 'You are knitted together in my mother's womb. You are fearfully and wonderfully made. Lord you have scheduled all my days before I was born.' She said, 'Well, what do you think that means? He said, 'I don't know.' Then she said, 'Don't you think that means that God scheduled all your days before you were born and he knew you were going to be my child?' He said, 'Oh, well, yes!'

"So I'm sitting there listening to her and I was just spellbound. I said to myself, 'Okay, God must have it all figured out. There is a child out there that could be ours with the last name of Ford and God has already scheduled out everything. Okay Lord, I think I can do this. If it's on your calendar, then I can do it.'

"I thought about it and pondered over the story a little while, then I said, 'But, Lord, here's the deal. You work in Tommy's heart first since we have not talked about adopting.' I knew it wasn't anything that Tommy was fired up about. Me neither really, but I knew that God had changed my heart.

"In the meantime, some real close friends, Bert and Julie Guy, had adopted a child. I filled in for Julie some at the pharmacy while she was on maternity leave. So I was able to observe their adoption experience."

When God is ready to answer prayer, He goes about it in His own way and not ours. He has a way of preparing one's heart for an answer

He wants to deliver. We may not realize until later how God is working, but His plan is always best. His schedule of deliverance should never be questioned. As Robin's heart was being prepared for adoption, God was at work in Tommy's heart as well.

"I didn't have a definitive incident like Robin had with Gerry's visit, but around Christmas time we began to receive Christmas cards from our friends with pictures of their children. I was looking at all those photos with kids and God just put a peace over me, a sense of calmness as if he put His hand on my shoulder and said, 'I have something in mind for you.'

"He just literally put into my heart and head the thought that maybe adoption was His plan for us," says Tommy with a lump in his throat when that defining moment came for him. "Of course, my first thought then was, 'How do I tell Robin?'

"My intention was to tell her on our bowl trip to Tampa. This was at the end of the 1996 season when we played Michigan in the Outback Bowl. My plan over the three days there was to tell her since we would be spending a lot of time together. As it turned out, our good friends Bryan and Pam Givhan went on the trip also and we ended up doing everything with them. With all the activities of the bowl game and during the trip itself, there was never enough time.

"Plus, I just didn't know how to tell her. It was like asking her out for the first date. I was afraid she would say no. I was so afraid of rejection."

So Tommy and Robin had separately accepted adoption in their own hearts but after many years of waiting for a child, it became difficult to concede with each other their full acceptance of adoption.

Robin makes a good point in saying that, "Adoption is something you don't need to talk each other into doing. You need to be on the same page about the issue or it can cause problems later."

Tommy struggled through the month of January and finally in February he prayed, 'God, I must do it. I need your help, guidance and wisdom to approach Robin on this.'

"So God gave me the understanding that if she said no, I would just drop it and not be upset."

Robin remembers the night of February 13, 1997, at home as Tommy mustered up the courage to tell her his thoughts. "Tommy said, 'We have got to talk about something.' So he gave me a 30-minute spill about what he felt like God had been telling him. When he finished I smiled and said, 'Well, where have you been? I have been waiting on you! God's already told me.'"

It was a Hallelujah moment for Tommy and Robin, a time of relief and a time of rejoicing after years of questioning and wondering.

Robin felt a great sense of joy and peace in her soul. "In a way it was almost like being pregnant. You had this sense of expectancy that God was about to do something big. I think the fact that God affirmed adoption in us separately was our way of knowing without a doubt that this is what He wanted us to do. We didn't have to persuade or talk each other into it. God did this individually in our own hearts and then brought us together on it."

Sadness had now turned to joyful hope. The next step was the adoption process, and God had been working this out as well. It is true, God does work in mysterious ways, His wonders to perform. To watch and observe "Godspeed" in action is one of life's richest treasures for a Christian.

"John Croyle had been the lone voice in the wilderness for me during the previous three years and perhaps even longer," says Tommy recounting the time. "He would ask me every once in awhile about us having children. I had shared with John our infertility and all we had been through. He had told me if we ever decided to adopt, that he would get me in touch with a good friend of his, an attorney in Birmingham that handled a bit of adoption work."

John was also from Gadsden and played football for Coach Paul Bryant at Alabama in the early 70's. Upon finishing Alabama, he started the Big Oak Ranch for unwanted, orphaned, abused and neglected children.

Tommy called John the next week to tell him that he and Robin had decided to pursue adoption. Within days, John hooked Tommy and Robin up with Bob Echols, who had been involved with many private adoptions and had also worked with the Lifeline Adoption Agency in Birmingham.

"We met with Bob and hit it off real well," says Tommy. "He told us some really crazy adoption stories, mostly when the birth mothers would change their minds at the last minute. He wasn't trying to scare us away; he was just being up front about the things that could happen. From the moment we made the decision and felt God was in it, we just didn't have any fear about it. As well, Bob had been the attorney for our friends Bert and Julie Guy, so that was comforting.

"Around the first of April, Bob called and said, 'I am working on a very complicated adoption case that may work out for you. It may be risky. In other words, it may take you right up to the last day and then not work out. I have told the birth mother about you and Robin. She seems to be interested. Are you at all interested?'

"It was an immediate and unanimous, 'Yes! Sure we're interested.' We knew there wasn't any harm in trying this possibility. What were we going to say? 'No, we'll go to the next possibility after waiting all these years.' So we assured Bob that we were all for pursuing this baby."

Tommy and Robin then began the 'home study procedure' and were connected with Lifeline to start the adoption process. Things really got serious at that point.

"Bob called a couple of weeks later and said the birth mother wanted to meet us," Tommy said. "So we drove to a designated place and met with her and Bob for about 20 minutes in a private conference room. We sat across the table from her and she told us that she was six months pregnant, and that it was going to be a boy. We had a good chat and we knew God was there leading us the whole way through."

Even though it was an awkward meeting, Robin felt at ease. "It was something I wasn't nervous about. I wanted to meet her and someday be able to tell my child that I met his birth mother and that she made the bravest decision she could possibly make. She gave life in this day and age where an abortion is as easily obtained as a tooth extraction."

Tommy expressed his feeling for her as well. "I told her, 'Whether or not we end up getting this child, we just appreciate the fact that you are giving him life.'"

Robin remembers that when Tommy said those words, "She looked at him and smiled."

It was a very good meeting even though it was a short one. Tommy and Robin felt good about her and they thought that she felt good about them as well. They said their goodbyes and departed, wondering if this child would really one day be theirs.

"During the next two months, we just sat around and prayed," says Robin. "There wasn't much we could do. God just delivered us from all fear involved. We would look at each other and say, 'Why are we not nervous wrecks?'"

Along the way there were little things that encouraged Tommy and Robin once they came to the decision to pursue adoption. Robin recalls one such incident occurring on Valentine's Day, the day after their first discussion about adoption. "My prayer warrior friend Pam Givhan came in to the drugstore the next morning and said, 'Robin, I just woke up in the middle of the night and the Lord had you on my heart. Are you okay?' I didn't tell her at the time that we had just made the biggest decision of our lives the night before. I told her later what we had done and she was so blessed. Her message meant a lot to me that day."

Another major blessing came to Tommy and Robin when they attended their first Fellowship of Christian Athletes camp in Black Mountain, N.C., the second week in June. One afternoon they visited The Cove at The Billy Graham Training Center just five miles away. Norm Sanders, Public Relations Director for The Cove and a native of Alabama, gave Tommy and Robin the grand tour. Norm is one of those souls blessed with a triple portion of personality and God's spirit. It doesn't take long before you feel like you have known Norm all of your life.

The tour ended up in the Chapel in the beautiful Prayer Room just below the tall steeple cross. "As we entered the Prayer Room, Norm asked, 'Tommy and Robin, is there anything that I can pray with you about?'" Robin remembers it with a laugh. "We looked at each other like, 'Well, since you brought it up, Norman, yes there is.' So we told him about what we were going through. He went straight to his knees at that round cushioned altar and prayed the most incredible prayer that has ever been prayed for two people that were about to adopt a child.

"We got up from that altar in tears and it was such a blessing to be prayed for in such a powerful manner that day. It really added to our belief that God was working in our lives. It was such a good feeling, too.

"Then during the women's Bible Study each morning at the FCA camp, Beth Evans was the leader. I thought that Anne Graham Lotz was going to be the speaker and I really came to camp excited about hearing Anne. But Beth was such a special speaker and the subject was, of all things, the story of Abraham and Sarah, whom God blessed with a child when she was 90 years old. Through our struggles, we just had that feeling that the waiting was about to come to an end."

The baby was due on August 15. Bob Echols would call periodically and let Tommy and Robin know that everything was going fine. Each weekly call was greeted with thoughts that there was an outside chance that the birth mother could change her mind. Even up until July 31st, Tommy and Robin had only told their families and Robin had shared the possible news with only a handful of prayer partners. They had always kept their infertility struggles and adoption procedures mainly to themselves.

Tommy recalls with great delight the ringing of their telephone. "On Thursday night, July 31, Bob called and said, 'Guys, I'm at the hospital and she, he called her name, has gone into labor. The baby is not premature but the doctor says it may be under a little stress and they want to go ahead and deliver it. Everything is okay. Don't worry.' That was around 8:30."

It was an awesome feeling for Tommy and Robin as they each hung up their phones and met in the hall and stared at each other. Their baby was about to be born and there was only one thing they could do. Pray.

"We just sat in the floor and Tommy prayed first," says Robin of that incredible moment. "He prayed for the baby's health, the doctors, the nurses, even the medical equipment. Then I prayed, 'Lord, we can't be in that delivery room but you can. Lord, just station your angel in that delivery room and watch over our child.' That was our prayer. It was an odd feeling knowing that your baby was being born and you were not there.

"We just prayed that God would station His angel there for us."

Bob called again at 10 p.m. to assure Robin and Tommy that everything was still going well and the birth was imminent. Then came the phone call that would forever change their lives.

"At 1 a.m., Bob called to say that the baby had been born at 12:15 a.m. on August 1," Tommy recalls. "He didn't have many details as to how much he weighed, how long he was or anything. He just said everything was fine."

"I thought I would stay up all night, but we went on to sleep and we slept pretty well," says Robin. "The next day was the longest day of our lives as we waited for more details about our baby.

"We didn't have anything ready in the house for the baby. It completely caught us off guard. We thought we had two more weeks to prepare," Tommy remembers.

Robin informed her prayer partner friends that day and by late that afternoon, Bert and Julie Guy were bringing over their baby things. Anna and Greg Solomon came over to set up a crib. Tom and Cynthia Walker brought food and baby formula. Pam Givhan brought a ham and toys galore, so many that Robin teased her about buying out the whole baby section of Toys R Us. It was a great joy to all their friends because their prayers were being answered also.

"It was like an old fashioned pounding," Robin reflects on the happy hours of anticipation. "Friends brought sacks of baby clothes, a bassinet, food, and everything we needed. One of the sweet moments was when Greg, busy setting up the crib, looked up and said to everyone, 'This is so exciting. It's almost like Christmas!' Tommy responded by saying, 'It *is* Christmas.'"

That Friday afternoon, the Ford's got the long awaited call telling them to be at the hospital the next morning at 10:30 to pick up their baby. Both were totally surprised that a baby would be ready to leave the hospital 36 hours after it had been born. They had anticipated a Sunday pickup.

"So we drove to the hospital and Bob Echols had to be out of state that day," said Robin, thinking he would hold their hands through it all. "Instead, Bob's wonderful paralegal, Libby, met us and guided us through the whole process. It was her first adoption experience also."

Tommy and Robin were led to the maternity ward with joyful anticipation. Years of praying for a child were minutes away. The nurse handed the child to Robin, who had endured until a baby of her own was placed into her arms. It was a moment of a lifetime.

Tommy remembers the scene well also. "I was as nervous as I could be. It wasn't that I felt something was going to go wrong. I've only been knee-knocking nervous twice in my life. One was when I got married and the other was when I held my baby boy for the first time. Knowing the awesome responsibility of raising a child was right there before me. Basically, we had only 36 hours notice, which makes adoption different from a natural pregnancy. In a pregnancy, you have nine months to prepare and plan.

"Libby handled all the paperwork and we literally walked out of that hospital with our baby in a borrowed car seat at 1:30 on that Saturday afternoon. The three of us, a family now, were on our way home."

Tommy and Robin had already decided on their son's name—John Michael—"John" after Robin's father John Rich and Tommy's friend John Croyle, and "Michael" after Robin's spiritual warrior brother-in-law, Michael (Mike) Griffin.

Only a handful of friends were aware of the Ford's adoption plans. The ones that knew eagerly awaited their return home. Tommy and Robin made a few calls when they got home late that afternoon.

Two special friends were Rich and Cheri Wingo. Rich is a former Alabama all-star linebacker and now a Sunday School teacher for young adults at First Baptist. Like Tommy and Robin, Rich and Cheri had undergone infertility, a miscarriage, and other similar circumstances before their children were born. So there was a close bond between the Fords and Wingos.

That night, Tommy placed a call to the Wingo home and got their answering machine. Tommy fondly recalls the message he left. "I wanted to pique his interest, so I said, 'Rich, I just want you to know that the *three* of us in the Ford family are doing really well.' Later that night, Rich called back and said, 'Tommy, what are you talking about? What's going on? Are you talking about you, Robin, Opie or Ellie?'

"I told him the whole story and he was stunned. We were prayer partners and had gone to many Promise Keepers conferences together and I know Rich and Cheri had been praying for Robin and me. Rich said, 'Well, man, we are coming over to see y'all tomorrow after church.'

"Sunday afternoon, the Wingo family came over to the house. We were back in our bedroom and they saw John Michael for the first time. I got a phone call and left the room."

Robin picks up the story. "They are ooing and gooing over him and Rich turns and says, 'Robin, Tommy said y'all had to go several hours away to get the baby. Do you mind telling me where he was born?' So I told him the town and the name of the hospital. He said, 'Do you know who delivered him?' I said, 'Well, it was a woman doctor.' I really didn't know her name. So I walked over and got the hospital papers out of the drawer. I read aloud her first and last name.

"Rich's face turned white as a sheet. He looked so stunned. He said, 'Robin, that's my first cousin and she's a wonderful Christian woman!' He called her full name including her maiden name – Wingo. Sure enough, I looked on the hospital papers and there was the name Wingo. So I just starting boohooing as I said to Rich, 'That's our angel! That's our angel that we had prayed for!' Rich was so moved that he turned away, walked over and looked out the window. The doctor who had delivered our baby was Rich's one and only first cousin. What are the odds of that happening?"

Tommy adds more to the amazing story and discovery. "The wondrous thing, too, was that Rich's cousin had been in that town for only six months. She was one of several doctors in her group that could have been on call that night, but she happened to be the one.

"When Rich later contacted her and asked her what she remembered about the delivery, she told Rich that she knew the baby was going to be adopted and that she had prayed in the delivery room that the baby find a good Christian home.

"We had prayed for an angel in the delivery room when we couldn't be there and God answered our prayer. It is so neat that the name Wingo is on our son's birth certificate. It was such a complete affirmation of God's love poured out on us. What an awesome blessing. It was like a miracle to us."

Through ten years of exhausting procedures, questioning and prayers in having a child, that slate of anxiety and pain was quickly wiped away as Tommy explains. "From the day we got John Michael, every single one of the disappointments, the bitterness, the impatience, the wondering why, the questioning God, every bit of it went away. It was absolutely like it got wiped away from our minds. The love that we have for our son and the circumstances by which he came to us so far outweigh all the disappointments we went through for ten years. They are just distant memories."

Robin makes a very important point on why God's way is always the best way. "I'm thankful that our plans didn't succeed. If our plan had succeeded, God's plan wouldn't have had a chance to. I look back now and am so glad that the IVF procedures didn't work for us. If it had, we wouldn't have this precious child today.

"Looking back, I wouldn't change my ten-year journey of waiting on the Lord for anything. I learned a great deal about myself and so much more about God. I learned that those years of praying didn't change God's mind – it changed me. I learned that His ways are higher than my ways. I look at my little boy's face and can't imagine life without him.

"John Michael is a living and breathing example of the sanctity of life. That birth mother could have easily aborted him and we wouldn't have him and all the joy and happiness that he brings to our lives."

At three years old today, John Michael has turned out to be a most adorable child. His loving parents have led him to love Jesus and Bible stories. He has such a charismatic spirit and an unusual loving heart as he greets friends of the family and other acquaintances. He is indeed an exceptional and special child and God gave him extra energy to explore life in all of its splendor and fullness.

And to Tommy and Robin Ford, he is an answer to prayer and a true miracle of a sovereign God.

CHAPTER SIX

CHAD AND LEAH GOSS

Chad Goss and Leah Monteith came to Alabama at the same time, had distinguished football and basketball careers respectfully, met at FCA, married before their senior year, and today are serving the Lord together.

It was August, 1993 when they arrived at The Capstone. Chad was a walk-on football player from Macon, GA. Leah came on a basketball scholarship from Centre, AL. Both discovered the Fellowship of Christian Athletes meetings their freshman year.

Chad was dating a member of the basketball team, who introduced him to Leah at an FCA meeting. It didn't take long for Chad and Leah to start seeing each other on a permanent basis. Their courtship grew and the summer before their junior year in 1996, Chad, the walk-on, worked all summer to earn money for either food or a ring for Leah.

When Chad reported for two-a-day workouts in August, he was hoping for a scholarship. "I knew there was a chance that I might get a scholarship because I had played the year before as a sophomore and had a good spring. I had saved up enough money the entire summer because I wanted to buy a ring for Leah and ask her to marry me.

"It was like, do I want to buy a ring or do I want to eat this semester? I just had to trust God. I told God, I believe that what you want for my life is to marry Leah. So I went ahead and bought the ring and was going to give it to her on the day she came back to school.

"When she came back, we had already had five days of two-a-day practices. So I took her to the Cypress Inn restaurant, our favorite in town, for lunch. Right there on the pier, I asked her to marry me and gave her the ring. That was between the two practices that day. So we had to put the celebration on hold.

"So I had taken a big risk. I went ahead and gave her the ring while hoping for a scholarship. The next day we had a scrimmage and I made a miraculous catch. It was just God. I think it was the play that sent me over the edge. The next day, Coach (Gene) Stallings said, 'Goss has fly-paper hands. Anything that's up in the air, he is going to catch.'

"On that play, I ran a post route on Fernando Bryant, who is now a starter for the Jacksonville Jaguars. Knowing I didn't have the speed to match Fernando, I ran down the middle of the field. Lance Tucker threw it up and I caught it with one hand. I actually pinned it up against my helmet with one hand. I was lying on the ground with the ball against my helmet. Our receiver coach Woody McCorvey raved over the catch later as we watched the practice film.

"The next day, Coach Stallings called four other players and myself into his office and gave us a scholarship. What a relief and what a blessing. I knew I could eat that semester and Leah had the ring I had worked for that summer. My worries and concerns were over," says Chad with a hearty laugh.

At Alabama it is unusual for a junior to be awarded a scholarship. Most are handed out to seniors. However, in Chad's case, no one was more deserving. His life growing up had not been easy.

When Chad was four years old, his mother Vicki was diagnosed with cancer and was told she had six months to live. She was only 22. Eighty percent of her liver had been removed, but it grew back and she was totally healed. Four years later, the cancer returned and all treatments were to no avail. She died on January 31, 1984 at age 27. Chad turned nine two weeks before her passing.

His two brothers and a sister moved in with his grandparents. Another blow would strike for Chad a year later when his grandfather died. He had been a healthy man all of his life. Chad loved him dearly and it was another great loss in his life. However, "Momma Goss," his grandmother, was a special lady and took good care of Chad, his brothers and sister.

Two other aunts, Lola and Gwen, gave the children much love and attention as well. However, a sister of Chad's dad, Jenice, would later become like a mother to Chad. Jenice had been best friends with Chad's mother, Vicki.

Sports became Chad's life especially between the ages of 12-14. In the eighth grade, he played football in the Macon Midget Football Association and scored 42 touchdowns. "People were saying that I was going to be the next great running back in the area," remembers Chad.

"Then I tore my knee up and I went from running a 4.6 time in the 40-yard dash to a 5.3 in six months. It was God's way of saying I'm going to make you depend on me. I had asked Christ into my heart when I was nine years old. I had an awareness of heaven and hell but there was no follow up for growth in my walk.

"When I was doing so well in football, I hung out with the wrong crowd. I began drinking alcohol and was doing things that the crowd influenced me into doing. So the knee injury got my attention."

Chad played high school football at Warner Robbins High School in Macon. They had won two USA TODAY national championships, so it was tough competition for a small 5-9, 165-pound quarterback. He was the starter as a junior and senior. In his final year, Chad passed for 1375 yards and Warner Robbins finished ninth in the nation. Chad also played baseball and was a three-year honor roll student.

"I sent video tapes to eight SEC schools," says Chad. "What is weird is that in the 1992 national championship game between Alabama and Miami, I was actually pulling for Miami because as a quarterback, I liked the way they threw the ball around a lot. I was pulling for Miami and I was upset because they had lost and Bama had won.

"Coach Danny Pearman of the Alabama staff contacted me. He said he thought I had ability but they didn't have any scholarships available. He believed I had enough ability to walk on and earn a scholarship.

"So I decided on Alabama. I walked on and had never seen the campus. Aunt Jenice and I came for orientation. She drove me to Tuscaloosa and I showed up for two-a-days with all the other walk-ons staying in Byrd Hall. There were 25 of us and maybe four of us graduated and stuck it out. I was the only one that got a scholarship."

Like Chad, Leah also grew up in Georgia. Her hometown was Rome until she turned 13. Her family then moved to Centre, AL. Leah loved sports and played basketball for fun. She loved picturesque Berry College in Rome and always thought it would be a good college to attend and play basketball.

Cherokee County High School had only beaten two teams the year before Leah arrived in Centre. With Leah on board, this team was about to orbit.

In her junior and senior years (1992 and 1993), Cherokee County won the Alabama Class 4A State Tournament. Leah was a true star. She set the 4A state record with 93 points in 1993. Her three-game totals were 29, 30 and 34 points, the latter in the championship game against Buckhorn. The Most Valuable Player award went to Leah, of course.

More honors followed. She was *The Birmingham News* 1993 Player of the Year and the biggest prize of all, 1993 "Miss Basketball" in the State of Alabama.

After scoring 2000 points at Cherokee County High, Leah was still thinking of Berry College and several other smaller schools. "Alabama and Auburn were the only large schools that showed an interest in me. I was really an Auburn fan. At that time, Auburn was basically a powerhouse," Leah remembers.

"I had gone to one of their basketball camps and I had gotten an award there. So I was just an Auburn fan. After my junior year, Coach (Rick) Moody spoke at our sports banquet. He had seen our championship game. In my senior year, Coach Dottie Kelso of the Alabama staff came to some practices and games.

"At that time, the coaches were saying that they knew I could score on offense. They were concerned about my defense." That proved to be funny for Leah to look back on since she turned out to be a fierce defender, one of Alabama's best ever.

"Our team went to an Auburn game that season and they showed me the locker room and everything. Basically right there on the court, Coach (Joe) Champi told me he wanted me to be playing for them. He pretty much offered me the scholarship.

"I was floored. I never in my wildest dreams thought I could play at Auburn. For me, it was like going to the pros.

"The next day I prayed about it. When I prayed I got this total peace that God wanted me to be at Alabama. The next morning I called Coach Moody and told him I wanted to come and play at Alabama." The decision had been made. Leah would play for Alabama and have a marvelous career.

Alabama had several guards and Leah agreed to be redshirted her first year. "Coach Moody called me in the day of the first game. He felt I would be wasting a year to play some and sit on the bench with so many junior and senior guards. So I understood and agreed to redshirt.

"That year was hard because we went to the Final Four. I dressed out for every game and did everything the team did. I just didn't play. I learned a lot which I think paid off."

The next season, Leah averaged 15 minutes per game which is good time on the court for a freshman. Leah saw action in every game.

It was the beginning of a remarkable feat in Leah's career. The 5-9 guard would play in every game in her four years at Alabama. It would be 129 games for an awesome accomplishment and a school record. She was truly a coach's dream. No injury sidelined her in that span.

What's more, Leah, wearing jersey No. 32 started every game as a sophomore, junior and senior. She also scored 180 goals from the 3-point range. However, her greatest contribution was on defense. She was one of Bama's all-time best defensive players.

Coach Moody would assign Leah to the opponent's best shooter when she was a sophomore and throughout her career. "I just loved playing defense," says Leah. "When I was a sophomore, I would guard Niesa Johnson in practice. She was our All-American and just an incredible player. So that helped me guard the best of our opposition."

Even when Leah was a junior, she declared on her page in the Alabama media guide: "When I play defense, I try to stop that person from scoring. It's like a goal for me, for a person not to score on me."

One of Leah's career highlights occurred her sophomore season against Maine's great player Cindy Blodgett. "Our team had lost to Maine up there when I was a freshman. Cindy got 30 something points on us. I remember sitting on the sidelines thinking, I wish I could go out there and guard her because I just knew I could stop her.

"My highlight came the next season when we played Maine in our Capstone Inn Classic. I got to guard Cindy and held her to four points. It was a great feeling. We won the game by 36 points." Blodgett went on to lead the nation in scoring with 27 points per game.

Leah contributed much to Alabama's great success on the court. The team reached the NCAA Regionals every year she was on the squad. In 1997, she was AP honorable mention All-American. She made a difference not only as a player, but as a spiritual leader as well.

To cap it all off, Leah finished her career as the most decorated academic player in Alabama's basketball history earning four Academic All-SEC honors.

Meanwhile, over on the football practice field less than a hundred yards from the Coleman Coliseum where Leah was practicing, Chad was getting killed as a scout team quarterback.

Ask Chad about his first year on the team and his reply would be, "I got destroyed. I was the first team scout team quarterback. We had a good scout team and our game day was every Tuesday. It was full pads and full go against the first team defense."

Chad's role was to be the opponent quarterback that week and run their offense. Some weeks he would be Peyton Manning of Tennessee, Eric Zeier of Georgia or Patrick Nix of Auburn.

"I had bloody noses. I was knocked senseless a few times. I got high-lowed every now and then by our defensive line. They poured through our offensive line like water. Their defense was ranked No. 1 in the nation against the run, pass and everything." The previous year, Alabama had won the national championship with a great defense.

"Coach (Mike) DuBose was defensive line coach. He would always tell them 'to run to me and through me,' and they did.

"I had started off dead last on the depth chart. I think I was the four-teenth quarterback. Our top quarterbacks were Jay Barker, Brian Burgdorf, Freddie Kitchens, Lance Tucker and it just went on and on. I eventually worked myself up behind Lance as some quit."

In that 1993 season, Chad got to dress out for two games. In prepa-ration for the Vanderbilt game, Chad scored six touchdowns running the Vandy I-Bone offense. Coach Stallings rewarded him by dressing him out in Nashville. It was the second game of the season. The other game was the Gator Bowl game against North Carolina.

Chad took his licks again on the scout team in 1994 at quarterback and now pass receiver. In the spring of 1995, Coaches Pearman, McCorvey and (Brother) Oliver saw his potential on specialty teams. Things were looking up for Chad.

As a sophomore in 1995, Chad saw action in nine games. He was on every specialty team and even returned his first collegiate punt for seven yards against Tennessee. He had 70 plays for the season. The biggest play came in the first game against Vanderbilt.

The play still excites Chad as he describes what happened. "We had planned this fake punt all week. I was going to sneak on the field and report to the refs. They said, 'Now Chad you run onto the field inside the (yard) numbers and tell the referees that you are reporting. Our offense was running off of the field so it kind of looked like I was going off the field with them. But before I got to the sideline, I stopped and lined up as one of the 11 men on the field. So nobody came out there to defend me.

"So that was called our 'spread punt.' When nobody on Vandy's team saw me to come over and defend me, I got excited. I'm thinking, I am fixing to score a touchdown! God, please let me catch this ball! I don't want to drop this ball wide open. The plan was, if nobody came out on me, our punter Hayden Stockton would throw it to me.

"The ball was snapped, Hayden turned and threw it to me. I caught it and I was running down the field with only one man, the punt return-er, between me and the goal line. I knew I could beat him, so I faked him out. He fell on the ground. Our sprint man on the other side of the field came across to block for me and, low and behold, his man tackled me. If he had not brought his man across, I would have scored."

The play covered 49 yards and it was the first catch of Chad's career. The Tide went on to score and won a close battle, 33-25.

As a junior in 1996, Chad had earned his scholarship and had worked his way into the rotation at split end. He was on all specialty teams including punt returner. "I had never returned punts in my life. Our other guys were dropping punts and one day Coach Stallings said in frustration, 'Can anybody out here catch a punt?' Coach McCovey said, 'Goss can. He's got the best hands on the team.' So that's how I began returning punts."

No doubt, one of Chad's worst nightmares in his entire young life, not just as a football player, came as a punt return man. It came at season's end in the Outback Bowl against Michigan in Tampa. Coach Stallings had already announced his retirement. A victory would give him 70 wins in seven seasons at Alabama. Everybody wanted that magical mark so badly for the well-liked coach.

Michigan was out front 6-3 at halftime. The third quarter was scoreless. With 12:13 remaining in the game, Dwayne Rudd picked off a Brian Griese pass and returned it 88 yards for a touchdown. Alabama was up 10-6. Two possessions later, Shaun Alexander raced 46 yards to make it 17-6 with 2:15 left to play.

Chad's nightmare was about to happen. Michigan was forced to punt. Chad was the lone return man standing on the 10-yard line.

"Their punter was going to try and punt it inside the 10 yard line. Well, I'm standing there at the 10. The rule is if you are standing on the 10 and the ball goes over your head, you let it go. If you have to take a step back, you let it go to wherever the ball is going to stop. You can't risk a fumble here.

"Anyway, I thought I had only taken one step back. Instead, I had taken about eight steps back and I fair caught the ball on the ONE YARD LINE. I didn't know it at first. I was just thanking God that I had caught the ball. The sun was right in my eyes. The ball was real high. Anyway, I caught it and I said 'Yes' with a sigh of relief you know.

"Well, the Michigan guys were laughing and I thought, 'What's going on?' Then I looked down and I was on the one-yard line. I just slowly dropped the ball because I knew what would be awaiting me at the sideline. I kind of looked to see if there was a clear line to the locker room because I was ready to hightail it there.

"I started jogging as slowly as humanly possible to the sideline. There was Coach Stallings staring daggers through me. His hands were on his hips just fuming. Everybody always likes to crowd the sidelines down on the field. The closer I got to Coach Stallings the more everybody just backed up and away. It was like the parting of the Red Sea. Now it was just Coach and me.

"He looks at me and I'm expecting a barrage of insults and every-thing because I deserved them. He looks at me dead in the eye with his bottom lip quivering and you could tell he was really ticked off. He said, 'Hey man, do you know how angry that makes me?' That is the last thing I expected. I was expecting him to ream me out.

"I said, 'Yes, sir. I know. I feel pretty bad about it myself.' Then he said, 'How can you be that stupid?' Then he goes into other things that he had taught us and he just keeps saying, 'How can you be so stupid?' I just had to stand there and take it. And then he just walks off.

"Then, he comes back to me and says, 'And hey, you're the guy that calls everybody up to pray, and you go and do something stupid like that.' Coach was always comparing things that came from outside at the heat of the moment. I had led the team in prayer for two years.

"Anyway, our team started punching the ball out from the one yard line. We avoided a safety and a turnover and punted the ball out. It was during that time that somebody tapped me on the shoulder and said Coach DuBose wants to talk to you. I walked over to him and he said, 'Chad, forget about it. Keep your head up. The game is not over.'"

Those were smart words from a coach who had already been named the next head coach at Alabama a couple of weeks before.

Michigan came roaring back with an 80-yard scoring drive in less than two minutes. With two points added to the touchdown, it was 17-14 with less than a minute to go. Michigan lined up for an onside kick to get the ball back and try to win the game.

"We're getting ready and they call in the Hands Team. I'm on the Hands Team and placed in the position of the person who has the best hands on the team. They place me right where they think the kicker will kick the ball.

"So we huddle up and I'm about to run on the field. Right before I run on the field, Shaun Alexander grabs me. He is a freshman at that time but we were close through FCA. He looks at me in the face and says, 'Man, you are going to catch this ball.' He says, 'You are going to get it. Be ready.'

"I ran out there and sure enough, the guy kicks the ball and it is bouncing perfect and coming right at Patrick Hape who jumped out there to try to recover it. He is between me and the kicker. The ball bounces up high and he being 6-5 jumps up and the ball tips right off of his hands and it's coming straight to me. It is like slow motion.

"I jump and lay out for the ball. I catch it, curl up and all of my teammates rush over and cover me up. We got unpiled and I jumped up and ran to the sideline with high fives for everybody. I'm so elated. Everybody goes crazy because we knew we had won the game.

"As I run to the sideline, Coach Stallings is standing there. He walks out onto the field and he meets me with a smile from ear to ear. He looks at me, shakes my hand and pats me on the shoulder and says, 'You're forgiven!'

"Since that time, I have taken a lot of ribbing from my buddies and I've had to tell that story many times. It sure wasn't funny then, but it is now and I'm thankful that it had a happy ending."

That was New Year's Day and the following May 24, 1997, Chad and Leah were married in Centre. It was the best catch Chad ever made. "When Rev. Phil Young married us," Chad says, "He said, 'Chad, Roll Tide and kiss the bride!'

"When we walked out of the church, they played 'Yea Alabama.' It was a surprise to Leah, but I was in on the setup. I didn't want her to cancel the idea. Everybody loved it."

By the time Chad's senior season had rolled around, he was a key player for the team. He had earned his spurs from those tough days as a battered scout team quarterback. Chad started every game at split end.

Highlights included a 35-yard one-handed touchdown grab from Freddie Kitchens against Kentucky at Lexington. ESPN ran the catch many times. Chad followed that with an end around touchdown pass of 40 yards that he threw to Quincy Jackson.

Moreso, Chad had followed in Jay Barker's footsteps as FCA leader and inspirational leader on the team. The team voted Chad the Charlie Compton Award recipient as the senior who had demonstrated the most outstanding Christian leadership. Chad received his award at the Calvary Baptist Church on Squad Sunday, a week before the season .

To know Chad Goss is to know a fast moving, free-spirited person. God blessed Chad with lots of energy. He is a risk taker and mischievous. He doesn't mind coming across the middle for a pass knowing that he may get clocked by a linebacker. He's a 'go all out' kind of guy in everything he does.

One of the smartest things that Chad did when he arrived at Alabama was finding the right kind of friends to hang out with. Guys like Jay Barker, Jason Cole, Roman Colburn, Mickey Conn, Matt Wethington, Lee Ferguson and Curtis Alexander were men whose faith was more important than football and academics.

Chad jumped right into Fellowship of Christian Athletes meetings every Wednesday night. Jay was the leader. Chad had made a true commitment to Christ at age 15 when evangelist Rick Stanley came to town and preached. Rick is the stepbrother of Elvis Presley.

The speakers at FCA and the fellowship deepened Chad's commitment. Jay led Chad, Curtis and Lee in a Bible Study every Tuesday night at eight for an hour. That was meaningful discipleship for Chad.

In the spring of 1995, Chad took over leadership of the FCA when Jay moved on. Chad would serve for two and a half years. His enthusiasm for the ministry helped reach out to more students at meetings. Crowds grew so much that meetings were moved from the Baptist Student Center Chapel to a much larger Allan Watson College Annex across the street from Calvary Baptist Church.

"FCA was the highlight of the week for Leah and me," says Chad. "Leah and I are so pleased that we met at FCA. That's so neat for us. The FCA meetings were like a pot of Christianity. It didn't matter what church you were affiliated with. It really bonded athletes together."

Leah remembers how "it was so great to invite teammates to FCA. They may not attend church with you, but they would go to FCA. Bringing friends to FCA increased your joy in reaching others for Christ."

Chad spoke approximately 150 times in the last three years in Alabama to different groups. Leah would join him many times and share her testimony as well.

Chad got his degree in Public Relations in May, 1998. However, a month before he became College Minister at the Church of Tuscaloosa, a new church in town. During that time, the church sponsored The Station, a Christian hangout spot on "The Strip" which is known for its student bar hopping.

"We had a huge ministry at The Station," Chad gladly recalls. "Some nights after home football games, we would have 350-400 students packed in there. We had a no drinking and a no smoking rule. We would have live Christian rock bands performing amongst the pool shooting and basketball on the outside."

In January, 1999, Chad and Leah moved to Centre where Chad became Youth Minister at the First United Methodist Church. Leah was girls' basketball coach at Tuscaloosa Academy that winter. In the fall, she became a sixth grade math and science teacher at Centre Middle School and coached the girls' basketball and volleyball teams.

Chad has since moved on to the National Auction Group in Gadsden as a marketing executive. He and Leah will always be involved in Christian ministry with youth. They have a heart for God who has blessed them far beyond their wildest dreams.

CHAPTER SEVEN

COACH MARK GOTTFRIED

You might say Mark Gottfried wastes no time. Eleven years after Mark played his last basketball game for Alabama, he returned at age 34 as head basketball coach with a beautiful wife and five precious children.

When he took the Alabama job on March 25, 1998, he brought with him a wealth of coaching experience. He had spent seven special years at UCLA and three as head mentor at Murray State.

At the tender age of 34, he became one of the youngest head coaches in the history of the rugged Southeastern Conference.

Mark also brought to Tuscaloosa a national championship ring. He was a full-time assistant for Jim Harrick when the mighty UCLA Bruins won it all in 1995. Mark was right in the middle of that fabulous team and success story.

The young coach has big dreams for Alabama, too. He is well on his way and in time, Mark will compete with the best teams in America.

When you consider the life of Mark Gottfried, one very important ingredient stands out. It is a part of Mark's life that is more important than basketball. That one aspect is the word "family."

Mark was blessed with two wonderful parents in Joe and Mary Gottfried. When Mark was born, his dad was the high school basketball coach in Crestline, Ohio, a little railroad town of 1,500 people. Mark's older sister was named Christie.

Mark's dad had the perfect job for his son. Joe moved around in the high school coaching circles in Ohio and eventually took the Ashland College (OH) job.

"I grew up in the gym," says Mark proudly. "Everyday when school was out at three o'clock, I would ride my bicycle to the gym. I would grab a basketball and play around as my daddy coached.

"I can still hear him say, 'Hold the ball, Mark, while I'm talking. You can dribble while they are dribbling. Hold the ball, Mark.'"

Church was also a meaningful part of Mark's young life, too. The family was always faithful and active in Roman Catholic churches

103

wherever they lived. Faith in God was instilled in Mark from the beginning.

Mark proved in college that he wastes no time when he met his wife Elizabeth and several years later started his own family.

"I can remember it as if it were yesterday," says Mark smiling as he recalled the night he met Elizabeth. "We were sitting in a Fellowship of Christian Athletes meeting in Bryant Hall. They passed around a clipboard where you signed your name, you know. Elizabeth was on the same row as I was. She was eight or ten people to my left.

"A good looking girl, she grabbed my attention and caught my eye. I got a hold of that clipboard when it came and I counted back to make sure what her name was. I managed to get over and meet her as we guys do in those kinds of settings. Then, after the meeting four or five of us went over to TCBY for yogurt next to the Bama Bowl and she was in the group.

"Alabama was playing Penn State the following Saturday on campus in football. I asked her to go with me, but she said her dad was coming over from Birmingham to attend the game with her. Elizabeth was just a freshman and I was in my third year. Anyway, we made a date for after the game.

"So after the game, I called her from the Bryant Hall lobby telephone. She was living in Tutwiler Hall where all the freshman girls live. That phone rang and rang and rang. No answer. I continued to let the phone ring and ring and ring. Finally, I said, 'I am going to call one more time.' This time, she was just getting back to her room and we went out that night. My car broke down on me, but we had a good time.

"I liked her so much that I asked her out Sunday, Monday, Tuesday, Wednesday and Thursday. Ken Johnson, one of my teammates, had a motorcycle. Wimp (Sanderson) would have killed him if he knew he had that motorcycle. So he let me borrow it and I took Elizabeth riding out to the lake. We'd go out there and walk around and talk. I fell in love fast."

So at this point in Mark's life, he had found his life partner. Marriage would follow. Only God knew that their family would, in a few years, bring such joy and happiness.

As a young boy, Mark's family made a deep impression on his choice of vocation as a coach. His dad, Joe, was the oldest of three sons. His second brother was Mike Gottfried. Mike was also a coach, but football was his game. Mark watched his Uncle Mike serve as head football coach at Murray State, Kansas and Pittsburgh. Uncle Mike had good success. Then he joined ESPN as a national game-day color analyst. Mike has been in the booth for several years calling some of college football's top headliner games.

Mark's dad had a first cousin named Jack Harbaugh. Jack coached football at Michigan and Stanford. His son, Jim, chose to play quarterback for Michigan and is now with the San Diego Chargers after several years in the NFL. Jim's youngest brother, John, coaches the defensive backs for the Philadelphia Eagles. Uncle Jack is the head football coach at Western Kentucky.

"In the summers as a young boy in Crestline, the Harbaughs and the Gottfrieds spent so much time together. In fact, our family houses were next door to each other. So Jim, John and I spent a lot of time together playing ball as kids.

"In fact, my dad can tell you that Crestline was a cradle for coaches. Many other men came out of Crestline and coached all over the place from that small town. Jim, John and I stay in close touch. We have always followed each others careers."

Mark's dad and Uncle Mike were the influences that began Mark's quest to be a coach when he was only eight years old. "The thing I remember about my dad and uncle in coaching was not their records, but more than anything, watching them develop these relationships with their players. I remember players constantly at our house eating ham sandwiches and just sitting there watching television.

"I remember when my Uncle Mike was the head coach at Murray State. One day he had all 80 of his football players holding hands singing, 'Love Lifted Me.' It was unbelievable. Those are the kind of things that got me interested in coaching. Plus, I was around basketball camps and later on as my dad coached in college, I got a first hand look at the recruiting process."

So once again, Mark wasted no time in choosing his vocation. Coaching got into his blood early and for good reason. Family had a heavy influence into his called profession.

Mark made a decision in the ninth grade about his own career. He decided to give up baseball and concentrate on just one sport. "I figured if I had a chance to be good, I needed to concentrate on one sport. Basketball was it," says Mark.

In Mark's last four years of high school, he found himself playing for three high schools in three different states… Ohio, Illinois and Alabama. Cliff Ellis, athletic director at the University of South Alabama, hired Mark's dad as Assistant Athletic Director.

So Mark spent his senior year at Mobile's UMS-Wright prep school, a military school for boys. "I wore a tie, gray pants and a blue shirt every day," says Mark with a smile. "It was a good academic environment and an interesting experience for me. I enjoyed it. Besides, it was just for one year."

Changing schools didn't slow Mark down in his skills on the court. He emerged as an all-state player averaging 22 points per game and five assists per game. In his career best game, he had 30 points, 16 assists and seven steals against Alba High School.

Recruiters found Mark's front door fast. Coach Mike Krzyzewski at Duke recruited Mark consistently and Mark enjoyed his visit to Duke very much. Other visits were to Ohio State, Alabama, Auburn and Mississippi. Ennis Whatley, an All-American guard, was at Alabama.

Mark chose neither of those schools. Instead he chose Oral Roberts University in Tulsa. "I look back on it today, and there is no doubt in my mind that God had his hand in my decision. Most people were scratching their heads. The ORU coach was Ken Hayes and he was the biggest reason I went there. He was a great Christian man and I had a good relationship with him. One day I woke up and I knew that was the school I was suppose to attend.

"Yes, I did receive many letters from Oral Roberts himself. He was active in recruiting. We became close when I went to school there. He took a high interest in the basketball program."

Even though Mark only stayed at ORU one year, he had an experience that made it all worthwhile.

"We had a player on team who was a walk-on who wasn't a very talented guy, but he was always reading his Bible. I would always wonder why he wanted to do that? Growing up in church, I had never really had any kind of daily devotion and had never read the Bible personally.

"One night we went over to a big crusade service they were having in the Mabee Center, the basketball arena. I sat up there and Oral Roberts himself made an altar call. I felt like it was something I needed to do. I had never asked Jesus into my life or understood what it meant. I had never understood the concept of grace to be honest. I had never understood that when we ask forgiveness of our sins, God forgives us of our sins as if they had never happened.

"So I felt convicted and just felt so good in my heart about going forward when Oral Roberts gave the altar call. Another basketball player named Sam Tanner was sitting next to me. He told me if I wanted him to walk down beside me, he would do it. And he did. Right there is when I gave my life to Christ."

So Mark had his answer on why he went to ORU. That Christmas, Mark's real reason for selecting ORU, Coach Ken Hayes, was fired. Turmoil developed inside the team. Players began to transfer. Mark began to look elsewhere.

Mark was serious in considering only three schools. One was Kansas where Larry Brown was the head coach and his Uncle Mike Gottfried was the football coach. The second was Tulsa, right there in town, where Nolan Richardson was head coach. The third was Alabama.

"Wimp (Sanderson) came out to see me. I had already visited Alabama as a possible place to transfer. Wimp got into a Marriott Hotel and he said, 'I'm going to stay in the Marriott until you tell me you are coming.' He had been out there a day or two. It was real cold. So I called him and told him to come on over.

"He took a taxi over to the campus. It was the funniest thing really. He got out with the scholarship papers. I signed them on top of the taxicab. We shook hands. He got into the cab and left for the airport."

In the fall of 1984, Mark enrolled at Alabama and moved into Bryant Hall. His roommate was Jim Farmer. They would room together for the next four years in Room 303. Sitting out a year was hard, but Mark realized the value of playing his fifth year at the age of 23.

"When I first moved in, I met Hoss Johnson, a big tackle on the football team who was an FCA leader. Rob Cain was a student worker in the dorm who became a close friend through Bible Studies that he led. Then there was Jeff Schulte, who was assigned to Alabama by Athletes in Action, an arm of Campus Crusade for Christ. Jeff was from Dayton, OH and a former Yale football player.

"To show you how God works, somehow Ray Perkins, our Athletic Director, had given Jeff permission to eat meals in Bryant Hall and be around the football and basketball players. Being that we had Ohio backgrounds, he kind of sought me out. Maybe he thought it was worth investing his time in me, so he discipled me through the scripture.

"As Jeff was pouring his heart into me, I gave him some resistance. A big, university campus was new to me. I was riding the roller coaster so to speak. But we became close and spent many hours together in the Bible as he taught me Christian concepts that caused me to grow in my walk with Christ. Outside of my family, no other man has had such an impact on me spiritually than Jeff Schulte.

"There were many, many times when Jeff was discipling me that he displayed tough Christian love. He kind of called a spade, a spade. He brought me to the carpet and said, 'I care enough about you that I am going to confront you where you are going to have to make some decisions. We are going to see if you are going to walk the walk.' So many times he brought me to the moment of truth where I had to take a good long look at myself and decide if I was going to be serious about my Christian faith or not. He really challenged me spiritually.

"You see, Jim and I had made our academic schedules around the soap, 'Days of Our Lives.' For four years, we both made sure we didn't have a class between 11 and 1 o'clock. We would eat from 11 until noon and then watch the show in our room at noon. And Jeff made it a point to come and sit in there and watch with us. I know later, he had no interest in that show. He would sit there and develop a relationship. We became awfully close and God used him greatly in my life."

Mark was also a regular at Wednesday night FCA meetings when the team wasn't playing. He recognized the value of his influence as a student/athlete and made himself available on many occasions to youth groups, churches, school groups and other such audiences.

On the basketball court, Mark started his final three years (1985-87) as Alabama reached the Sweet 16 in the NCAA Tournament all three seasons. He played with future NBA players such as Derrick McKey, Keith Askins, Michael Ansley and his roommate Jim. Those were three of the best years of basketball in Alabama history.

During his senior season, Alabama had 28 wins, the most in school history. The team was SEC champions and won the SEC tournament in Atlanta. Mark made 81 three-point field goals that year. He had eight against Vanderbilt, which is a school record shared with Alvin Lee. It was the first year, fortunately for Mark, for the three-point shot in the NCAA.

Mark also earned Academic All-SEC honors and was named Bryant Award Winner as the University's top scholar-athlete of the year. It was quite an honor. Mark was drafted by the Detroit Pistons in the seventh round and was cut prior to the season. "I had decided that if I didn't make the NBA, I wasn't going to try other leagues. I felt like as an adult right out of college, I wanted to be around Christian men on a daily basis. So I played on the AIA (Athletes in Action) team my first year out. It was one of the best decisions I have ever made."

In January of 1988 as Mark was with the AIA team, he flew back to Tuscaloosa for an important duty. "Elizabeth was still in school and I surprised her when I came in. I took her to the parking lot of Bryant Hall, the place where we had met four years earlier. We got out of the car. I pulled out a ring and asked her to marry me.

"So we got married on August 20, 1988 at the First Presbyterian Church in Tuscaloosa. Neither of us attended there. Her family had moved from Birmingham to Atlanta. It seemed natural that we marry in Tuscaloosa. Dad was my best man. Jim and Jeff were in my wedding."

It would take patience and a test of faith, but exciting days were just around the corner for newlyweds Mark and Elizabeth.

Several months prior to their marriage, Mark had already contacted several colleges about being a graduate assistant. The Pistons had asked Mark to play in their Los Angeles summer league. Coach Jim Harrick had been named the UCLA coach in April. Mark applied for his G.A. job even though he didn't know him, but Harrick knew Coach Sanderson and other people in Mark's family.

"In July, Coach Harrick called my mother in Mobile looking for me. He didn't know I was in Los Angeles. So even without a car, I made my way over to his office to see him. He told me he would be making a decision soon. Meanwhile, Wimp offered me his G.A. job and sort of put the pressure on me to take it. He knew I was getting married. Elizabeth had an apartment and it would be so easy for me to move right in as his grad assistant.

"With Alabama on the semester system, Wimp needed to know by August 28. UCLA was on the quarter system so Coach Harrick was not in that big of a hurry to make a decision. I felt if I had an opportunity to start coaching at UCLA, I said I'm going for it. So I told Wimp no and waited for about a month.

"So Coach Harrick called and offered me the position. When I told him later about passing up Alabama and waiting for him, he told me, 'You're crazy!' So after the first of September, we got into Elizabeth's MGB and drove to Los Angeles. I didn't know anybody out there except Coach Harrick."

It seemed that God ordained Mark's steps to UCLA, a college basketball mecca. What a place to start your coaching career and three weeks after you are married!

For the next seven years, UCLA reached the NCAA tournament. Mark worked his way from a grad assistant to a full-time assistant and recruiter. The 1994 recruiting class was the nation's top class. Nine players Mark helped coach went on to NBA careers. Mark's last season capped it all as UCLA won the national championship in Seattle.

If that wasn't enough, while at UCLA Mark had the privilege of getting close to the Wizard of Westwood, Coach John Wooden. "I met Coach Wooden the first fall I was at UCLA. Jim took our staff out one morning. We went by and picked up Coach Wooden and took him to breakfast. It was a place near his condo much like a Shoney's. I remember at first being so intimidated. But there we were having breakfast and here's this legendary coach eating his pancakes and wiping syrup off his chin. I'm thinking this is John Wooden, perhaps the greatest basketball coach of all time. He's just like the rest of us.

"But I got over the intimidation. That didn't last long. From there, Coach Wooden invited us to drop by his place any time. Drop by, sit down, and spend an hour. So I took advantage of the invitation and went by to see him dozens of times. For many years, Elizabeth and I lived out near him and many times I would stop after practice and talk. I'd call and say, 'Coach, I'm stopping by.' He'd say, 'Come on. I'm here.'

"We'd sit and talk. More than anything it was philosophy of coaching, teaching, life, family and spiritual things. There were very little x's and o's. There was very little about out of bounds plays and zone defenses. That was one-tenth of what we talked about.

"He's so wise, yet so humble. I'd ask him a question about discipline or something. Then he would always tell me a story. 'Well, Mark, in 1964,' and then he would tell me a story and there would be a moral to the story. Today, I treasure those times with Coach Wooden. There is no way I can measure the wisdom he gave me and the confidence that was instilled in me by spending so much time with him. I thank God for it."

After the 1995 national championship, Mark was ready for a head coaching opportunity. He had turned down some prior offers, but Murray State's offer was right for Mark. He brought in Tom Kelsey, whom he knew from AIA days, and Philip Pearson, a former Crimson Tide player, as assistants.

For the next three seasons, Murray State won the Ohio Valley Conference championship. The first team went to the National Invitational Tournament and the last two were in the Big Dance, the NCAA tourney. Mark's team fell to Duke by only four points in the first trip and, as fate would have it, Jim Harrick's Rhode Island team eliminated Mark's second team in the NCAA. Mark's third team at Murray State posted an incredible 29-4 final mark.

Meanwhile, basketball wasn't everything in the life of Elizabeth and Mark. They were married three years before their first child, Brandon, was born in 1991. "Brandon and Mary Layson were born in the UCLA Medical Center. When we moved to Murray, Elizabeth was seven and a half months pregnant with Cameron. Then Aaron and Dillon followed while we were at Murray," says Mark proudly.

"The five children came within six years of each other," says Elizabeth who had other aspirations as a youngster that were far from motherhood. "My dad was a pilot and I grew to love planes as a very young girl. When I was in the second grade, I dreamed of being an astronaut, getting into the space program and going to the moon.

"In the eighth grade, I set my sights on going to the Air Force Academy to be a jet pilot. I did pass up a nomination to the Academy as a high school senior in Birmingham. I came to the University of Alabama on a Presidential Scholarship and did participate in the ROTC program for four years.

"It was during my freshman year that I became a Christian, so that made it all worth while. Right after Mark and I met, we went to a Burger King one night and he asked me a surprising question. He said, 'If you died, do you know where you will go?' I knew I didn't have a right relationship with Christ and doubted if I would go to heaven. So a short time after that, I prayed to receive Christ into my life. My involvement in Campus Crusade helped me so much in discovering a new life in Christ.

"As it turned out, my plan was certainly not God's plan. I didn't know he wanted me to be a Mommy and a coach's wife instead of a jet pilot. I found that His plan is always so much better than ours."

Elizabeth was the oldest of five children herself, but there were 15 years between her and the baby. Five children in six years kept a beautiful young woman like Elizabeth busy. She can casily be mistaken today for a coed on campus.

"It wasn't anything we planned. We just kept getting pregnant quickly after each child. I love how close our children are age wise. There are many benefits. They play together. They are friends and have the same friends their age. Plus, it is easy to pass the clothes on down," says Elizabeth with a laugh.

When out in the public, Elizabeth says the comments are about the same. "People will say, 'Are all five yours?' 'Are any of them twins?' 'My, you have your hands full, don't you?'

Elizabeth's mission was easy to discover, being blessed with five children just six years apart. The ease with which she manages her gifts from God is most admirable. She is also so devoted to Mark in his profession and gives him her full support at every home game with cheers and applause.

"God's plan is always perfect," says Elizabeth. "His will is done and that's what I wanted."

"Elizabeth is an unbelievable mom. She is unbelievable," says Mark boastfully in re-enforcing his point. "She is strong enough to handle five children. She is just tremendous with them and I'm so blessed to have such a supportive wife as a coach and such a tremendous mother for our children.

"When we are out in public, people are usually shocked," Mark says smiling. "People will sometimes ask, 'How do you do it?' Elizabeth and I have always loved kids, so we are thankful unto God for the beautiful kids he has given us. We are truly blessed. There is no question about that."

When Mark replaced David Hobbs at Alabama, he was virtually the only coach the Alabama fans wanted. He was a former top player for Alabama. He was young. He was successful at a Division I-A school. He had the UCLA experience. Athletic Director Bob Bockrath got hundreds of pleas from the Alabama faithful to hire Mark.

The state media jammed the Alabama media room when Mark was announced as head coach on March 25, 1998. It was remarkable what Mark had experienced and accomplished over the past 11 years. Now he was overjoyed to be back at his alma mater as head coach at the age of only 34. You couldn't write a better script.

Standing by his side was his vivacious wife Elizabeth who had three children in diapers. That had to be an NCAA record for a new Division I-A coach.

Becoming a part of the athletic family, Mark's presence was like a ray of sunshine to the athletic program. He gave the athletic program the lift it needed after a 4-7 football season and a losing basketball campaign. His first recruiting class was in the nation's top ten. He was a welcomed coach and fans couldn't have been more thrilled with Mark.

Highlights of Mark's first year included a 62-58 victory over Kentucky in Tuscaloosa, home and away wins over Arkansas. His team won its first SEC tournament game over Georgia and earned an NIT tourney bid, losing to Wake Forest in Winston-Salem.

An even better recruiting class followed. Some had the group in the nation's top five.

However, Mark created a classic moment in Alabama basketball history when he brought dozens of former players and coaches in on

August 27-28, 1999, for "The Legends Weekend." Returning were seven decades of players from the first 1934 SEC championship team, the wonder team called "The Rocket 8" in the 1950's, the great SEC championship teams of the 1970's, plus outstanding NBA talent of the 1990's.

It was a grand ole time at the Friday night banquet and 10,000 turned out in August to watch Alabama's finest players compete in a basketball game on Saturday night. Mark brought the Alabama basketball family back together in one spectacular weekend performance. The former players and coaches couldn't praise Mark enough for a once in a lifetime player reunion.

Mark's second season at the helm was devastating with numerous injuries to key personnel. Many starting lineups included four freshmen and a junior. However, young talented troops were gaining invaluable experience in the tough SEC for next year and the next. It was a year of patience and preparation for better days ahead as the team finished with a disappointing 13-16 record.

In Mark's third Tide recruiting effort, he and his staff collected some of the South's finest talent. Most of the recruiting experts rated prize recruit Gerald Wallace of Childersburg, AL as the finest prospect in the nation. It would be a first such honor for Alabama to attract the nation's best.

Soon after Mark settled into his new office in Coleman Coliseum, he made a suggestion that validated his heart and interest in other men in the department. It authenticated some of the reason why the young coach had raised the attitude level since he arrived.

Mark approached three or four staff and fellow coaches about having a Bible Study one morning a week. Five or six men in the department began to meet for Bible Study every Tuesday morning from 7 until 8.

The place was Mark's staff meeting room. It is not your typical staff meeting room. For 24 years, it was the office of Coach Paul 'Bear' Bryant, located on the second floor of Coleman Coliseum. At first, different staff or coaches would lead the Bible Study for a month at a time. After a year, Rob Cain, a local youth pastor close to all the athletic staff, became the regular Bible Study leader. Rob has since joined the Billy Graham Evangelistic Association and works in Franklin Graham Festivals. However, he still lives in Tuscaloosa and conducts the Bible Studies when he is in town.

After two years, an average of 15 men meet each Tuesday morning at 7. As many as 21 have crowded into Coach Bryant's former office. Rob presents a Bible Study gut check to the men every week. The meeting is also a time of prayer for those in need within the department and among family and friends.

The Bible Study has met all of Mark's expectations. "The Bible Study has challenged me every week as I know it has all the other men," says Mark. "It has helped keep our compass pointed true north. It has been real encouraging to watch other guys and see their faith grow deeper and take steps that maybe they wouldn't have taken without the Bible Study.

"I felt when I got here that my responsibility was much deeper than just winning games. From the position I'm in, I wanted to help facilitate guys in their spiritual growth anyway I could. I feel strongly that is something God wanted to have done and I feel like the men who are coming are making a statement about what is important to them."

Mark's perspective on being the coach at Alabama is clear also. "For me, obviously I want to win. I want to win the national championship like every other coach. That is a burning desire, just the competitive nature that is inside of me.

"Probably in the last ten years I have started to realize just how important it is to use the position God has given you to have an impact upon people. Primarily, that is your players. Outside of your players, there are people you work with everyday, plus your community.

"It can't be just about winning. I look at older coaches that are retired. It seems like we boil down their careers to one statement many times. Well, he was a good motivator or a good coach. He was a good offensive mind. He went to the NCAA tournament. He ran the high post offense well.

"You hope that your players look back on the relationship that you had with them and the impact you made upon their lives. That's one thing I witnessed from Coach Wooden. Every player that came through there, that I met at UCLA, talked about what an impact he made upon their lives.

"I'm young in my career as a head coach, but already I have players from Murray State who will come by and talk about our times together. If you don't have that relationship where you have the opportunity to dig into somebody's life, then you have really missed it as a coach. You have really missed it."

You have got to believe that Mark is going to make his mark on countless lives in his career.

You wait. You watch. You'll see. Plus, he wastes no time.

CHAPTER EIGHT

COACH CHARLIE HARBISON

He's known as Coach Cheese. His players revere him as their big brother or maybe their father. He's their spiritual leader. He's their accountability partner. He's a friend that they admire and respect.

Who is this man? Who is this Coach Cheese? His name is Charlie Harbison. He coaches the defensive backs at Alabama. He's a special kind of man. He's a special kind of coach.

Every day before practice, Coach Cheese has prayer with his 25 or so defensive backs. Every day after practice, his players gather up for prayer again. There is a tight bond among Charlie's players.

The players and Coach Cheese have a mutual affection for one another. It all started with a man who has a deep and abiding faith in Almighty God.

He got the name Cheese in high school because, yes, he does love cheese. Equally, his chipper attitude and smile contributes to his taste for cheese. So Coach Cheese fits. In fact, he prefers that players call him Coach Cheese. He loves the close rapport with his players. He likes to hear "Coach Cheese."

Coaching is ministry to Charlie. He treasures the opportunity to mold young men's lives. He loves to give guidance. He thrives on giving them counsel and direction through God's word. He welcomes the opportunity to be a role model as a Christian man.

Charlie is 41 years old in a handsome 6-1 frame. He grew up in Shelby, NC. He was the fifth of 13 children. He was on his way to the Navy Recruiting Office the day he was contacted by Gardner Webb College to play football. After his first game as a freshman, Charlie started at left cornerback for four years.

The Buffalo Bills drafted Charlie in the twelfth round in the 1982 NFL draft. He was cut just before the season began and went on to play two years for Boston in the United States Football League. Since he was playing in the spring months, Charlie became a student coach for Head Coach Ellis Johnson at Gardner Webb in 1983.

That contact with Coach Johnson would later lead Charlie to coaching positions at Clemson and Alabama. Coach Johnson came to Alabama as Defensive Coordinator from Clemson in 1997. Charlie followed his friend Ellis to Alabama in December of 1997.

Charlie tutored some fine defensive backs during his three years (1995-97) at Clemson. Brian Dawkins of the Philadelphia Eagles made All-Pro in 1999. Dexter McCleon was an All-Pro safety for the Super Bowl champions St. Louis Rams in 1999. Leomont Evans plays for the Washington Redskins.

Then after his first year (1998) at Alabama, the 1999 NFL draft paid Charlie quite a compliment. Antiwan Edwards of Clemson was the 24th first round pick and Fernando Bryant of Alabama was the 25th pick in the first round. Both had been coached by Charlie.

Leaving Clemson was tough on Charlie, but the opportunity to coach at Alabama was too big to pass up. The tough part was leaving his players. They had drawn so close.

"Ellis Johnson had recommended me to Coach DuBose. It was early December and Clemson was going to a bowl game. I decided to take the job. My coach at Clemson, Tommy West, asked me to tell my players about my decision to leave Clemson for Alabama.

"The players came in like we were going to have a meeting. I said, 'Guys, I have something to tell you.' I told them that sometimes in life, you have to make some tough decisions. I told them that I have made a decision about something and I have prayed about it.' They still didn't have a clue as to what I was about to say.

"So I told them I had taken a job at the University of Alabama and I would no longer be coaching here. Everyone looked at me stunned. I was nervous myself because we grew together. We were a family and had gone through some tough times together.

"I started crying and some of the guys started crying. I hugged on all of them. One of the players, David Edwards, hugged me and started crying and wouldn't let go. Robert Carswell did the same thing. I told them that in their lives they would face tough decisions and that the Lord would lead them in the right path. We never know where it might be. One player left and went down to the weight room. He couldn't say goodbye to me. He wasn't being mean, he just couldn't do it. We were all so close. It was a tough separation."

Coming to Alabama was a dream for Charlie. He had watched Alabama play on television many times from North Carolina with Keith Jackson calling the games. Charlie felt blessed to be on the Alabama staff.

Charlie felt that God had ordered his steps to Alabama. After meeting all the coaches, it came time to meet his new guys, his new defensive backs at Alabama.

"I remember saying to them, 'Guys, thank you for letting me be part of you. I'm just who I am.' I told them things that I expected out of them and things they should expect out of me.

"Then I told them this, I said, 'Listen guys, I love God. One thing I do is give God the glory in everything I do. I'm not doing this for someone else to know.'

"I was leading them up to this particular point. I said, 'If any of you don't agree to it, you can step out into the hall for a minute and you can come back in. I said, you have a choice. I said, I am going to pray before we start today and before every practice. And after practice, we are going to pray too. We will start our day with prayer and we will close it with prayer.'

"I said, 'This is just like tithing. We will give God the first part of our day. He has blessed my career. He has blessed you guys with the opportunity to play college football and get a degree. You can't do it by yourself even though some of you think you can.'

"So from that first day in my two years at Alabama, we have started each practice with a meeting of just my secondary guys like all coaches do with their positions. I have never had a player to step outside of the room while we pray. I tell them that God has blessed them with talent and we have got to make sure that we give Him the glory. Don't look for self-gratification. Understand that it is God that causes you to excel on the field.

"So we begin each meeting with two or three verses of scripture and then we pray. I like to read from the book of Proverbs because it has such wisdom. I'll call on guys to come up and read from Proverbs. Then I will ask, 'What do you think God is trying to say to us today?' It doesn't take but a couple of minutes a day.

"Then I will say, 'Who wants to lead in prayer today?' Someone raises their hand and comes up. This is a brief few minutes, but it makes a world of difference in our meeting and preparation for practice. Our attitude is right. We develop singleness of purpose. After our scripture and prayer, then we go right into practice. It makes everything go so much better on the field that day.

"Then after practice, we come together on the field. I will call on certain ones to pray. I pray sometimes and they will volunteer to pray. It is amazing some of the things our guys say in their prayers.

"When I pray, I will usually start out by saying, 'Father, in the name of Jesus I thank you for a day that we have never seen or lived before. Father, give us all recall that we can remember what we learned in the meeting and out here on the football field today. Also, Father, give these men recall on what they have learned in the classroom today, so they can recall it and put it on paper when they have their tests. Father, thank you for covering us today and making us free from injuries. Bless these guys as they study tonight. Give them a sweet sleep to refresh them for tomorrow. Protect their families. Dispatch your holy angels over us all.

"I will pray words like that and then when they pray, they will often times say the same things.

"I also believe in praying the Word back to God. I will pray Psalms 91. I will read the verses right there in our huddle. Those verses are so powerful. Some of them say, 'He who dwells in the secret place of the Most High shall abide under the shadow of the Almighty. I will say of the Lord, He is my refuge and my fortress. He shall cover you with his feathers, and under His wings you shall take refuge. For He shall give His angels charge over you, to keep you in all your ways. I will set Him on high, because He has known my name.'

"I tell the guys, this is like a covenant we have with God. Then later on, early in the season when the secondary was taking a beating, we were fine. We knew the power and armor of God was on us because we had prayed Psalms 91 back to God.

"We just kept on going through the tough times. Everyday, I would just tell my guys, don't fret, don't fret. We work and play as unto the Lord, not unto man. Man will fail you, but God won't. I tell them that God has us here for a reason. God has a plan and a purpose for each one of you here.

"I tell them, it all depends on us making the right choices. Don't make a wrong for a wrong. It doesn't make a right. It is like Coach DuBose says and I got it from him. If one man falls, we all have got to get that man up. If a man does wrong and falls short, we can't push him down. We've got to lift him up and get stronger together.

"This past year (1999) with Fernando Bryant gone, we stayed even closer than the year before. I hope we get stronger because the guys now understand me and know what I am about. They're understanding my approach in teaching them.

"Sometimes I lose my cool on the practice field. I tell guys all the time, 'Don't lose control of your spirit.' If you lose control of your spirit, it is like a city with broken down walls. Satan will come in and steal and rob.

"I've lost my control of the spirit on the field and when I have, I hear from Tony Dixon and Marcus Spencer. They will say, 'Coach Cheese, don't lose control of your spirit.' Now they are not joking. They look at me. They call my hand. I like that. I will take a step back and I will walk off. I will get myself calm and I will go back because they are right.

"They are my accountability partners. Because if I say it, I have got to walk it. Many times Tony and Marcus will come to me and calm me down. They will say, 'Coach Cheese, you know better.' It might be during a game and somebody makes a bad play. They will check me and get me back into focus to where I am suppose to be. And those two guys I respect a great deal.

"Those two guys have had to play under adversity. They have had to play with younger players and sometimes they had to overplay to cover for those young corners. So we work together. In the heat of the game, we stay focused on what God has taught us during the week. It works. It is the only way I know to coach my guys and be one together."

"When game day comes, we find us a corner in the dressing room and we say our prayer just like we do before practice. After the game, we will come together like we do after practice and pray to God. We have our team prayers, but we include our own prayers just like we do at practice," says Charlie who is deeply sincere and convicted. Players respond. They have a special bond that Charlie has created among them with the Lord's spirit.

Charlie would be the first to say that his faith has not always been what it is today. There have been hardships. There has been heartbreak. There have been low times. There have been things he has done that he would never digress back to again.

From childhood, Charlie was raised in a Christian home and church was important. "My mother gave me a small pocket Bible and I read it," says Charlie. However, at 12 years of age, Charlie experienced his father's death of heart failure at home one day while his mother was away working. Even today, it is still a tender subject for Charlie to discuss. It was the saddest day of his life. His father was only 39. It saddens Charlie that his father never got to see him play ball or coach.

After college and several years in the World Football League, Charlie got married and had two fine boys, Charlie and Stedman. Charlie coached at Lincolnton High School in North Carolina and worked the midnight shift at a steel plant that made roller barrons. Charlie drifted from his faith as he was stretched to make ends meet for his family. After five years at the steel plant, he returned to coaching with the Charlotte Barons of the WLAF league in 1990, then to the Raleigh-Durham Skyhawks before becoming the wide receivers coach at Gardner-Webb in 1992. At Gardner-Webb, Charlie coached his baby brother, James, who was an outstanding receiver and defensive back. GW also won the Division II national championship in 1992. James was the MVP on defense.

After a year at UTEP, Charlie joined the Clemson staff as the secondary coach. His friend, Ellis Johnson, was Defensive Coordinator and brought Charlie in on the staff. Tommy West was head coach.

Along the way, Charlie and his wife divorced. Low times shackled his personal life. However, at Clemson, Charlie found the Lord again. This time it was a powerful movement of God that took place in Charlie's life. God placed in Charlie's path a godly lady named Gloria Allen who was a secretary in the athletic academic center at Clemson.

"I was looking for happiness in all the wrong places," says Charlie. "Then God humbled me and when I came to brokenness, I came to myself and was led back to God. I wasn't a bad person, but good people just don't make it to heaven unless they accept Jesus Christ into their heart. I had been a Christian earlier in my life, but I had backslid.

"Then I met Gloria who was working in the academic center. She was a ray of sunlight. She always had a glow about her. The power of God was in her life and she would always give me a kind word and the kind word she would give me was scripture. It was a check in my spirit and I knew that she was the kind of lady I needed for a wife. At the time, I wasn't thinking it would be Gloria, but someone like her.

"I was doing okay in my career, but there was something still lacking. I was unhappy. I realized that it wasn't a wife I needed. Moreso, I needed to rededicate my life back to Christ. So Gloria invited me to church one Sunday. I was single again and had not chosen a church.

"So I went to church with Gloria. I got there and the spirit of God moved and I enjoyed it. People loved on you. As a coach on the Clemson staff, I tried not to let people know I was a coach. So I would slip in right before the service began and would leave before it was over.

"This is where I met my spiritual mom, Mrs. Doris Rice. She noticed me and would sit with me near the back. She would watch me and put her arm on me and say, 'Son, everything is going to be all right.' She didn't know what I was going through, how much I missed my boys who I loved so much. She said she would be praying for me and we became close. Her husband had passed. She was an elderly lady. It was like she took me in as her son. She was like an angel watching me.

"Every Sunday, it was a joy to see her. We would talk about the week. She would bake me cakes. To this day, we stay in contact and I go to see her when I go through Clemson. She has even visited Gloria and me in Tuscaloosa."

Through Gloria and Mrs. Rice and his new church, Charlie was getting back on spiritual tracks. He was happier, but he was on the verge of a spiritual awakening in his life. It came one April night in 1997.

"People thought I had it all together. I was a football coach at Clemson. Football is huge at Clemson, too. I was my usual, friendly self to people. However, when I got back to my apartment at night, it was a time of despair and loneliness. I was a different Charlie there. My spirit was often times low.

"Then one night I came home to my apartment. I was so tired. I was in my bathroom and I broke down. I said, 'God, I'm tired. What do you want to do in my life? Help me. Help me because I want to be able to please you. I'm tired of this way of life.'

"I would come home at night and just sit and drink beer. I would try to drink my problems away and that is no way to do it. You have to do it with God. Then God visited me that night.

"I started praying and a calmness came over me. Then I went to bed real late and I began thinking about all I was going through. I wasn't sleeping but just thinking about all I was going through and how I wanted to be freed of all this misery.

"As I was lying there on my bed, from my left came what seemed like a puff of air from someone that appeared to be standing there blowing on me. It happened three times and the last two times, I just inhaled. I don't know why I did. I took a deep breath and inhaled that breeze.

"At 4:30 that morning, I called my pastor Bill Reinhart and Gloria and told them what happened. I was crying and they told me the Holy Spirit had visited me. A powerful movement of God was present in that room and it moved into my heart. I know this. My life has never been the same since that experience.

"Immediately, I had no desire to drink. I opened every can of beer in my refrigerator and poured in down the sink. Things in my house that weren't Christlike, I got rid of them. I started to clean my act up. I had to clean myself up. I didn't want to judge anybody. I quit going to some places that a Christian person doesn't need to be.

"Then when I was with people who said, 'Let's go here or there,' I would say to myself, 'I don't need to go there.' I have no desire to go to former places. I had a choice now and I started to take a stand.

"Another clear sign of God's visitation that night was an eagerness to learn more of God's Word and to enjoy reading the Bible. I had a hunger for the scriptures. Through all of this, I have had greater boldness. Wherever I go, I pray that people will see the power of God in me. I always pray that what I speak are His words and that my actions demonstrate His power. My desire is that people see Him in me.

"When I started to take a stand, I started with my defensive backs," says Charlie who was filled with new joy and excitement which Christ had given him. He acted on God's power in his life immediately in his own mission field.

"They looked at me like lightening had struck me. It was like going into a dark room and turning the light on. They saw a big change in me. That fall when we gathered for two-a-day practice, I told the guys, 'Listen, no more profanity in here. It is going to start with me.' They knew how I was. I would curse on the football field. They saw me change. I started prayer in our meetings also.

"I said, 'You may not agree with it and if you don't, you can step outside a couple of minutes while we have a prayer.' No one ever left. I prayed before meetings. I cleaned my mouth up and I made them clean their mouths up when they were around me. They checked me and I checked them. It was like accountability to one another. They responded. We prayed in our position meeting before practice and then again after practice.

"No one knew we were doing this and I didn't do it for anyone to know. We gathered on the field after practice and put our hands together and prayed. If I had done something wrong during practice and lost control of my spirit, I would ask for their forgiveness right then. They had to see me ask for forgiveness, so they would learn how to do it.

"I loved my guys. I would give them tough love. God says, 'You spare the rod, you spoil the child. They grow up in shame.' I really feel like I had become a better coach for Tommy West. I really feel like I was a better staff member. I never wanted to be a selfish assistant coach. I always wanted to be a team player. I always wanted to be a blessing to my peers and players and if not, I needed to move on."

After that 1997 season, Charlie moved on only because God "ordained his steps to Alabama," as Charlie puts it.

Romantic interests between Charlie and Gloria didn't begin until several months after they became acquainted. However, Gloria had been used mightily by God to help Charlie find restoration in his faith. At Clemson, she was an encourager to Charlie and prayed for him daily.

"I prayed that God would visit Charlie in the night," says Gloria whose cup is always full of the Lord. "God gets your attention in the night because you are quiet and still. So when he had that visitation from God that night, it thrilled my heart. It was an answer to my prayers for Charlie. He woke me up that morning at 4:30 and what a joyful experience that was for me also.

"From that day to this, his life has been radically different, a 180 degrees complete turn. He has been hungry and that's the part that has caused him to grow. He devourers spiritual things. He's open to truth. People get saved and they get stuck. They stay right there. They never grow; they never go on and produce fruit. They just stay saved and then they go on and be with Jesus, too. But some people get hungry spiritually and those are the people that go on and fulfill their destiny and purpose in God."

When Charlie moved on to Alabama, he and Gloria would talk every morning and evening by long distance. They not only grew in love, but they were prayer partners. Every phone call always included prayer for one another.

So on June 26, 1999, Charlie and Gloria married. They then experienced a very unusual honeymoon. They were married on Saturday and on Monday they checked into the Fellowship of Christian Athletes Coaches Camp at Black Mountain, NC. They spent their honeymoon at FCA camp.

But hold on, there is much more to this story. Ellis Johnson and his finance, Caroline, also attended the FCA camp. So for the camp week, Charlie and Ellis roomed together and Gloria and Caroline roomed together. Says Gloria, "If it is going to enhance the Kingdom of God, then it was worth what we did even though we had just been married. It was their first FCA camp and that meant more to us than being together as newlyweds."

Charlie laughs at the kidding coaches gave him during the week. They would say, "How about Coach Cheese. He takes his wife to FCA camp on his honeymoon?"

Their first year of married life has been a honeymoon in Christ. "Gloria is my prayer partner," Charlie is proud to say. "She is my accountability partner. We pray together. We read scripture together and talk about it. When I get down, she is quick to tell me, 'You know better.' Before I know it, she has given me scripture and covers me with prayer and I'm not down long."

Another venture that has enriched Charlie's life has been the FCA Coaches Camp at Black Mountain. Even before he met Gloria, Charlie would take his sons to the camp each June. They have built memories together at the camps. The June 2000 camp was Charlie's fifth consecutive experience.

"Clyde Christenson, a coach on our staff at Clemson, encouraged me to go. So my boys and I went. Being that I was separated from them, it was our time together and it drew us closer together. It was the best time for me also. You were around Christian coaches and their families and you were fellowshipping with brothers and sisters in Christ.

"When you are there, it is like being refueled. It refuels me for the season. You get the Word, you sing, you praise God, you play ball together and you hear from coaches and what their past year has been like. I've heard such men as Tom Osborne, Brad Scott, Dean Smith and many others. Tony Dungy and his family of the Tampa Bay Buccaneers have been there every year. What a blessing he has been to me.

"It is amazing that you see certain men at camp only on television or across the field coaching against you. Then, we are all together as one big family, God's children praising God. There is no who's the best and who's the lowest. We are on the same plain. God is not going to ask us how many games we won, but how many souls we won for the Kingdom. He will ask, 'What seeds are you sowing?' God says, whatever seeds you are sowing you will reap. FCA Coaches Camp changed my whole prospective on coaching.

"You build relationships also. Throughout the year, you will get notes from coaches in your huddle group saying, 'I'm praying for you. I saw you play last week on TV. Continue to give God the glory. I can't wait to see you at FCA camp next year.' "

In Charlie's office is a display of several past FCA monthly magazines for his players to pick up and read. *Sharing The Victory* magazine is not the only inspirational piece in his office. On his desk are gospel tracks entitled, "Do You Know This Man?" The track shares a simple message of how one may receive Christ into his life.

As a Christian coach, Charlie has acquired wisdom and leadership that may be helpful to other coaches. His thoughts are filled with spiritual power and consideration.

ENTHUSIASM FOR COACHING: "I have joy. The Lord has blessed me with doing something I love to do. I wear it on my sleeve. I am not going to put God in a box. I really feel like my players are an extension of me. If I am going to be out there on the practice field, I am going to be a warrior for the Kingdom. I want to make sure that when I do something, I am going to do it with all my might. I do it as unto the Lord. I am not going to do something halfway for God.

"Plus, I want to make sure I do my best as a coach. I don't want to be a hindrance but a blessing. I want to be a blessing to Coach DuBose, a blessing to the staff and a blessing to the University of Alabama. I want to be a blessing to the players. If they look out there and see that I am dejected and not enthused, they will think, 'Well, Coach Cheese, he is just going through the motions. I might as well go through the motions, too. If it is okay with him, why wouldn't it be right for me?'

"Some days I have the fear that I will go out there and not feel good. But when I am prayed up, I will go out there and boom, God has blessed me and picks me up. Everything doesn't always go right, but you can correct things with a purpose and a good attitude. The players will receive it."

PLAYER MOTIVATION: "I get on to my players. Sometimes they will say, 'Man, Coach, you are pushing me awfully hard.' I will say, 'Listen, do you want to be average? If you want to be average, you should never have come here. We are going to win the national championship. You have a part of this. Everybody has a piece of the puzzle. If your piece doesn't fit, the picture is not complete. Everybody has a role. Know your role and be the best at it.'"

COACH-PLAYER RELATIONSHIP: "I prefer that players call me Coach Cheese. If someone calls me Coach Harbison, that is not me. I'm just one of the guys. I love to be in with the guys. We can laugh and I can love on them. They know when it is time to work and when it is time to play."

THE DEFENSIVE BACKS CAUGHT ON NATIONAL TELEVISION IN PRAYER BEFORE THE GAME ENDED WHEN ALABAMA DEFEATED FLORIDA 34-7 FOR THE 1999 SEC CHAMPIONSHIP: "The Lord had blessed our guys with such a great performance. We always pray after the game, but I knew when the game was over, it was going to be a wild celebration on the field. It would be hard to get together after the clock ran down. It was certainly done not for people to see us. I said, 'All right guys, let's give God the glory, right here, right now!

"The presence of God was all over those guys. I just thanked God for the season, for the performance and for protecting both teams from injury. I prayed for safe travel for our team and families. I prayed for our opponents. I don't want one of their players to be harmed. That's some-body's son. I am not going to sow that bad seed. So we asked God to cover everyone and we just thanked Him for blessing our team and using us to glorify His name. We just gave Him the glory."

COACH MIKE DUBOSE: "Coach DuBose has been a blessing to me. He is my brother in Christ. When he admitted to his improper relationship before last season started, I was upset. It wasn't so much at him because I have failed before. I don't judge because the measure you judge, the same measure will be judged unto you. I was upset because I began to fret about my job. I wasn't blown out of the water, but God restored my spirit right away.

"When Coach DuBose rededicated his life and came back to Christ, God ordered his steps. I believe that the Lord orchestrated last season to show the world His handiwork. Coach DuBose is a strong man and he's going to be a strong man of God. He can change so many people's lives through Christ. He has and he will continue. I look at his fruit. The man is genuine. Only God can change a man like he has Coach DuBose. I love the man and he has been a blessing to me and my wife. We are brothers in Christ."

FAVORITE SCRIPTURE AND LIFE GOAL: "My ambition is to be a coordinator and if the Lord blesses me to be a head coach some day, so be it. But I don't ever want to walk out of God's will. If the opportunity comes up, I will pray about it. Then I will turn to my favorite scripture, Proverbs 3:5-6. 'Trust in the Lord with all your heart and lean not into your own understanding. In all thy ways acknowledge Him, and He shall direct thy paths.'

"That's scripture I hang my hat on. When I rededicated my life back to Christ, I had to quit leaning on my own understanding and lean on God. I had to trust Him. I live by the spirit and die by the flesh. Everyday, I have to make my flesh die and let the spirit lead and guide me. What I do is between God and me. If I go out here and publicize it, I am not doing it as unto the Lord, but unto the people.

"I want to make sure that when I go before the Throne, that God will say to me, 'WELL DONE.'"

When you consider the spirit of God that lives in Charlie's life, you get the feeling that God will welcome Coach Cheese with a big smile and an enthusiastic "Well Done."

CHAPTER NINE

COACH ELLIS JOHNSON

When a pre-season physical exam notified Ellis Johnson that he had Hodgkin's Disease, his faith in God from childhood left him concerned, but unshaken.

One thing the Alabama defensive coordinator learned from the shocking news was that he had a gift of faith that every person should have when calamity strikes. Ellis knew that he wasn't afraid to die.

Ellis received Christ into his life at a young age and faith in God was instilled in him. Therefore, at age 41 when he took a physical exam in August, 1993 before the football season and discovered he had cancer, Ellis was prepared spiritually. He knew if the cancer took his life, he would go to Heaven. He had that blessed assurance.

That is real security when you consider that the greatest fear of most people is the fear of dying.

Ellis was born into a strong Christian family. His grandfather Johnson was an ARP (Associated Reformed Presbyterian) minister. Ellis claims that his mother, Ernestine, was the strongest Christian that he has ever known. She attended Converse College on a music scholarship and was captain of the field hockey team.

There were eight children in his father's family. All but one graduated from Erskine College, a Presbyterian school in South Carolina. Therefore, church came first with the Johnson's and everything else had to get in line. Ellis had listened to hundreds of sermons by the time he left Winnsboro, SC, for The Citadel in 1970.

Coach Gene Stallings invited Ellis to serve as Outside Linebackers Coach when he came to Alabama in 1990. Three years later, Alabama players and coaches were wearing national championship rings. Alabama won the cherished national crown in 1992. Ellis and the defensive side were the best in America. The 34-13 Sugar Bowl victory over Miami was one of Alabama's truly great wins.

Now the time had come, August that is, to prepare for defending the title. Prior to two-a-day practice, each coach took a physical exam. Thank God for physical exams!

Ellis recalls the physical that day as merely a routine procedure.

"It was one of these deals where I went up to the DCH Hospital to get the pre-season physical. The doctor, Dr. Ann Lewis, started asking funny questions. I had some symptoms that had been going on for three to six months. I was losing weight, but that was not unusual for that time of the year. It wasn't a drastic thing like I should have known something was wrong," recalls Ellis.

"Irritation of the skin had occurred around my lymph nodes. It wasn't to the point that you would say, 'I've got a problem here.' At the exam, something showed up on the chest x-ray that looked a little unusual. I was sent down for a CAT scan and they brought me back that afternoon. Dr. Lewis hit me with it real bluntly. She said, 'You have a mass in your chest the shape of a football!'

"Hindsight, as she explained the diagnosis to me, revealed for six months, someone medically could have diagnosed the disease. But it really had not gotten, I guess, to an advanced stage.

"I was obviously right on the edge of having some serious problems," says Ellis who had always been healthy and free of any health related complications.

"I was never a great athlete, but I was always fairly successful in sports. At 41 years old, you kind of do what you want to do. You may not excel at everything you take up, but you can do it. Then, something like this happens and it brings you back to reality. Nothing has ever been really difficult for you. You have had to work hard, but you've always kind of physically been fine, you know.

"Then when something like this happens, it is like, 'Well, you've got the wrong guy. It must be this other guy down there.' It is the kind of thing that when you first hear it, it makes you realize that you better appreciate every day. Life is just that unpredictable."

Ellis was coaching the outside linebackers at the time. So in a matter of a few hours, his life was drastically changed. His thoughts suddenly changed from the new freshmen reporting in, being ready to teach defensive schemes and deciding who was going to replace NFL draftees: John Copeland, Eric Curry, Antonio London, Antonio Langham and George Teague. His mind suddenly changed gears to his own body and well being.

"That afternoon, Dr. Lewis told me that they didn't have a way of knowing what it was yet. It could be benign. It could be malignant. So J.D. (Dr. Askew, team physician) and I came back over and told Coach Stallings.

"The next morning, they checked me in and did a needle biopsy. They go in with a lasperator between the ribs and get a little piece of that tumor. It takes about two or three days for them to analyze with a needle.

"That time of waiting for the result was the hardest time. You just have to wait and pray. The other tough part was that we had already started practice. I told Coach Stallings that I didn't want to be around the football scene and the media until I found out what this was.

"So I was sitting around the house. Your mind is just turning over. You don't know what it is. Finally, the doctor came by and told me that it was a malignancy."

Further testing was needed and Ellis checked in the next day at the Kirklin Clinic in Birmingham.

"They did a frozen biopsy first thing the next morning. Before I got back into my room and in that bed, they knew it was malignant. It takes a few more days before they can say exactly what cell type and to be more specific with you. People get confused about cancer. Its location doesn't tell you what you have. It's more complicated than that.

"For four or five days, you have so many things going through your mind. You try to be patient. You think of the worst and you believe for a complete recovery. I've never had a problem with death because of my faith. It is hard for me to deal with something when I don't know what I am dealing with. That really was the hardest time.

"Finally, they told me I had Hodgkin's. They would have to do more definitive testing. They wanted me to come over (Birmingham) and get with Dr. John Carpenter. He would be my chemotherapy oncologist. Dr. Merle Salter was my head oncologist.

"I stayed there in the hospital for a day or two and that was all the time I was ever in the hospital. I would get treatments as an outpatient."

Next for Ellis was finding out what he could and couldn't do with his coaching responsibilities. Those decisions registered heavily on his mind. Practicing twice daily is a crucial time in preparation for the season. The players, coaches, students and fans are in great anticipation for the season to begin. Ellis was now faced with an altogether different challenge. He had to attack cancer while he was teaching his linebackers to attack the opposing team's quarterbacks.

"I asked the doctor, What can I eat and what can I do?' He said, 'You can do anything you want to. Just don't open that surgery up.' I said, 'Okay.' So I came back and told Coach Stallings exactly what was going on.

"The response I got from Coach Stallings was so important to me. He said, 'You do what you can do, as much as you can do. Don't do anything you can't do.' I said, 'Well Coach, if you need to put Lorenzo (Ward, graduate assistant coach) on the field and take me off, I understand.' He said, 'Hey, I'm not worried about that.'

"Staying busy and staying in my routine was very helpful with my mental attitude. I did fine through the chemotherapy until the last two treatments. I had six rounds of chemotherapy that lasted about six months. I would go over to Birmingham three days in a row. The first day I got four drugs, the second day I got two drugs and the third day I got the same two drugs. I took mine with the IV procedure.

"That would knock the white cell count to the bottom. Basically it is poison to try and kill the tumor. I would feel bad from the treatments. There were days when I would have to go home and rest awhile. I know that was a tremendous load on our staff because I had not been able to do 100 percent of what I had been doing. Mike (DuBose), Bill (Oliver), Jeff (Rouzie) and Coach Stallings being understanding and taking some of my load was very important to me during a tough time.

"I would go for treatment once a month. You would have to wait until your white cell count built back up before you took the next treatment."

After the third round of chemo, Ellis was given some very good news. Through prayers from his God-fearing family and the Alabama family of friends and with medical treatment, the tumor had deteriorated from the size of a football to the size of a golf ball or baseball. It was a most unexpected blessing to see his condition begin to improve in such short order.

There was another important turn in the whole matter that was in Ellis' favor.

"If the growth had been benign, they would have had to go in there and cut the tumor out because it would have kept growing. Since it was malignant, the chemo treatments killed those cells that were out of control. My tumor was in the chest cavity and thank goodness it wasn't attached to anything. So everytime I would go in for treatment, they would do an x-ray or CAT scan. I guess the cells deteriorate as fast as they multiply, I don't know. They do the testing to see if they are on the right protocol, to see if the medicine is doing the right thing.

"That was obviously a positive sign. It seemed like everything that happened along the way was positive and encouraging. I think my state of mind helped too, but it seemed like I kept getting good news."

When Ellis returned to the practice field after his initial testing, he never missed a game and only missed one or two practices. It was remarkable how he managed to take treatments and perform as a coach in a major football program.

Alabama won the first five games over Tulane, Vanderbilt, Arkansas, Louisiana Tech and South Carolina before a 17-17 tie with Tennessee in Birmingham. Then the Tide defeated Mississippi and Southern Mississippi and lost to LSU in a close battle in Tuscaloosa. A win over Mississippi State and a 22-14 loss in Auburn still put Alabama in the Southeastern Conference championship game in Atlanta. Alabama lost to Florida 28-14 for a season record of 8-3-1. A Gator Bowl berth against North Carolina awaited.

At this juncture, Ellis made a surprising decision with the condition that existed. After the SEC championship game, he took a position coaching linebackers at Clemson.

"I consulted the doctors and they told me it wasn't unusual to move your treatments. So I went to the Greenville Cancer Center in Greenville, SC and was referred to Dr. Lewis Terry. He did my radiation oncology and that consisted of about 30 treatments. These treatments were such that you could take one every day if you held up okay. So I took them all within two months."

At this point, Ellis had completed all of his treatments. He would have a checkup every three months, and then it became every six months.

Over the next three years, Ellis remained at Clemson under Coach Tommy West. He was Defensive Coordinator for the last year in 1996. When Mike DuBose took over as head coach at Alabama the next year, Ellis accepted his invitation to replace him as Defensive Coordinator. Ellis then returned to Alabama and continued to get checkups every six months.

In returning to Alabama, Ellis saw the Crimson Tide defense come into its own in the last five games of the 1999 season, including the SEC championship game against Florida. During this span, the rushing defense held opponents to an amazing 28.0 yard average per game and only 221.1 yards of total defense was given up per game.

When Alabama stunned Florida 34-7 to win the SEC Championship, the Crimson Tide defense held Florida to several all-time lows under Coach Steve Spurrier. Florida could only muster six first downs, seven points, 83 passing yards and an unheard of 114 yards of total offense. Florida was 0-for-9 on third down conversations and in the fourth quarter Florida gained just two total yards of offense in nine plays.

So how is Ellis today?

"Everything is fine," says Ellis who feels so blessed that his cancer was caught in the early stages. It has not affected or slowed down his career in any stretch.

"The only problem I have had is the location. Because of where it was, I had a little heart damage probably attributed to the radiation. They make a lead template for you and each person has his or her own when they go in for treatment. It blocks the major organs the best it can. But I did have a little bit of heart artery damage. I did have an angioplasty right before the 1997 season.

"It's funny, Dr. Ann Lewis came to the rescue again and caught it on the treadmill in the pre-season physical. I didn't have a clue that anything was wrong. She spotted something while I was on the treadmill. They brought me in the next morning and one of my major heart arteries was about 90 percent blocked. They cleaned it out and everything has been fine. They are assuming it was from radiation which is pretty common. You can get scar tissue with radiation in that area.

"I have to be careful because I consider myself a heart disease patient. There is no guarantee it was the treatment that caused the blockage, but everything else looked so clear and that treatment probably led to the problem.

"Honestly, the biggest concern I have now is not reoccurrence of Hodgkin's. The chance of relapse on Hodgkin's is very, very low. I am almost seven years out now and that has passed a milestone percentage wise. All of these things are just statistics, of course. I need to be more concerned about my heart than the cancer.

"Overall, I'm very fortunate when you consider life and death. I'm fortunate because there are many forms of cancer. I had the lightweight if you catch it early. It can certainly be deadly, but it is one of the most treatable cancers there is right now.

"I remember something Dr. Salter told me when I went over to the Kirklin Clinic when it first happened. She said, 'You are going to be fine. You are most likely headed for problems when you are 70 or so. I will tell you this, you are fortunate in many aspects in what you are dealing with. We have come a long way in cancer treatment. I will give you an example. If Pat Trammell were coming in today as you are, he would still be alive.'"

Pat was Coach Bryant's outstanding quarterback who led the

Crimson Tide to a national championship in 1961. He died at the age of 28 in 1968 of cancer just as he was starting his career as a medical doctor.

"That example is why my pet project is St. Jude's Hospital for Children in Memphis. I give because I know now that the money is working. It is a slow fight and a tough uphill battle, but all you have to do is to hear that statement to know that the money and the research has helped people. And I'm one of them."

Today when you see Ellis Johnson, you see a handsome man whose hair has already turned gray and he looks the picture of health. He's 48 years old and he would tell you he has a prize position in college football, coaching as Defensive Coordinator for the Crimson Tide. The future looks most promising for Ellis.

Though he coaches in a tough man's sport and teaches young men to play with reckless abandon, cancer has a way of sensitizing a man and teaching him to look inward for peace, comfort and strength.

"I have a philosophy and it may not be 100 percent, but I don't think that things like this in life necessarily build character or faith. I think they **reveal** what character and faith you have. I know that's what I discovered in myself through cancer.

"I have been able to deal with all of this because of the way I was raised. I certainly didn't get this strength from being an athlete, going to military schools, or coaching football.

"My grandfather was a Presbyterian minister and was very strict. I always laugh to hear stories about his eight children. They were cutups and funny as they could be. They are all in their 80's and 90's now. He had a big influence on me and our entire family in knowing what a true Christian was. I wish I could have known him, but he died before I was born.

"My mother's brother, Rhett Sanders, is a very special person in my life. Christ being my Savior was explained to me as a seven or eight-year-old. I consider myself one of these spoiled Christians. I've had it pretty easy. I didn't have to go through some major crisis and have somebody introduce me to Christ at the age of 27 or something like that. I was told at a young age and I am very thankful for that.

"Rhett Sanders is very special to me. He lost his mother as a child and my mother practically raised him. She was more like his mom than his older sister. He lived with us when I was a small child. He was an evangelist preacher. I helped him build a Bible camp when I was in the third grade.

"We've always had a good Christian influence, discipline and great role models in my home and family. So that's something I've always had to lean on. Taking on the challenge of a major health issue or losing a loved one or anything else may be real hard to go through. But I've always felt those things reveal what character and faith you have. It certainly has caused me to be more at peace with my faith.

"The problem I have is that I get off track too often. When it came to a situation like cancer, it occurred to me that I'm not afraid of dying. I'm afraid of not living. I want to live life as a Christian should. I'm not ready to go. Like everybody, I have more to do. I don't want to leave yet. But I have no problems with death. I know where I am going."

To be born into a Christian family is worth more than anyone can measure. If Ellis was not a Christian, his response to cancer would have been much different. Perhaps, fear of dying would have shaken his life to the point of great mental anguish and worry. Perhaps his recovery would not have come as quickly and as smoothly as it did. But his faith in Jesus Christ and His power, made a huge difference when the trial came.

Ellis's father, John Johnson, was the son of a Presbyterian minister. He graduated from Clemson, an all-male military college and Ellis's mother, Ernestine, graduated from Converse College in Spartanburg.

So it was pretty much expected of Ellis, his three brothers and a sister to attend college.

Ellis was in the third grade when his oldest brother, John, enrolled at the West Point Military Academy in New York. John was an outstanding football player for Army and made All-East as a cornerback. Amazingly, Ellis' second oldest brother, Oliver, attended West Point also and played outside linebacker and defensive end for Army. They were at West Point during the 60's when the Army-Navy game was about the biggest national game played each year. It was always on national television. John and Oliver played for coaches Dale Hall, Paul Dietzel and Tom Cahill.

Both John and Oliver were Christian young men who set quite an example for younger brother, Ellis. They offered Ellis coaching, that was profitable to Ellis as a youngster. John and Oliver went on to complete 30-year careers as Army officers.

Ellis played football, basketball, baseball and ran track in high school. As a ninth grader, his dad took him to see Clemson play Alabama at Clemson on Oct. 28, 1967. "I noticed that Coach Bryant was leaning up against the goal post and was signing autographs as the team was warming up. So I told my daddy, 'I'm going down there to get his autograph.'" Ellis still has that program with Coach Bryant's signature on the front cover in his desk today. It is a prize possession.

His goal was to play football at Clemson. However, his best scholarship offer was to The Citadel in Charleston and he took it after giving up the opportunity to attend West Point. A month later, his brother, John, became the Head Freshman Football Coach at Army and tried to coax Ellis into enrolling at West Point.

However, Ellis went on to The Citadel and played on the freshman team and even joined the basketball team in the winter. Freshmen were not eligible to play on the varsity team at that time. At the semester split, John talked Ellis into enrolling at West Point. He wanted Ellis on his team and felt a degree from West Point was good for his career even if he didn't have a full military career. So Ellis enrolled at West Point the next fall and had to start all over as a freshman, a mandatory rule at the Academy.

The Viet Nam war had just ended and attending a military academy at that time was not as highly regarded since the war was so unpopular. After one year at West Point, Ellis transferred back to The Citadel where he graduated in 1975. Ellis knew he didn't want a military career. Students did not have to sign a military contract at The Citadel, and Ellis was much happier there. Ellis played outside linebacker and defensive end and already knew he wanted to be a football coach. His high school coach, Joe Turberville at Winnsboro High, had made a profound influence upon Ellis and his desire to be a coach. He was also a Citadel graduate.

His first coaching job was as a graduate assistant at The Citadel. Bobby Ross was the head coach. "I learned more football from Bobby Ross in one year than in my first ten years of coaching," says Ellis. "Some things I do today organizationally and structurally in my work habits, I still attribute to him." Ross went on to become the head coach at Georgia Tech and is the Detroit Lions head coach today. Others on that staff went on to become head coaches such as Red Parker (Clemson), Frank Beamer (Va. Tech), Jimmy Laycock (William & Mary) and Cal McCombs (VMI).

"I wouldn't give a million dollars for the six years of coaching experience I had in high school," Ellis points out. "It helped me to be a better teacher, a better coach and it has really benefited me in recruiting." Ellis coached at Gaffney (SC) High School and was head coach at Spartanburg High in 1980-81. Then he joined the staffs at The Citadel,

Gardner-Webb College, Appalachian State, East Carolina and Southern Mississippi before his first tenure at Alabama in 1990.

"I have worked with so many good people in all of these places and have gained from seeing things done in coaching in many different ways," says Ellis. "I have worked at all levels and have learned so much about coaching philosophy and x's and o's that has been of great help in my coaching career."

Having never been at any one place more than three years caused a hurtful situation to occur in Ellis' life. He has experienced two failed marriages through the perils of coaching.

Ellis explains the downside of what the demands of coaching can bring. "It has been hard to experience two unsuccessful marriages because I grew up in a family filled with stable marriages. Those things hurt and thank goodness there have never been any children involved in either marriage. As much as it was some of my shortcomings, the demands of moving and relocating can eventually take its toll on a marriage. There is an old expression that says 'It takes a special lady to be a coach's wife.' It also takes a special man to be a coach's wife's spouse.

"Making many moves puts a strain on a marriage. It is important for young coaches and their wives to fully understand the demands and time that coaching requires. There are 14-hour days and there are times when you have some free time away from work. This is a lesson for every marriage no matter what the profession may be. When it comes to coaching, the husband and wife need to know the demands, see it and understand that before they get into it. It's hard."

Through the struggle, Ellis has found happiness in his marriage to Caroline Courie, which took place on February 19, 2000. "Caroline loves football more than I do," says Ellis with a big smile. "She was working in the athletic department at Clemson when we met and understands our profession very well. She just loves it and has enjoyed getting into Alabama football, too. We are so pleased to be expecting a child in December."

Through the grace and mercy of God and a loving companion, Ellis has discovered a new lease on life and a deeper love and purpose for life itself.

"It (the cancer and successful treatment) has made me a better Samaritan for others in their time of need. I've never been a real communicator, but it has made me a much better person with other people who are going through sickness. When I visit with my aunts, I am more in tune with their feelings and realize the inspiration I can be to them.

I never knew how encouraging a kind note or phone call can be to people until I received so many, many expressions of love from people.

"It was unbelievable the outpouring of concern I received. The day I returned from the Kirklin Clinic and surgery, two good friends, Coach "Lefty" Johnson and Steve Nuttall, drove seven hours to visit me and drove back that night. My brother John flew from Virgina to South Carolina and picked up my father, and drove seven hours to see me. My sister, Martha, and brothers, Oliver and Ridgeway, filled my days with phone calls and notes. I got letters from friends I hadn't seen in 15 years.

On that 45-minute trip to Birmingham for treatment, I felt sorry for myself. When I arrived, I saw plenty of people who didn't receive that kind of support. It is easy to feel sorry for yourself, but I have found that someone else has always got it tougher."

Hanging in his office is a calendar from St. Jude's Hospital for Children in Memphis. "It is one thing for a mature, grown man to experience pain and go through treatments yet regain good health and have all the support I've had. Then I thought, how in the world do innocent children who are five, six and seven years old endure cancer and the treatments? It is a source of inspiration for me to support the great work they do at St. Jude's. I toured the facility one time and it was really impressive. I donate to several cancer causes but St. Jude's is kind of my pet project. These kids are my heroes!"

Ellis has never forgotten another source of inspiration. "Since I have moved around so much, my church membership is still at Bethel ARP Church in Winnsboro and I still send them my monthly contribution. That may change soon as Caroline and I are deciding on a church in Tuscaloosa, but the Bethel congregation will always be special to me."

Through the influence of a praying family and thousands of friends, Ellis has experienced God's healing upon his life. "Too many people think they shouldn't have problems or they think it is somebody's fault that they have them. If you don't have faith in God, you can't understand why life is not perfect.

"I'm one person now alive who wouldn't have been 30 years ago. My trial has not been as trying as others I've seen, but God has blessed me and I'm grateful to Him."

Ellis says that during his deepest concern for his health, a dear friend sent him a verse of scripture that meant the most to him. She was Virgina Townsend, the mother-in-law of his uncle Rhett Sanders. It summarizes Ellis' journey through 48 years.

It is the familiar verse from Isaiah 40:31…"But those who wait on the Lord shall renew their strength; they shall mount up with wings like eagles, they shall run and not be weary, they shall walk and not faint."

Ellis has waited upon the Lord and his strength and life have been renewed.

CHAPTER TEN

KERMIT KOENIG

You are 42 and the doctor says you have two years to live with treatment. It wasn't the kind of news Kermit Koenig expected to hear shortly after becoming an assistant basketball coach at Alabama in the summer of 1997. After 20 years of coaching, coming to Alabama and the Southeastern Conference was a dream come true for Kermit.

When Kermit and his wife Sharron received the news that day at the M.D. Anderson Clinic in Houston, their thoughts shifted suddenly through the shock and the tears that flowed.

The dream job exhilaration a few weeks earlier had now turned to the stark reality of life and death for this husband and father of two bright daughters.

Kermit's improbable story of his discovery of cancer is one for the books. Someone was looking out for Kermit. Changing jobs had become a blessing moreso health wise than for the coaching basketball.

Kermit had been assistant basketball coach nine years at Mississippi College in Clinton, MS when he was hired by Coach Dave Hobbs on July 1, 1997.

The opportunity to coach at Alabama meant everything to Kermit. "It felt like I was reaching the pinnacle of what I had always wanted," says Kermit. "You always think the grass is greener on the other side. Well coming from Mississippi College, a Division III school, to Alabama was a big step for me.

"Alabama had just been in the NCAA Sweet 16 the year before I got here with Antonio McDyess and there were nine or ten Alabama players in the NBA. At that time, it was probably the second best job in the Southeastern Conference.

"I thought, Man, I have finally made it. I was so pleased, so proud and so happy. I had been struggling in my profession and now things had turned around for me.

"For the two previous years, Sharron kept saying, 'You just don't seem happy.'

"The reason was because we had been in Division II at Mississippi College and had finally worked our way to the national tournament. Then the school decided to move down to Division III without any scholarships the two years prior to my coming to Alabama."

Sharron had noticed a difference in Kermit's attitude. He had become edgy. He didn't seem to feel good or look right. She wondered what he was searching for? Sharron kept telling Kermit that he didn't seem happy where he was.

"At the time, Sharron was spiritually much closer to the Lord than I was," Kermit recalls. "However, we had a Monday morning coaches Bible Study and it meant a lot to me. Our head coach Mike Jones was a solid Christian man. It was a pleasure to work with him. He is the best.

"There are two people in my spiritual life that have made the biggest difference. Mike Jones is one of them and Sharron is the other one. I have always been a fairly strong believer, but at the same time, I had not come to the point of totally releasing myself. I just wasn't that open with my faith. If someone asked me, I would say, 'Sure I am a believer in Christ.'

"We were active in our church and I had attended two Fellowship of Christian Athletes Coaches camps that were a real spiritual boost to me. The camps helped me to be much more open with my faith and caused me to be more aware of where I needed to be spiritually as a husband, father and coach."

At the 1996 FCA camp, Kermit found himself in a huddle group led by Coach Tony Dungy (Head Coach of the Tampa Bay Buccaneers) and Dal Shealy (President of the FCA). There was a basketball coach from Alabama at the camp also. Kermit and Rick Moody, the Alabama women's coach, got closely acquainted.

A year later, it was Rick and Kermit's friend Bob Marlin, a member of Coach Hobbs staff, who recommended Kermit for the vacancy at Alabama. Kermit took the "restrictive earnings coach" position at $15,000 less than he was making at Mississippi College.

Sharron was a nurse and would get a job in Tuscaloosa. Their house sold in 24 hours after failing to sell twice previously. They laughed when the job came because they had just purchased a shiny red car that would go well at Alabama. Affirmations for a move were abundant.

"It was like there was a reason for us to come to Tuscaloosa," Kermit reflects. Little did they know what was ahead. Their lives would change drastically. There was a reason for the move, but not what this young and excited family expected.

Kermit dove into his work at Alabama with a passion. His family joined him a month later. Life couldn't be happier for the Koenig family.

Then on August 28, a fire alarm went off.

"We were up in Bob Marlin's office where the basketball coaches offices are in Coleman Coliseum. Bob (men's assistant) and Mike Murphy (women's assistant coach) and myself were ordering new shirts from a tailor whose name is Don Reese," Kermit remembers in detail. "In fact since I was so new on the job, Don had come for the first time to see the coaches. I just happened to walk into the room. I had no idea I would be ordering any shirts that day.

"Mike and Bob were going to order custom made shirts and because of my salary cut, I was just going to order two shirts. I had gained some weight. So I said to Don, 'Why don't you measure me just to make sure. I know I have gained some weight, but I wear a 15 and a half shirt. He took his tape, measured me and said, 'I got you 16 and a half skin to skin.'

"Then I thought to myself, 'That doesn't sound right. I know I have gained some weight, but I haven't gotten that big.' I was still working out and still running. I had never worn any shirt larger than a 15 and a half in my life.

Without saying anything to the men there, Kermit reached up and felt his neck and he knew something was wrong.

"That afternoon, our family went to Coach Hobbs's lake house. We came home that night and I was deeply concerned. I said, 'Sharron, feel my neck.' We went into our bedroom and being a nurse, she had me lie down. She felt my neck and with sudden alarm she said, 'O God. We have got to see a doctor in the morning!'

The next morning, Sharron called Dr. Jimmy Robinson's office since he was the team doctor. Being new in town, the family had not been to see a doctor yet. Sharron's persistence paid off with the person that answered. The office receptionist did not know the Koenig's at all.

When Sharron called, she further explained, 'I am a nurse myself and there are huge knots all up and down my husband's neck. I am really concerned!' The receptionist told Sharron to bring Kermit in and they saw Dr. Robinson that day. He immediately sent Kermit through a CAT scan and MRI.

While waiting for the tests results, Dr. Robinson gave Kermit some antibiotics. Kermit thought it was perhaps infection and it wasn't anything bad. "I just kept saying, I am going to be all right," says Kermit who had been healthy all of his life.

"Initially they were thinking it was lymphoma," Sharron remembers. "It took about a week to get the diagnosis back. I knew by then that they were hoping it was lymphoma."

Whether it was her nursing or spouse intuition, Sharron had what she describes "an extremely uneasy feeling about Kermit for about two years. To me it was the Holy Spirit speaking. It started out like a whisper, a little notion until it just built and snowballed in my thoughts."

Kermit recalls Sharron telling him over that same span that there is "something about you that doesn't look right, something is not right. Are you looking for a new change in direction, or what is going on?"

"So when the Alabama job came up, I asked her what she thought and she said, 'Let's go.' How many times will your spouse be ready to make a move that quick? I think she felt this was going to solve a lot of my unsettled actions and feelings at the time. Maybe even the way I looked," Kermit said with a smile.

Even with the new post at Alabama, Kermit still wasn't the old Kermit that Sharron expected to see. "A month after arriving at Alabama, Kermit still wasn't himself," says Sharron. "You could see that he was tired, real edgy and still just not himself. Kermit is real happy-go-lucky, always happy. He was not that way and I thought, boy this hasn't fixed it. Something is not right."

A week after Kermit saw Dr. Robinson, the tests came back. The news would be far worse than they had expected.

It was a week after Labor Day on a Monday. Dr. Robinson called Sharron at home to let her know the results were in. "He didn't want to tell me over the phone, but I insisted that he tell me," says Sharron. "He told me that the tests showed that Kermit had cancer but further tests would have to follow to know just how far along it was. I'm a nurse but when it is your husband, it is devastating news. I immediately called Kermit at the office."

"I answered the phone," Kermit remembers well. "She said, 'Kermit, you have got to come home now.' Then I said, 'What is it? It's bad isn't it?' Then she repeated, 'You have got to come home now, Kermit!' And then she just started crying.

"I got home and she met me at the door and we held each other. What was so unusual is that my father was there from Louisville. He had just arrived with my car that had broken down when we were there Labor Day weekend. My dad is a strange kind of dude. He doesn't always act like he knows what's going on, but he knew something was going on at this time with us.

"Sharron asked if we could just be alone. Then she told me that I had cancer. We didn't know what kind or how serious it was. So we went upstairs and told my dad. He said, 'Well, let's find out what kind it is and let's beat it. Let's find out what type it is, treat it and cure it, and you'll be alright.' It turned out well that he was there just to say those words.

"So we went to see Dr. Jimmy that day and he said he didn't know what type of cancer I had because they could not locate the primary tumor at that time. So he sent me to see Dr. James Walburn, an eye, ear and throat specialist in Tuscaloosa. He checked me out. He said, 'I don't know what to tell you for sure, but I am going to send you to see Dr. Glenn Peters at the Kirklin Clinic in Birmingham.'

"Two days later, I saw Dr. Peters and he did a biopsy by running a tube up my nose. In that process, they found a tumor less than an inch long just beneath the left side of my nose at the base of my nasal cavity. If you think of your head as a ball, the tumor was right in the middle. The tumor was at the base of my skull but was not attached to my brain."

Sadly, Kermit and Sharron found out that it was a Stage 4 tumor, which is the highest level in cancer progression. The cancer had mastastisied, which means that it had begun to spread in other areas of Kermit's body, particularly the lymph nodes. Dr. Peters told Kermit and Sharron that his cancer was called "naso pharyngeal."

Still, there was hope for Kermit. "They told us that there was a cure for this type of cancer," says Sharron. "They can't say that about many types of cancer, but they said they knew a cure for this cancer. Even though Kermit was still fit, he was a little overweight, which worked to his advantage. So many patients begin treatments when they are so thin, but Kermit had more strength to draw from."

The following week, Kermit began to take 38 radiation treatments to his neck and nasal cavity. In conjunction with those treatments, Kermit was assigned three 96-hour periods of chemotherapy once a month. Kermit also took susplation and a 5 FU drug that was so potent that the nurses had to administer it with gloves on.

Says Kermit humorously, "I thought, man, if they have to wear gloves to protect themselves because it is so powerful, what is it going to do to my neck and nasal cavity! However, we were pleased that the treatment was available. We believe that God also works through medicine to cure diseases. We were thankful for the treatment, but it really zapped me physically.

"They told me that I was going to feel like they were trying to kill me," says Kermit. "However, if your body can withstand the treatment, there is a chance they can cure you. They also told me that ten years prior, there was only a 10 percent chance of survival. Now there is a 65 percent chance of being cured with this type of cancer."

For the next three and a half months, Kermit endured the powerful radiation and chemo treatments at DCH Hospital. That took the place of coaching basketball and enjoying his new dream job a half mile down the hill at Coleman Coliseum on Paul Bryant Drive. He would go to the basketball office and practice occasionally and work, but only as his strength would allow.

Despite being fed 3000 calories a day through a tube in his stomach, Kermit lost 50 pounds, going from 210 to 160. More discomfort resulted in ulcers that covered the inside of his mouth. His saliva glands were affected so severely that he always had to have warm salt water with him everywhere he went. The treatment even led to third degree burns on his shoulders and upper back.

The basketball season started and Kermit would think that he had enough strength to go to the gym and help. He would stay awhile until he had to leave with just enough strength to get back home and in bed. It was frustrating for Kermit.

With the toll that treatment was having on Kermit's body and the disappointment in not helping to coach, there was yet good news for Kermit. He was announced cured in late December. There was no tumor and no signs of cancer, praise God.

The treatment had worked but moreso, God had answered the prayers of hundreds of people that had Kermit on their prayer lists. Kermit and Sharron maintained a strong faith in The Almighty throughout those four months. The battle had been won for now but the prayers continued.

The tube was now removed from Kermit's stomach so he began to eat again and learned to swallow without saliva. Little by little Kermit got back into his coaching duties while adjusting physically after taking a pounding from the four months of treatment. On December 28, he traveled with the team to the All-College Tournament in Oklahoma City for his first road trip in his new job.

Alabama without Antonio McDyess, who had exited after his sophomore year for the NBA, was struggling. Disaster for Coach Hobbs and his staff came on January 18 at Auburn. Alabama lost 94-40. Still the team regrouped and had some impressive wins including an amazing 76-62 win at home against that same Auburn team two and a half weeks after the first meeting. Still, it was not enough as Coach Hobbs and his staff were to be replaced after the season.

Kermit and Sharron's test of faith had now moved into another direction. Job security was at stake. When coaches are let go, their contracts usually run for a few months until they can relocate.

Meanwhile, from January through May, Kermit was doing okay. His hair was coming back. He was gaining weight. He started running and exercising again. He even got in a game of golf that he loved every now and then.

"In May, I started getting back pains," Kermit recalls. "I thought it was just an old basketball injury that reoccurred while exercising again. It was time for an MRI anyway, so Sharron suggested we have it checked out. To our great disappointment and surprise, the diagnosis revealed that the cancer had moved to my liver and my bones."

The first week in June, Kermit and Sharron flew to Houston for a week of tests at the M.D. Anderson Clinic. "You are there all week and you don't know anything until they give you the results on Friday," says Kermit. Before the doctor spoke to Kermit, he called Sharron in and showed her Kermit's x-ray that revealed his liver full of tumors. She also saw where the cancer had spread to the bones of Kermit's legs, pelvic area, ribs and shoulder.

"The doctor came out to talk to me," says Kermit, "and I asked him two words, 'How long?' He said staring in my face, 'Two years with treatment at best.' Then he just turned and walked away. I suppose he goes through this all the time with people. He made his announcement and left after a brief consultation. It was like, okay, let's go have lunch.

"So we were left standing there and I just started crying. It was quite a blow after thinking I had beaten the cancer one time. Still we had God to lean on and family and friends to help us plus the wonderful medical support in Tuscaloosa."

To add to the hurt, Kermit's mother died that week in Louisville. She had heart failure which stemmed from stomach cancer. So Kermit and Sharron flew to Louisville from Houston to bury his mother and bare his own sad news to family and friends.

On July 5, Kermit started a new type of treatment. It was a three-day treatment in the hospital for every four weeks. A new experimental drug was prescribed for Kermit. He responded well. Again, medical treatment, God's power through prayer and Kermit's positive outlook was going to lead to another supernatural breakthrough.

In January, 1999, the doctors only found two spots, maybe dead tissue, on Kermit's liver and his bones were stabilized. Miraculous results were Kermit's again. Doctors were surprised and thrilled for Kermit.

At that time, the doctors decided to allow Kermit's body to rest and regroup from all drugs and treatment. They did until the cancer returned to his liver and bones again in March. So at the end of the month, the doctors put Kermit on two new experimental drugs called gemcitabine and topotecan. The drugs, given a 30 percent success rate, worked amazingly well for 14 months until May of 2000. Kermit had been on the experimental drugs longer than anyone known to be taking them had.

During a periodic checkup, the cancer showed up again in two new spots of his bones and liver. "It was obviously disappointing to get the news after the other drugs worked so well for 14 months," says Kermit who maintains relentless hope for a complete cure. "With cancer, you keep experimenting with new drugs and treatment that research continues to provide. You hope that someday there will be something that will cure you completely. So this time, the doctors gave me three choices of treatment and this time we are going with a drug called navalbine."

Kermit began taking the new drug in June and with prayer and reliance upon Almighty God, he hopes for a complete cure someday.

As far as his job, his coaching staff friends moved on to other jobs as Coach Mark Gottfried came in to replace Coach Hobbs. "Athletic Director Bob Bockrath told me to seek another job but if I couldn't find anything with the condition I was in, they would find a place for me in the athletic department. I can't say enough for the kindness and understanding that Bob displayed to me in my situation as well as Dr. (Andrew) Sorensen, Finus Gaston, Debbie Warren, Sarah Patterson and Mike DuBose. When David Hobbs was on his way out, he asked the University to take care of me. What a gesture that was on his part. They and so many others in the athletic department have been wonderful to me and my family."

On December 1, 1998, Kermit was assigned to Bill Farley's staff in Athletic Development. Kermit works approximately six hours a day until he has to rest. He maintains a regular family schedule, enjoys playing golf and otherwise lives life as normal as possible.

His weight and hair have returned and no one can tell that Kermit has ever had a problem physically by looking at him. "I feel good," Kermit says for all he has suffered. Even with the return of cancer in May, Kermit feels no different than when the drugs were working.

So what has Kermit learned from his three-year ordeal with cancer and about life itself in the past three years?

"Deep in my heart, I always felt there was a reason for my coming to Alabama. In fact, there were three. First, it was as a basketball coach to help the program. Second, it was to have a Christian influence upon the team. Third, I would later learn that the medical support here was much greater for what I needed. God knew what was ahead for me.

"You know, if I had stayed at Mississippi College, I wouldn't have discovered my cancer as soon as I did here. It was certainly a blessing when I was measured for those shirts that day in the basketball office the first month I came to Alabama.

"The doctors look at me now and shake their heads. We get up each day and are thankful for every day. I kick myself when I catch myself thinking I am having a bad day. There are no bad days for me.

"All I have is today. There is no clue that I have tomorrow, next week or six weeks. I have learned that we are all planters and doers. All we have is right now. The bottom line in life is right now."

Sharron with her strong faith trusts God completely. "We don't think that God gave Kermit this illness. We know that He gives us what it takes to take care of it. Sometimes people think that God gave us this to teach us something. It is just not so. God's grace abounds with all of this treatment."

For Sharron and Kermit, two scripture verses, which are posted on their refrigerator door, have sustained them the most. Jeremiah 29:11-13 says, "For I know the thoughts that I think toward you, says the Lord, thoughts of peace and not of evil, to give you a future and a hope. Then you will call upon Me and go and pray to Me, and I will listen to you. And you will seek Me and find Me, when you search for Me with all your heart."

The other is Isaiah 41:10 which says, "Fear not, for I am with you; be not dismayed for I am your God. I will strengthen you. Yes, I will help you. I will uphold you with my righteous hand."

The Koenig's have also learned that you have to allow other people to love you and do good things for you, even when you feel you can never repay them. The outpouring of love from the Tuscaloosa community was overwhelming to a family brand new to the area. Strong support has come from numerous churches other than their beloved Christ Episcopal Church downtown.

Kermit has accepted many opportunities on behalf of the cancer society to speak at half times of basketball games and other places. He has encouraged people to give financially to cancer research and has told his story numerous times.

On June 25-26, he was the main force behind the "Coaches Vs. Cancer" golf tournament at Pine Tree Country Club in Birmingham. Coaches from several states including some SEC head coaches accepted Kermit's invitation to participate and fight cancer. Kermit has not only been strong for his own sake, but for the sake of others as well.

Sharron always intended to get a nursing job when she came to Tuscaloosa. Her job turned out to be taking care of Kermit instead. In recent months, she has begun work at the Physicians Weight Loss Center in Tuscaloosa.

Daughters Katie (12) and Kelly (10) are exceptional kids who have been picked already for the Duke University Talent Identification Program. Katie has already scored a 28 on the ACT test and Kelly a 16 on the aptitude part. In May, Katie was one of 300 kids from 16 states who attended the Duke TIP seminar. She was given a medallion and Kermit and Sharron were told "How to Lead Kids with High IQ's."

While growing up in Louisville, Kermit was raised in the church. His mother was secretary of the Church of the Advent Episcopal Church and his dad was the custodian. They lived in the rector's home.

"Ever since I was a little boy, I have always prayed the same prayer my mother taught me to this day. Every night I pray that prayer and then I follow through with my family and a list of other family, friends and concerns. I ask the Lord to help me do what I need to do to stay here," says Kermit who never loses his great spirit and sense of humor.

For Kermit, that day-ending prayer has taken on a deeper meaning:

"Now I lay me down to sleep,
I pray the Lord my soul to keep.
If I should die before I wake,
I pray the Lord my soul to take."

"I'm living on borrowed time," says Kermit. "God has been so gracious. I've got too much to do to leave. I have these three queens to take care of. Still, I am going to trust the Lord. I have complete faith and trust in Him for whatever life holds for me ahead."

Every day is a holiday for Kermit. His cheerful spirit and outlook on life is an inspiration and a blessing beyond belief.

Thank God for people of faith and courage like Kermit Koenig.

CHAPTER ELEVEN

BILL MCDONALD

Friends of Bill McDonald jokingly refuse to ride with him. The veteran football athletic trainer has had more scrapes with death and serious injury than Indiana Jones.

For that reason, friends are afraid some catastrophe is going to happen if they ride or hang out with Bill.

Bill has been an athletic trainer since the eighth grade. He was Head Athletic Trainer at Georgia Tech from 1974-1987 and at Alabama from 1988-1999. He has treated thousands of injuries. It seems that Bill was born to be an athletic trainer.

Yet in Bill's life, he has experienced several incredible clashes off the football playing field dealing with death and life threatening injuries. Had he not been trained to deal with traumatic physical disasters, some people may not be living today, including Bill himself.

Of greater significance, had it not been for a strong faith in Almighty God, Bill could be confined to an insane asylum because of the tragedy he has seen. He acquired a strong faith in God from Christian parents from the time he was born and raised in Carbon Hill, a small community in northwest Alabama.

That faith enabled Bill to not panic but to trust God in several very serious and painful mishaps. Any other person without Jesus Christ in his or her life would likely be a mental case today.

On June 5, 1997, Bill was doing something he greatly enjoyed as a Christian layman. It was the tenth men's summer mission trip he had organized to help construct a church building. This particular mission was for a rural church called Freedom Baptist Church in Ranburne, AL. This small town of 500 people is located in northeast Alabama and two miles from the Georgia line. Freedom Baptist had 100 members and the pastor was Rev. Jackie Taylor.

Seventeen members of Bill's Northport Baptist Church in Tuscaloosa gave a week of their time to help build this new church. Most of the men had been on previous building trips. Two young men were on their first mission trip with their fathers. Bill was in charge.

Two other building projects were canceled, causing Bill to scramble for the Ranburne church project within three weeks of building time. As always, before the men departed in vans for Ranburne that Sunday afternoon, the group circled together, held hands and prayed that God would give them a successful mission and safety for the trip and work project.

No one could ever imagine what would take place five days later that would affect their lives forever.

"On Monday the work began in earnest and much was accomplished the first day," Bill recalls vividly. "Some of the men in the host church were there at different times of the day to work. By Tuesday, flooring and framing were finished and roof trusses were ready to be installed."

The trusses were 50-feet long, 12-feet high and 132 of them had to be installed on two different sides of the building. Wednesday was the day the trusses would go up. They had to be raised by a crane to be lifted into the proper position.

As scheduled, the truss installation began that morning. By late Thursday afternoon, there were only 20 trusses left. Everyone was excited as the job neared completion, especially the five men working on top of the trusses. The trusses were 12-feet off the ground and the men were working four to six feet higher to make sure that the trusses were braced together properly.

Then disaster struck. As Bill explains, "I was one of three men working underneath the trusses handing up bracing materials and other items as needed by the men on top. As I was bending down to pick up a bracing board, I heard a sound that my father had described to me whenever a coal mine had a cave-in. It was a sound of cracking and breaking timbers as they begin to fall.

"When I heard the sound, I knew immediately that the trusses were falling. I realized that they could only fall in one direction and I tried to go opposite that direction. I do not know how many steps I took before a truss hit me in the face and chest.

"I immediately went down, curling up into a fetal position and expecting the remaining trusses to fall on top of me. In a few seconds, it was over. Trusses had fallen all around me but none had fallen on me. God had protected me.

"I knew I had a possible broken nose and a cut on my head that was causing me to bleed profusely. I called for help immediately because I was unsure whether the bleeding was coming from my nose or from a severe cut on my head. One of the men indicated that most of the bleeding was from my nose.

"After slowing down the bleeding, I began to evaluate the injury situation of the other men," says Bill who always served as an athletic trainer on mission trips for cuts and any minor injuries that sometimes would occur in a building project.

"I will never forget the faces of those men as they lay injured," says Bill. "Eight of our crew were covered with heavy trusses and all with significant injuries. At that moment, I thought that some of the men might die. I prayed for them and asked God to help me to assist them until help arrived.

"As I evaluated the men, more help miraculously arrived. We were 25 miles away from a trauma hospital in Carrollton, GA. Help just seemed to come from everywhere and anywhere. After I had checked on each man, there were two people assisting each injured man.

"I began to feel better about our chances until I heard someone yell that one of the men had a rod that went through his leg and into his chest. He had significant internal injuries. When I arrived at his side, I was informed that he had been knocked from the building onto a rod sticking up from the crane truck below. It had pierced through his left leg and embedded into his right upper chest.

"He was Byron Sprayberry, one of our men. He was 42 years old. Before I got to him, he and a young man lifted him from the rod. He was in such an awkward position on that crane truck, that they lifted him off the rod freeing him from it. They had taken a great risk. The rod had gone through the fleshly part of his leg barely missing his bone.

"Byron had profuse bleeding in his leg and had an open chest wound. At that point, I was afraid Byron was going to die before we could get him to the hospital. All of a sudden, Byron looked over at me and said, 'You look awful.' I knew then that God was not going to let him die."

With so many injuries, Bill requested that the paramedics transport the men to the nearest trauma hospital even though it was farther away from other available help. Several ambulances were required to get the men to the Tanner Medical Center in Carrollton.

"It certainly proved to be a great hospital for all the injuries. Even though Byron and another one of our men, Billy White, had suffered the most severe injuries, everyone, thank God, survived this unbelievable crashing down of over 44 trusses. Six of the eight men hurt were from our church and two were from the host church."

Other men from Northport Baptist who were injured were Max Davis, Mark Landers, Berneal Ellison and Bill.

The mens' injuries included fractured upper legs, fractured arms, multiple facial fractures, fractured pelvis with spinal injuries, fractured heel, fractured ribs, knee injuries, and numerous cuts and bruises. The injuries were severe and only the grace of God prevented the loss of life.

Pastor John Nixon of the mens' church in Northport rushed to Carrollton with other family and church members to assist and be of help. Most of the men were hospitalized for several days before being transported back to Tuscaloosa for further medical help.

All of the men, except for Billy White, have overcome their injuries through rehabilitation including Byron Sprayberry. In the disastrous falling of the trusses, every bone in Billy's face was broken and both arms were broken. He has undergone several surgeries and is still reha-bilitating. He has improved enough to return to his work. Billy is known as a great prayer warrior and has always been a stalwart church leader.

After the unfortunate crashing of the trusses, it was discovered that the trusses fell when the crane accidentally hit some of the trusses in place, causing them all to crash to the ground.

"I never once heard a man ask the question, 'Why did God let this happen?' says Bill. "I never heard one indicate that he wished he had not made the trip or would not ever go again on another mission trip.

"Although none of us understands why it happened, we all have experienced God's love and power in uniting that church, that commu-nity and our own church as well. Two days following the accident, work began again by local church members to build God's church at Freedom Baptist."

The following year on June 28-July 3, 1998, the same Northport Baptist men returned to Ranburne to complete the building of the church and to be present for its dedication.

"It was quite an emotional time for our men and their people," says Bill. "It was a time of great fellowship and emotional healing for both groups. We believe it will always be a special place for God's people there to worship. We are so thankful that there was no loss of life in the tragic accident. We know that God was there for us. That's the only way we can explain it."

Growing up in the small town of Carbon Hill, Bill was the second son to Joe and Dorothy McDonald. Bill's parents were pillars of the First Baptist Church. Dorothy was the church organist and pianist and Joe was an adult Sunday School teacher. The family was in church every

Sunday morning and evening and attended a prayer meeting on Wednesday night.

Joe was a fine high school athlete, as was Bill's older brother, Joe Karrh. Therefore, Bill acquired a great love for athletics early on as well. However, a "rigid flat foot" on his left foot caused Bill problems as he tried to play football, basketball and baseball. That eventually led to three fractured ankles and finally surgery as a high school junior.

In the summer of 1960, going into his eighth grade year, Bill took a student course for athletic trainers. This would become his involvement in athletics for years to come. So in the eighth grade, Bill became a trainer-manager for Carbon Hill Head Basketball Coach Wimp Sanderson. In 1961, Coach Sanderson became a graduate assistant at Alabama and was named assistant basketball coach in 1963.

When Bill entered the University of Alabama in 1964, Coach Sanderson's influence led Bill to an athletic trainer position in basketball and football during his college career with Coach Jim Goostree. Coach Hayden Riley was the head basketball coach and Coach C.M. Newton was a graduate assistant working on his doctorate. Coach Paul Bryant was the football coach, of course. Bill got his Health, Physical Education and Recreation bachelor degree in 1967 and his master's degree in 1968.

Bill and Dian were married in 1967 after a courtship that began as college sophomores. They both had attended high school together but never dated until college.

An incredible series of misfortune began to occur in Bill's life soon after his college years. His athletic training experience would be highly tested.

In the summer of 1968, Bill took a high school coaching and teaching job at Clarkston High School in Clarkston, GA., near Atlanta. Athletic training was also included. Like many coaches and teachers, Bill sought a summer job for additional income. Bill was hired by the Clarkston Baptist Church as Youth Director for the summer.

On one particular week, the pastor took a group to Israel and the associate pastor took a group to a conference in North Carolina. Bill was left in charge at the church. A family called the church office wanting someone to come to the hospital to pray for their 12-year-old son. He was having surgery to repair a heart defect. Bill rushed over to the hospital to pray with this family who was not active in any church. Following the surgery, Bill also sat in the intensive care unit with the boy and his parents.

A few hours later the boy died. Bill prayed with the parents in the hospital chapel and they asked if he would handle the funeral arrangements and conduct the service. With the help of a local Baptist associational missionary, arrangements were made and Bill conducted the service.

"I was only 23 years old, but the Lord gave me the strength to minister to this family as best as I could," says Bill. "The family did start coming to the church. It was quite an experience for me and so unusual that it happened with the pastor and associate pastor being away at the same time, when I was the only one available to help."

This was only the beginning of a rash of serious mishaps that Bill was going to face.

The following year in one of Bill's physical education classes, another tragedy struck. "One of my students and basketball team members was passing the ball to one of his teammates and immediately collapsed to the floor. I realized that he was in cardiac arrest. I proceeded to send class members for help and started CPR to this young boy who was only 13.

"The police and fire rescue unit arrived in minutes and took over the resuscitation efforts. He was moved to the hospital where all efforts failed. He died really when he first collapsed. I summoned his parents and got them to the hospital. The young man's brother was my first high school student athletic trainer and was now a freshman at Georgia. I drove to Athens and informed him of his brother's death. Again, the Lord was right there with me to give a young coach and teacher strength to minister in a tough situation."

Five months later in August, 1969, Bill awoke one Saturday morning in a cold sweat. "The Lord had revealed to me that my father was going to die a tragic death sometime soon," Bill sadly recalls. "I woke up and it was like an audible sound from the Lord that said, 'Bill, something is going to happen and your daddy is going to die a tragic death.'

"The feeling was so strong that it woke me up. I didn't know where it came from, having had no previous thoughts of this revelation. I contacted my family to see if something was wrong with my dad. Nothing was wrong and he was in fairly good health. I contacted my pastor at Clarkston. I didn't know how to interpret it. I was confused."

Bill told his mother and brother of what he had experienced. His father, who was 61, was not told of Bill's concern for him. Only Bill's pastor offered to help with prayer and counsel as a friend.

"Two weeks to the day on a Saturday morning, I received a phone call from my mother telling me that my father had just burned to death in a trailer fire at the lake. We had a trailer on Smith Lake and Dad had spent the night alone. Mother was to join him on Saturday morning after work.

"That morning when she awoke, something told her that something was wrong at the trailer. She drove immediately to him and when she arrived, all she could see was the smoldering remains of the trailer. She could see his bones laying up on the springs of the mattress."

Bill's premonition two weeks earlier had become a stark reality. It had cushioned the tragic loss a tiny bit. "God had prepared me to be able to deal with the situation and to help my mother cope with this tragic accident," says Bill. Again for Bill, it was another traumatic occurrence in such a short period of months.

The cause of the fire was never discovered. There was suspicion of a possible robbery that led to the fire. Nevertheless, it was a tragic chapter in Bill's life.

Bill's next tragedy would come six months later in February, 1970. It would involve Bill. He was 24 years old.

While pulling out of his driveway to go coach a basketball game, a big yellow blur went by almost hitting the front end of his car. It was a school bus rounding the curve. Thinking they had missed colliding, Bill felt the bus bumper on the back of the bus slice down the side of his car like a big can opener. The bumper had sliced a big hole down the firewall side of his car. Bill felt a piece of metal that had hit his leg.

"I immediately put my hand down to check my leg and felt a hole big enough to cover my hand," Bill recalls that shocking jolt. "Blood was spurting everywhere and I tried to stop the bleeding with my hand and belt. I was alone. Just as I started to cry out for help, the Lord sent a police car over the hill that just happened to be patrolling the area.

"The policeman was calling for an ambulance. But I told him I was an athletic trainer and I knew an ambulance would arrive too late. So he put me into his car and rushed me to the hospital.

"About the time I arrived, another policeman was being brought in who had been shot. I was lying on the table in the room next to the policeman, but I was not getting any medical attention. I happened to hear the nurses saying that I was the person who had shot the policeman.

"I quickly told them that I had been in a car accident and was rushed there because I was bleeding to death. I told them what was going to happen if they didn't do something fast.

"They immediately began to work on me and I was in surgery for the next several hours. I recovered, but my leg had permanent damage, which is why I have a limp today. Obviously, that accident could have been a lot worse for me, but again God was looking over me and I am so grateful."

Two weeks after the accident, Dian began to have labor pains with their first child. Bill was in a cast up to his hip and unable to walk without crutches. Dian had to carry her bags to the hospital with Bill unable to help.

"Upon arriving at the hospital, the nurse thought I looked so bad that she brought a wheelchair for me, also. So Dian and I traveled down the hall together in wheel chairs to the labor room. So our first son, Scott, was born while I was in a cast and on crutches," says Bill with a slight smile.

In January, 1972, Bill became Assistant Athletic Trainer at Georgia Tech and was made head athletic trainer of all sports in 1974. Bill seemed to be granted parole from disaster for awhile but more was yet to come. It came in 1982 and this time it concerned Bill's mother.

"My mother was diagnosed with inoperable lung cancer. Georgia Tech was playing Tennessee in Atlanta on television that fall Saturday. After taping the team, I received a call from the Brookwood Hospital in Birmingham. They said my mother was not expected to live through the day.

"Coach Bill Curry told me that I had to go and that the team would be in good hands with my assistants. Upon arriving at the hospital, I found mother watching the game on TV, looking for me on the sidelines. She had improved tremendously. So I watched the game with her and had a good visit. We won the game 31-21 which was an uplift for our situation as well.

"On the following Wednesday, Coach Curry and the team presented the team ball to me on behalf of my mother. I had planned to call her later that night, but on the way home after practice, the Lord just revealed to me that I should call Mother as soon as I got home.

"I called her and said, 'Guess what Mother, Coach Curry and the team presented you with the game ball today to honor you for your courage. They are concerned for you.' Mother replied, 'That's great. Tell them thank you for me.'

"At that very moment, she started coughing and died while I was on the phone with her. I am so grateful that God allowed me one last opportunity to speak with Mother even though she died while I was talking to her on the telephone. Rarely would that happen to anyone, but it was quite a way to lose your mother. She had only been diagnosed with cancer for 10 weeks before she died."

Four years later in November of 1986, Bill would experience yet another very serious clash with tragedy. It came when Georgia Tech went to Athens for the big rival battle with the Georgia Bulldogs.

As Bill describes, "We were leaving Sanford Stadium on the Georgia campus after our brief Friday afternoon workout. We were staying in a motel in Commerce, GA which was 35 miles away. I noticed that two of our student trainers had gotten into the patrol car, which was in the police escort for the team buses. I instructed them to get out and get on a bus because I knew it was safer. The cars sometimes speed back and forth in an escort to cut off traffic and it can be dangerous.

"Upon arrival at the hotel, I noticed that the police car was not with us. I heard on the state patrol car radio that there had been an accident and our police car was involved. We immediately had a team meeting and had prayer for the two men in the car.

"An hour later, a state trooper came to Coach Curry and me and told us that both men had been killed. The police officer was Gary Beringaus, a close friend of mine, fishing buddy and roommate many times on game trips. The other gentleman was Jim Luck, our associate athletic director and former baseball coach. You can imagine the shock it presented to our team and, of course, it was national news.

"I was asked to participate in Gary's funeral service. Once again, the Lord was always there to help me deal with this tragic situation and to minister to this mother and her three sons. God's grace is always sufficient in every situation no matter how difficult the situation may be. He will always get you through it."

In January of 1987, Bill reached his collegiate goal of returning one day to Alabama as Head Athletic Trainer. He became involved in Northport Baptist Church soon thereafter. He started the mission building projects the next year, which led to the scary accident at Freedom Baptist Church in Ranburne in 1997.

Bill has always been a very confident professional as an athletic trainer. On July 1, 2000, Bill received the Distinguished Athletic Trainer Award, the second most prestigious award given to men in the training profession.

His dry wit and humor have been most beneficial through all of his many tragedies which have occurred away from the football field.

Probably his best known line among friends concerns the game of golf. "If I go to hell, they'll probably make me play golf every day," Bill says with a big laugh. Bill enjoys a game of golf every few months in charity and alumni events, but to play every day would be hell to Bill.

Twenty-five years ago, Bill felt the Lord calling him out of athletic training and into fulltime mission work. After turning it over to the Lord with prayer and counsel, God showed Bill that he was already on the mission field. He has worked with over 16,000 young men and women during his lifetime. They are Bill's mission field.

In reflecting back over the unbelievable clashes with death and severe injuries, Bill says, "It is very difficult to understand why all of these events have happened to me. I can only say that God has always been by my side in every incident. Each one helped me to deal with the next mishap.

"I like the verse in Philippians 1:21 that says, 'For to me, to live is Christ, and to die is gain.'

"I know this. All I am, all I have, and all I hope to be, I owe to the Lord. He's been my constant companion through it all. He never fails."

Now you know why friends tease Bill about riding with him or being around him. You never know when something serious might happen.

For sure, when you are around Bill, you know that the Lord is always near.

CHAPTER TWELVE

COACH RICK MOODY

Rick Moody is a guy who will always remember the day of his senior prom.

His prom day was not remembered for a white sport coat and a pink carnation. It was not remembered for dance music, a decorated gym or even a pretty girl for his date.

In fact, Rick almost missed the Grove Hill Academy high school prom. The afternoon of the prom, Rick was helping his dad with an installation job in a house out in the country from Grove Hill where they lived. Grove Hill was 80 miles north of Mobile on Highway 43. Population was 1,500. Rick had done many installation jobs. It was his Dad's business, putting installation in houses.

In a rush to get home so Rick could polish himself up for the prom, the fast moving truck hit some sand, missed a curve and turned over on its side. The front windshield was shattered. Rick's dad climbed out through it but Rick's leg was pinned underneath the truck. There was no solution but to go after help.

Rick's dad walked one and a half miles with a broken bone in his back before he found some construction workers. They rescued Rick by using some of their equipment to lift the truck off his leg. As Rick lay there, gas and oil were dripping on his back. So while risking the danger of the truck catching on fire, fortunately, he was spared of such a disaster. Still, Rick was petrified.

So to the hospital they went, but Rick had not even suffered a broken ankle although it blew up to the size of a softball. Rick refused to miss the prom, so he picked up his date on crutches with his best friend Mickey Lindsey and his girlfriend. The prom went fine. Rick was full of conversation and explanation about his afternoon mishap.

After the prom, Rick volunteered to drive Mickey's dad's brand new Buick. Then, there was a curve that the car approached and went through. Rick was two for two on curves on his prom day. Pain pills caused Rick to doze off. Only the screams of his three companions woke Rick up as he saw a telephone pole coming at them. Rick hit the brakes in time to stop an inch in front of the pole.

Prom day for Rick was quite eventful. It was a foretaste, in many ways, of other traumatic experiences that life would bring in the path of Rick Moody. He always managed to keep going strong. In fact, he was forced to play a doubleheader baseball game the day after the prom. His dad was the coach. His feeling was, if you can attend the prom, you are going to play these baseball games, too. So Rick took his place at second base, balloon ankle and all.

Full of grit, energy and enthusiasm, it takes a lot more than even a pickup truck to keep Rick down. He's a true competitor. He's self driven. He demands everything an athlete has to give. That's the reason he has become one of the nation's most successful Division I women's basketball coaches.

Along the way, he has met with two head on collisions that would test any person with great faith in God. To know Rick is to know a man who takes his faith very seriously. How seriously? You can find him teaching his adult Sunday School class on Sunday morning at 8:30 a.m., even though there's a tough SEC opponent to face at 2 p.m. that afternoon. That's pretty serious. Rick has done it plenty of times.

To know Rick Moody and his all out approach to coaching, being a husband and father, teaching Sunday School or fishing for bass, a glimpse from his background explains it all.

Rick was born and raised in Mobile. No, he didn't grow up in a suburb, but with his family of five boys and one sister, Rick actually lived on a dirt road on the outskirts of town. Rick was the third of the five sons and his lone sister was the baby of the family.

Rick's father made a living by placing installation in houses. He was fully engrossed in athletics with the boys after the work was done, however.

"My daddy coached all of us in baseball, RA (Royal Ambassador church basketball) and Little League football," says Rick fondly recalling his upbringing. "I remember so many times, my dad and I and all the other kids that were playing ball would go and watch the Mobile Bears in the summer.

"During the football season, we packed up in a station wagon like sardines and went to high school football games every Friday night. Every Saturday afternoon in a smoke filled room, our family would watch Alabama play on TV or listen to the game on radio, whichever one it would be on. The smoke came from my dad's cigar smoking. So

Coach Mike DuBose always meets in the shower room with his captains before each game. Shaun Alexander gets instructions before Alabama beat Florida 40-39 in overtime in Gainesville early in the 1999 season.

Shaun Alexander slashes for yardage on the way to the Southeastern Conference Championship in a stunning 34-7 victory over Florida.

Shaun counsels a young man who came forward at the Franklin Graham Festival in Coleman Coliseum on April 30-May 2, 1999.

Shaun scored more touchdowns and ran for more yards than any player in Alabama history.

Mike and Polly DuBose at their daughter Juli's wedding day February 5, 2000. Left to right are Mike, Polly, the groom G.W. Keller, Juli and her brother Michael.

Coach Ronnie Cottrell is Assistant Head Football Coach and Recruiting Coordinator, who devotes time to FCA and Chapel plans for the players.

Coach Mike DuBose was the 1999 SEC "Coach of the Year."

Ronnie and Jean Cottrell

TIDE PRIDE Director Tommy Ford with his wife Robin and their Godsend blessing, John Michael.

Chad and Leah Goss were outstanding Alabama football and basketball athletes who met at FCA.

Coach Mark Gottfried returned to his alma mater as head basketball coach 11 years after graduating.

The Mark Gottfried family of five precious children make quite a team: Front row, Cameron, Mary Layson, Aaron and Brandon. Back row, Mark, Elizabeth and baby Dillon.

Charlie and Gloria Harbison

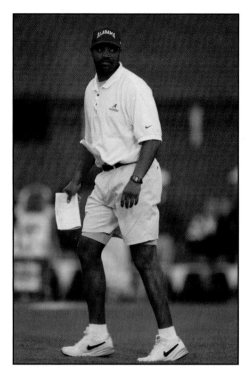

Coach Charlie "Cheese" Harbison, the
Crimson Tide's spirited defensive
backfield coach.

Coach Ellis
Johnson is the
outstanding
Alabama
Defensive
Coordinator.

The Kermit Koenig
family standing in
front of the Duke
University Chapel
in June,
2000…Kermit,
Katie, Sharron,
Kelly, and Kenneth,
dad of Kermit.

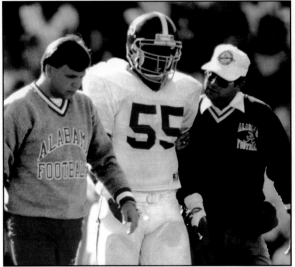

Head Athletic Trainer Bill McDonald (right) and student trainer Tim Bush escort Derrick Thomas (55) off the field when he played for Bama.

Bill and Dian McDonald

Coach Rick Moody coaches the Alabama women's basketball team and is a Sunday School teacher for adults.

Dottie Kelso, while serving as assistant basketball coach with Coach Rick Moody, died suddenly on September 18, 1993 at age 31.

Rick and Sandra Moody with their son Ben

Betty Palmer has coached the women's golf team since 1988. She and David are the proud parents of Katie.

David and Sarah Patterson have coached three Alabama gymnastics teams to national championships.

FCA leader Ryan Pflugner was always aware of God's hand upon his life.

Ryan Pflugner

The Alabama baseball team has prayer before and after each game. Andy Phillips and Nate Duncan instigated the prayers. Coach Jim Wells is in the center.

Andy Phillips was the most celebrated baseball player in Alabama history and a dynamic Christian and FCA leader.

John David Phillips

John David Phillips started the first four games of the 1998 season at quarterback. His Christian maturity and character was a total inspiration in the midst of adversity.

The Robert Scott Family: Left to right, Robert, Rahshaé, Robert Rahmun, Cynthia, and Daniel. Robert was assistant basketball coach and died of cancer on May 9, 2000 at the age of 42.

Men's golf coach Dick Spybey with wife Mary and son Rick. Dick was the 1992 National Coach of the Year.

Kevin Stephen came to Alabama from Trinidad as a decathlon athlete in 1993. His remarkable story resulted in receiving a kidney transplant from his sister Pat on August 11, 1999. This photo was taken a week after the transplant procedure.

Baseball coach Jim Wells has led Alabama to six straight NCAA appearances and to three College World Series, averaging 48 wins a year.

The Jim Wells Family left to right are Melissa, Lisa, Drew, Jim and Lauren.

Evangelist Billy Graham met with first year leaders of the Alabama Fellowship of Christian Athletes on April 26, 1965 in Paul Bryant Hall. Mr. Graham came to Tuscaloosa to preach in a one night service in Denny Stadium. Left to right are trackman Eddie King, tackle Richard Cole, sports information graduate assistant Wayne Atcheson, Mr. Graham, center-linebacker Paul Crane and quarterback Steve Sloan.

Billy Graham is shown preaching in Denny Stadium on April 26, 1965 in preparation plans for a Crusade in Montgomery the following June. Mr. Graham preached in a raincoat to 15,000 people and had to end his message after five minutes due to heavy rain and severe weather.

In June, 1965 early Alabama FCA leaders attended the FCA Conference at Black Mountain, NC with notable speakers and athletes. Front row, L-R, are Jerry Claiborne (Virginia Tech coach), Eddie King, Steve Sloan, Richard Cole and Wayne Atcheson. Second row, L-R, are Dickie Bean, Loren Young (FCA staff), Paul Anderson (world's strongest man) and Bill Wade (Chicago Bears).

The No. 18 picture has been the "trademark photo" of FCA nationally depicting the movement's key theme of "Influence." No. 18 is David Dean, younger brother of Alabama defensive back Mike Dean (1967-69). David looks on to his brother's huddle group at an FCA conference at Black Mountain, NC in 1967.

Billy Graham and his evangelistic ministry has had a profound impact upon the Alabama family and FCA through the years. On May 14-21, 1972, Billy Graham and his team held a Crusade in Birmingham at Legion Field. On the platform for one service was front row, L-R, Mrs. Mary Harmon Bryant, Coach Paul Bryant, Joe Namath (Alabama, New York Jets), Coach Tom Landry (Dallas Cowboys) and Mr. Graham. On the second row was Scott Hunter (Alabama, Green Bay Packers) and Mike Kolen (Auburn, Miami Dolphins).

Squad Sunday at Calvary Baptist Church began in 1964, the same year the Alabama FCA was organized. This picture was taken at the 1984 service. Pictured left to right are Wayne Atcheson, John Erickson (FCA National President and guest speaker), Paul Fields (Charlie Compton Award recipient), Coach Ray Perkins (Head Football Coach) and Dr. Allan Watson (Calvary pastor). Dr. Watson called the first meeting of the Alabama FCA in September, 1964 held in his church at Calvary.

At the Alabama-LSU game on November 5, 1988, the Alabama FCA huddle was recognized prior to the game for its twenty-fifth anniversary. Pictured left to right are Dr. Charlie Barnes (FCA advisor 1964-73), General Dick Abel (National FCA President), Steve Sloan (Athletic Director), Howard Cross (FCA huddle president), Wayne Atcheson (FCA Advisor 1985-present) and Dr. Gary White (FCA advisor 1973-85). All FCA Presidents since 1963 including James Jeffrey, John Erickson, General Dick Abel and current president Dal Shealy have visited the Alabama FCA for various events.

Following the 1988 Alabama-LSU game in Bryant-Denny Stadium, FCA President General Dick Abel led both teams in the post-game prayer.

All Squad Sunday services are special occasions as was the 1991 service.
Pictured left to right are Dr. Bruce Chesser (Calvary Baptist Church pastor),
Hootie Ingram (Athletic Director), John Mark Stallings, Coach Gene Stallings
(Head Football Coach), Martin Houston (Charlie Compton Award recipient)
and John Croyle (Big Oak Boys and Girls Ranches founder and guest speaker).

Dr. Gary White
was the Alabama
FCA advisor
from 1973-85 and
his wife Susanna
was a community
Bible leader for
women. Susanna
died of cancer on
September 11,
1990 at age 47.

Jay Barker was known as
a Christian role model in
1990-94 as much as being
the winningest quarter-
back in Alabama history.

The ladies in author
Wayne Atcheson's life
who have supported him
through his years of
involvement in
FCA....Wayne, Amy,
Elizabeth and Barbara.
Wayne and Barbara met at
an FCA Conference in
Estes Park, CO in 1971.

Franklin Graham, son of Billy Graham, held a West Alabama Festival in the Coleman Coliseum on the University of Alabama campus on April 30-May 2, 1999. Some 4,000 volunteers participated in the three-night Festival services. An average of 17,000 people attended with the overflow crowd seated in the indoor football building. Franklin's team, headed by Festival Director Wendell Rovenstine, led in the 10-month preparations that resulted in 3,800 decisions for Christ. Many FCA athletes, coaches and athletic staff participated as counselors, choir members, ushers and numerous other roles.

Jay Barker (7) and his closest brothers in Christ started getting together for prayer in the shower room as they awaited pre-game warm-ups. The "Shower Prayer" has continued as players dedicate their talents back to God. This 1993 photo includes Tony Johnson (5), Mickey Conn (40), Chad Key (19), Tommy Johnson (10), Roman Colburn (84), Jay, and Eric Turner (39).

many men smoked in that day and we didn't think anything about it, even in our home.

"Then, every Sunday afternoon, it was a ritual to watch 'The Bear Bryant Show.' It was Golden Flake and Coke at our house at 4 o'clock. It was 'Great Pair says the Bear' in our living room. You did nothing. You planned nothing. At 4 o'clock on Sunday afternoon it was quiet at our house. It was like the world stood still for an hour. We watched every minute of Bear Bryant and Alabama football."

Growing up, there were two people who had a profound influence upon Rick. They were his dad and mom, Joe and Joyce Moody. "The main thing I learned from my dad was that we had to work. Dad had an installation business and his boys were the employees. In the summer months, we would get up at 3:30 and 4 o'clock in the morning trying to get into a house before it got too hot.

"We had an old pickup truck that was converted into a work truck. Gosh, I remember those hot summer days and freezing mornings in the wintertime. There wasn't enough room for all of us to get into the cab, so some of us had to sit in the back. It was brutal.

"The thing I remember about that business the most was my dad being a man of such integrity. We had to do it right. When we worked on somebody's house, those people had to inspect the job before we could leave. If it wasn't right, we made it right.

"Dad was always incredibly respectful. It was 'yes, ma'am and no, ma'am' and 'yes, sir and no, sir.' It didn't matter how young or old the person was. If they were younger than he was, he treated them all the same. That taught me some valuable lessons that I have taken with me throughout my life."

Rick's mom contributed to his life in an altogether different fashion. "My mother was the person who got me into church, thank the Lord. She was the spiritual person in my family who got me involved in youth retreats. There was a retreat center near Biloxi, MS named Past Christian Camp Retreat that the youth of Cottage Hill Baptist Church attended. It was one of the most spiritual moments of my life. We sat around a bonfire on the beach singing, 'Kum Ba Ya.'

"It was soon after a retreat there that I went home and walked down the aisle at Cottage Hill and accepted Christ as my Savior. I was baptized by Brother Don Watterson. Of course, my mom was real involved in the music of the church. She had me in choir. We went on choir tours. I thank God for my mother's spiritual guidance. Our church had 200 or 300 on Sunday. Today, Cottage Hill has two or three thousand on Sunday morning. It was such a good influence on my young life."

Rick attended high school at Davidson High which was in the top division of the state. Even though he was small in stature, Rick was still out for football and basketball in the eleventh grade. One of his best friends would one day be a star quarterback at Alabama and have several outstanding years in the National Football League.

"At Davidson, Richard Todd was one of my best friends. We played baseball and football together. He stayed at my house and I stayed at his house. He broke more bats one summer in baseball, so much so that the City of Mobile was going broke trying to keep our baseball team in bats. My dad coached us. It was wonderful growing up.

"Richard and I were in the same class. He was the quarterback and I was one of the down the line quarterbacks." Rick hung in there on the football team but basketball was his better sport.

At this juncture in Rick's life, trouble found itself brewing on his high school campus. "Things got really rough in Mobile. That was when segregation was taking place. They had the National Guard coming to our high school to keep riots from taking place. I had some kinfolks in Grove Hill. They had just started a new school called Grove Hill Academy. They contacted my dad and wanted to know if we would consider coming up there and going to school. They even offered me a scholarship.

"So, my whole family moved to Grove Hill. Then at the Academy, I became a three-sport star! I played football, basketball and baseball. With my athletic ability and with my size, the smaller school was perfect for me. It was good for my confidence to experience the thrill of competing in three sports," says Rick.

All four children still left at home attended the Academy and Rick's dad moved his installation business to Grove Hill.

The summer after high school graduation, Rick met his future wife Sandra who was from Thomasville, just 16 miles away. They met at the amusement park at the T intersection in Gulf Shores. Rick attended Patrick Henry Junior College in Brewton while Sandra was a senior in high school.

"I guess you would say we were going steady," says Rick. "At Patrick Henry, I was dating other girls while she was seeing no one at her school. Then when she joined me at Patrick Henry, I found out that she had a date with a boy in Thomasville. So when she had a date with somebody else, it was like sticking a dagger into me. From that point forward, I never dated anybody else. She gave me a dose of my own medicine."

Rick played basketball his two years (1972-74) at Patrick Henry. Then he moved on to Troy State and graduated. Sandra followed. Two weeks after Rick's graduation, they were married on August 14, 1976.

Having already fully decided on coaching years before, Rick's first job was as basketball coach and physical education teacher at Meigs Junior High in Shalimar, FL, near Ft. Walton Beach. Fortunately for Sandra, Troy State had an extension school at Eglin Air Force Base nearby and she completed her degree there.

After one year at Meigs, Rick moved over to be the junior varsity coach at Choctawhatchee High in Fort Walton Beach. The varsity coach was Coach Benny Gabbard. "This high school basketball coach taught me more about basketball in two years than the rest of my 22 years combined. He was amazing," says Rick.

"We had phenomenal success and then I became the basketball coach at Fort Walton Beach High School. It was a great job. Two years later, I worked in a BC All-Star Basketball Camp in Milledgeville, GA. When the camp ended, they had a girls' camp and they needed somebody to stay and help. So they asked me to stay, although I had never worked with females before. I needed the money."

Rick didn't know it, but the University of Alabama was just around the corner.

"I was working that girls' basketball camp and I looked on the end of the bleachers and saw the head women's basketball coach of the University of Alabama sitting there. It was Ken Weeks. I melted. All of a sudden, those Sunday afternoons and Saturday afternoons of Alabama and Bear Bryant flooded my mind. I was still such an avid Alabama fan. So I took the opportunity to go over and introduce myself.

"We spent some time together and before the week was over, he offered me a graduate assistantship. I quit my job, sold my house and came to Alabama with $10,000 equity money. Sandra was teaching at Meigs and we were making $50,000 a year, which was a lot of money at that time. That system was one of the highest paying in Florida.

"So we came to Tuscaloosa with me as a graduate assistant, Sandra with no job and both with a lot of faith. My daddy always taught me that if I get an opportunity, even if it is at the very bottom of the scale, and you do a good job, try to be the best ever at that position, then people will recognize that and it will turn into greater opportunities. I believed it.

"To be honest, I was hoping to get up here and be around Wimp Sanderson and the men's basketball program. Hopefully, they would recognize my work ethic and coaching ability, and I would eventually get on with their staff. That was my real goal but God had other plans.

"In all of this, the amazing thing was to have a wife who would believe in me like Sandra did. We moved to Tuscaloosa on faith and right before school started, she got a job at the Tuscaloosa Academy making $6,000 a year. She was making about $18,000 down there at Meigs. So it was quite a sacrifice to be at Bama."

Rick joined Coach Weeks in 1981 and in three years the women's program was turned around. "The 1984 team was one of the best teams in the history of this program. We went to the school's first NCAA tournament and had the Tide's first All-American player in Cassandra Crumpton, who is one of my assistant coaches today," Rick says.

When Ben was born on June 15, 1984, all savings were depleted and the family income forced Rick to leave Alabama and take the varsity boys' basketball job at Guntersville (AL) High School. Rick went from his assistant coach salary of $14,000 to $35,000 at Guntersville. Family had become top priority over the college post at Alabama. It turned out to be five wonderful years of coaching as his 1987 and 1989 teams reached the state tournament.

"One night at 11 o'clock, I got a call from Wimp Sanderson," remembers Rick with keen recall. "He asked me if I wanted this job (women's head coaching position)? I was shocked. Lois Myers had resigned. But fortunately, Sarah Patterson was a good friend of mine from my previous days there. She was women's administrator. Wimp was a good friend and he was in a position of influence. Steve Sloan was the athletic director.

"So the move that I made from Fort Walton Beach High School to Alabama and establishing relationships with Sarah and Wimp proved to be one of the greatest things I have ever done. Without that, I had no shot in getting this job.

"Honestly, as much as I loved Alabama, we also loved Guntersville. Ben was getting ready to go to kindergarten. We were well entrenched in Guntersville, plus it had 69,000 acres of the best bass fishing in America," says Rick, an ardent fisherman, with a laugh. "We also had some wonderful friends. However, we prayed about it and asked God to show us some signs and he did. God really opened doors."

Rick believes that it takes at least three years in high school or college to get a program turned around. In his third year at Alabama, the team was in the NCAA tournament with a final 23-7 record and had recruited some great players. However, Rick, in his fifth year in 1994, had Alabama in the NCAA Final Four, an awesome accomplishment. You couldn't have written a better success story.

Much of that success came with the first phone call Rick made when he was considering the Alabama head job. "Before I took the job at Alabama, I knew I had to have some good help. I could not do it by myself," Rick is quick to point out. "I called Dottie Kelso, who was at Decatur High School as a junior high coach. When I was an assistant in 1984, we had recruited Dottie and I knew what kind of person she was. I knew about her faith, her personality and her work ethic. She was the first person that I thought of. I called her and asked her if she would consider coming with me if I took the job. Like a duck on a June bug, she jumped all over it.

"So my first staff was me, Dottie and Sherri Smelser. We were so close. It was unbelievable. We had a wonderful time recruiting and developing this team into one of the nation's best."

The road to the Final Four in Richmond, VA was paved with overwhelming emotional roadblocks. Rick would face enough hardship in one year to last for an entire lifetime. Yet his faith guided him on in spite of two cases of heartbreak along the way. They would involve the love of his life, Sandra, and assistant coach, Dottie, who was the true spirit of the team.

"The 38 years prior to the time Sandra discovered a tumor, my life had been very simple," says Rick. "It seemed as if my marriage, my family, my career had been on a steady course that kept carrying me forward. That goes for my love for the Lord as well as my desire to serve Him with my life."

On a Tuesday evening in September of 1992 after Rick had departed for bed, Sandra did a routine self-breast examination and felt a lump in her breast. The next morning she told Rick and a doctor's appointment was arranged.

"That afternoon we were on the coliseum floor taking team pictures when I was sent word that Sandra was in my office and very upset," recalls Rick. "I made a beeline to the office and a preliminary diagnosis indicated that it was indeed cancer. Sandra was virtually a basket case. The following Monday, they did a biopsy. Sitting alone in the waiting room, the doctor came and told me Sandra's tumor was malignant. I hit my knees right there in the waiting room when the doctor came in and said to me, 'I'm sorry, it's malignant.'"

A radical mastectomy was performed the next day on Sandra who was only 37. Recruiting was already in progress and practice for the upcoming 1992-93 season was about to embark. It was a very trying time for Rick. However, Sandra's attitude eased the burden.

"My wife virtually attacked the cancer itself," said Rick. "Her positive attitude and the aggressiveness with which she went about taking chemotherapy and the other treatments, I guess was the most inspiring thing I've ever seen. During the basketball season through the NCAA tournament, I could not be present most of the time she was taking medication. When I called her, she never gave any indication that she was sick. She would pick me up. She has been the most inspiring person I've ever known. Sandra did not miss more than 10 days out of school the entire year as an 11th grade history teacher at Northside High School.

During that season, Rick's team posted a 22-9 record and lost 74-73 in overtime to North Carolina in the NCAA Mideast Regional tournament at Chapel Hill. With Sandra's health as a concern, it was nice to have a team that won consistently.

One year after Sandra was diagnosed with cancer, more stunning news came into Rick's life. On Wednesday, September 15, 1993, Rick was fishing the day before home recruiting visits became official. He was in Demopolis fishing with a friend, Bobby Knowles. His wife Linda was secretary to Coach Gene Stallings.

"When we returned to the truck, there was a note on the windshield from the police department that said call the athletic department immediately. I called Linda and she said that Dottie had gone into the hospital to have some tests run and had gone unconscious. I suddenly recalled many times when Dottie had headaches and would have to go home with migraines. Little did we know just how serious Dottie's condition was.

"I asked Linda if she was dead and she said, 'No, but you need to hurry.' We were 50 miles away from the DCH Hospital. Finally, we got to the hospital. I went in and held her hand and started talking to her. I felt if I could just get there, she would respond to me and would make it. I asked her to respond to me in some form or fashion. To move her hand, to squeeze my finger or to do something to let me know she heard me. I got no response.

Dottie was pronounced brain dead on Thursday, the day after it was discovered that a cyst in her brain had burst. On Friday, her family agreed there was no hope for Dottie and the life support was removed. On Sunday afternoon 3,000 people gathered in the Coleman Coliseum basketball arena as Dottie lay in an open casket on the basketball floor for her memorial service.

Dottie was 31 years old and single, but had a special fellow that she planned to marry in the near future.

"To eulogize Dottie, a person I cared for so deeply, was the most difficult thing I've ever had to deal with. When I give a talk, I usually write notes. This is the only time I wrote everything out and read it. It was hard to give Dottie up. She was a wonderful person and like a big sister to all of our players. As recruiting coordinator, she was responsible for most of them being at Alabama," says Rick, still finding it a tender subject to discuss.

Ironically, eight days before Dottie was stricken, she had shared her faith in Christ so beautifully at the Alabama FCA Huddle meeting before 120 athletes. She had been scheduled to speak one day after she was buried, but due to a cancellation, Dottie agreed to speak two weeks earlier than scheduled.

So in God's divine providence, Dottie's last opportunity to share her faith was made possible. Her life was a daily witness of the Christian faith, and her sudden passing had a mighty impact on the Alabama campus. A few months later, a tree was planted in front of Coleman Coliseum in memory of Dottie.

For Rick, September, 1993 was one of the lowest points of his life. Yet six months later in March, 1994, his Alabama team was in the Final Four. "We went from the very debts of despair to the very tip of the mountain top. To reach the Final Four, we defeated Oregon, Iowa, Texas Tech (previous season national champions), and Penn State (ranked No. 2 in the nation). We lost to Louisiana Tech by three points in the Final Four, barely missing the national championship game."

Through the difficult times, Rick continued to teach his adult Sunday School Class (ages 27-41) at the Tuscaloosa First Baptist Church and serve as a deacon. Rick took a class of ten people that now averages 55 in attendance each Sunday morning at 8:30 a.m. If he has a home game that afternoon, Rick still stands before his class that morning and delivers the lesson.

"Teaching that class forces me to stay in the Word and it forces me to live my life by the Word," says Rick whose reputation as a teacher is highly regarded.

Rick is also a regular speaker in churches when his schedule permits. Also, the Fellowship of Christian Athletes Coaches Camps at

Black Mountain, NC have been a highlight in Rick and his family's life many times. Rick has made great friendships at the camps and he has taken away a greater sense of purpose in coaching.

One of the most important things to Rick and his coaching has been Devotion Time before every game his team plays. "Of all my years at Alabama and the great wins we have had, some of my greatest and most memorable moments have happened before the game was played in our Devotion Time," says Rick with a humble heart. "To see young ladies break down and share their innermost feelings about their faith, their difficulties, and struggles, there have been some cherished moments. I believe that it carries over onto the court, too."

As for Sandra eight years later, her life goes on as if cancer had never struck. "We are Winnie the Pooh fans in our family. Sandra reminds me a lot of Tigger. She bounces here and there full of energy and enthusiasm. Her health is good. Her whole outlook is that *she is living with cancer and not dying with cancer.*'

"Besides, God has used Sandra time and time again to counsel others with cancer. She is still teaching world history at Northside High also," Rick says proudly and thankfully.

As for Ben, he's a delight. Ben started on the varsity basketball team at Northside last year as a ninth grader. "His real passion is golf, but he can shoot the basketball well, too," says his father Rick.

"Already, Ben has expressed a desire to be a minister. One day I asked him if he really thought he wanted to be a minister. He's just in the ninth grade. His reply was, 'It doesn't matter what I think. If God is calling me, I have to do it.' So when he said that, I didn't say another word. With that kind of answer, I let it alone."

Rick's spiritual summation concerning Sandra's cancer and Dottie's passing away so suddenly has good wisdom for trying circumstances.

"I believe God has allowed things to happen to really put a spotlight on me. I truly believe with a clear understanding that people are watching you all the time. They want to see if you are going to be as strong a Christian as you claim to be.

"Through it all, I trust that God has been glorified because without Him, life would be a disaster. Our strength comes from God. We can trust Him no matter how tough life can be. He never fails, thank God."

Rick's dream of coaching at Alabama came true through God's divine plan and blessing. In response, Rick has coached totally unashamed of the great God he loves and serves.

Indeed, he truly shines for Christ in the spotlight.

CHAPTER THIRTEEN

COACH BETTY PALMER

You are 33 years old. You coach the women's golf team at Alabama. You are in excellent health.

Then over the next seven years, you have three major surgeries. Two are cancerous. What do you do?

For Betty Palmer, life was good. She grew up in Tuscaloosa as Betty Buck, the daughter of a prominent family. Her dad was a well-respected man, Circuit Court Judge James D. Buck. The third of three children, Betty wanted for nothing.

Dolls and golf were her great interests growing up. At Tuscaloosa High School, she was a standout prep golfer.

She began college at the University of Arkansas. She loved it there, but transferred to Alabama after two years to play golf for Coach Conrad Rehling. As a collegian, Alabama won four tournament titles and played in the AIAW National Championship Tournament for four straight years.

Betty loved Alabama football, the rich tradition and Coach Paul "Bear" Bryant as well. She grew up watching Alabama win national championships. She was so happy at the Capstone.

After graduating in 1982, Betty had many good opportunities to pursue. Ann Marie Lawler, the Alabama Associate Athletic Director for women, made her a graduate assistant in golf. A year later, Mississippi State made her their assistant golf coach. Betty was a mere 24 years old. She moved on to the University of Georgia the next year in a similar position.

She joined the private sector in 1985-87 serving as the assistant professional at Horseshoe Bend in Roswell, GA. In 1987-88, Betty became the first female Tournament Director for the American Junior Golf Association. Two of the juniors at that time happened to be Tiger Woods and Phil Micholson.

Then on July 24, 1988, Betty came to Tuscaloosa for Coach Rehling's retirement tournament. Her threesome consisted of Cecil

Ingram, Jr. and a friend of his whom she had never met. His name was David Palmer.

"It was not a setup by Cecil," says Betty. "They were just good friends from Birmingham. Besides, all during the round, David's boxer shorts were constantly coming out and he was always having to correct this problem. So it was not love at first sight! It was like laughter at first sight!"

It was a special month for Betty, though, as she received a call from Sarah Patterson to become head coach of the Alabama women's golf team. She replaced Dick Spybey who took over the men's program when Coach Rehling retired.

It was a dream come true for Betty. Once again, life is good and all is well. Meanwhile, several months passed by when David and Betty had their first date at the Pizza Hut. That was February and in May they were engaged. They were married on December 9, 1989 in Christ Episcopal Church, Betty's church in downtown Tuscaloosa.

Ironically, David and Betty were born two and one half weeks apart in 1959. David was the son of a Southern Baptist minister in Morristown, TN. He graduated from Samford University in computer science and was in Tuscaloosa working for Southland National Insurance Cooperation.

David and Betty were a great match. They were so compatible. They rarely had a disagreement. One of their few disputes encountered though was when Betty tried to give David a golf lesson one day. Otherwise, a good marriage has been their delight. Stay away from golf lessons for David and the marriage was well in tact.

Their lives took on added joy when God gave them a baby girl named Katie on February 3, 1993. Betty was 33 at the time and the Cesarean section birth was a normal procedure. Later on however, it would become a part of added physical trauma that Betty would endure.

No matter how good life can be, you never know what lies ahead. Betty was about to find out.

In April, 1994, Betty had a routine Pap smear examination. Every day thousands of women have such exams. "The doctor's office called and told me to come back in because something didn't look right," remembers Betty, whose mind tried to refuse that phone message. "Something was not as clear as it should be.

"Well, I hesitated about going back. In fact, it was several months. I took one of my options, which was to forget about it or ignore it.

Maybe I had always been in such great health that I didn't want to hear of any bad health news. I felt fine."

Betty waited until December 21 before she was checked again with another Pap smear. That resulted in a biopsy for further testing. Then on January 6, 1995 Betty got a shocking phone call from Dr. Gordon Bryars, an OBGYN in Tuscaloosa.

"I was at the office. It was a Friday afternoon about 3 p.m. It was cold and rainy outside. It was a gloomy day anyway," remembers Betty vividly. "The phone rang and it was Dr. Bryars. He said, 'Betty, I have looked at the lab report. Get in touch with David and come to my office as soon as possible. I'm concerned about your report. We need to talk about it today!'

"When you hear news like that from a doctor, it is like you don't hear anything. Everything was a big blur. It came as such a shock, especially when you feel fine. So I got in touch with David and we got to Dr. Bryars' office right away.

"He explained that this looked like cancer and that he had already set up an appointment for me to see Dr. Ed Partridge at the UAB Hospital in Birmingham on Monday morning. After receiving the hard news, we made our way home. Our entire world had changed and caved in on us within one hour on that Friday afternoon. That weekend was a 'living hell' as we waited for Monday."

David also had feelings to deal with as well. "There is nothing worse than finding out on Friday that your wife has cancer and you can't see a doctor until Monday. Betty had been told that she could have a complete hysterectomy. Naturally, we were concerned for her.

"Still during the weekend, Betty considered the fact that if she didn't make it, she wanted me to remarry and have someone to raise Katie, who was only two years old. You immediately think of the worst that could happen as you pray for the best."

Monday morning finally came as Betty and David made the one-hour drive to Birmingham to meet with Dr. Partridge. Betty still felt good physically.

"Dr. Partridge brought us into his office. He had all of the lab work slides and he was real straight and up front with us," says Betty. "He said, 'You have an early Stage 1 cervical cancer. I am going to operate in two days. You have one day to get your affairs in order for surgery and recovery time. You have a 70 percent chance of overcoming this cancer, should it be in the lymph nodes and a 95 percent chance if it is contained.'

"When he said that, it made me feel better. Having had a C-section with Katie gave me some experience with surgery. So we went back home and I got things in order at the office and at home the best I could in one day."

Word spread rapidly in the athletic department, in the community and at Calvary Baptist Church where they had been attending for a year. Betty and David were greatly encouraged when they heard of numbers of people who were praying for Betty. David's mother is especially known as a prayer warrior, and Betty felt so much strength from her faith and prayers.

Wednesday morning at 6 a.m., Betty was wheeled into the operating room. Only five days had passed since she got the dreadful news on Friday.

"Even as I was being wheeled down the hall for surgery, I had no pain," says Betty. "I couldn't tell that anything was wrong with me. I was working hard as a golf coach and as a mom to Katie and wife to David. I just didn't feel like I should be having surgery for anything."

The anxious time for surgery proceeded. Betty would have a complete hysterectomy and a complete cervical procedure to try and remove all signs of cancer.

"I go through the surgery and the first voice I hear is my brother Roger, who is a doctor in Gadsden. My family always called me Liz. I could barely hear him say in my right ear, 'Liz, it was contained. They got it all. You are going to be okay.'

"What a blessing God had given to me and our family. It took a lot of prayer, but I had a lot of prayer going up for me. We had only been at Calvary Baptist for a year, but those people offered so much prayer for me. While I was home recovering for six weeks, they supplied our family with all the food we needed.

"I found out that such Christian support aids the healing process as much as anything. Sometimes it is easy to think that people have grown callous in our society and do not have concern for each other. It was quite the opposite for me. People were so supportive and encouraging. I couldn't have made it without them.

"David had just begun his second semester working on his doctorate. So I was concerned for his studies, but everything worked out for him.

"Then God had already prepared us in another special way for this time when I couldn't do anything for myself, much less Katie and David. A year before the surgery, Mother moved into a house next door to us. So when I was out of commission, Mother was there to take care of Katie. What a blessing from God!"

For Katie at age two, "Momma was sick." For David and Betty, their faith and the strong support of family, friends in the athletic department and community, plus their church got them through. "I never questioned God about why this happened," says David who developed a strong trust in God as a 'preacher's kid' growing up.

"There is some shock in there, but my faith in God remained solid. There were times when I thought if Betty doesn't make it, I was somewhat adjusted. Betty, as a golf coach, is on the road about 100 days a year. So I had that experience of keeping Katie when she was away. Still, I felt that everything was going to be okay and it was."

Six weeks later, Betty was back to work. Her cancer had been contained. She would see her doctor every three months for the next year and every six months thereafter. For now, Betty was cleared of cancer.

As golf coach, Betty's team had done well. Her team had been runner-up in the Southeastern Conference in 1991 and 1994. She was SEC "Coach of the Year" in 1993.

Betty had also served as vice-president of the National Golf Coaches Association from 1993-95. Later, she became a member of the Board of Director's of the Southeastern Amateur Team Championship. Locally, she became a board member for the Tuscaloosa Big Brothers/Big Sisters organization, and serves at her daughter's school, Tuscaloosa Academy.

"So after I recovered from the surgery, my faith and spiritual life took on greater meaning. I also thank God for modern medicine and doctors like Dr. Partridge and Dr. Bryars who have the skills and wisdom to promote life. I have shared with many people how God has spared my life and what a blessing He has been to me," says Betty.

Betty's cancer surgery had taken place in January of 1995. Four and a half years later, Betty was to receive another doctor's call and more devastating news. This time, it came about in a different way.

Severe lower back pains struck Betty on June 7, 1999. "Naturally, it scared me so much that I called my brother Roger. He said it sounded like I might have a kidney stone. He told me to see the doctor right away. So the next day, I was x-rayed in Dr. (Jimmy) Robinson's office.

"While the nurse was x-raying me, I noticed that she was looking at the x-ray over and over again. Finally, she said, 'There is something on your kidney. I can't see your kidney. There is something blocking its view.

"That added to the anxiety and concern. The next day was Wednesday and they scheduled a CAT scan. I had to drink those horrible liquids and the scan was set for 2 p.m. I went home. At 3:45 the doorbell rang. I was home alone as Katie was in a summer program and David was at work.

"It was Dr. Robinson at the door. I knew he was leaving with the baseball team to Omaha and I didn't sense anything wrong until I opened the door for him. He said, 'I've come to give you some bad news.' So we sat down in the den and he told me that the CAT scan had revealed a large mass attached to the lower right part of my liver. 'It doesn't look good,' he said. He told me it appeared to be a form of cancer on the liver.

"He also said, 'I have made an appointment with a liver transplant specialist for you on Friday morning in Birmingham.' It almost sounded like a broken record. Once again, the big blur came back. I knew my mother next door couldn't take this news. So I had Dr. Robinson go with me to her house and had him share the news with her. Once again, I have found that it is good for another person to hear distressing news like this when it concerns you. It is difficult to comprehend such dreadful news without your mate or someone close to you.

"The next morning, my brother Roger flew in. He took the CAT scan x-rays, held them up into the light outside on our deck and said, 'I'm not a radiologist, but I do not see the worst part of it. Maybe it is not as bad as they think.'

"On Friday morning, David and I walked into the Kirklin Clinic in Birmingham to see Dr. Devon Eckoff. For some reason, I was acting real business like. Let's get this over with. The pains had left me. I knew I had a kidney stone and it had passed. I was feeling fine. But thank God for the kidney stone. Without it, we would not have discovered what Dr. Eckoff was about to tell us.

"He looked at the x-rays and said, 'It's got to come out.' He studied it again and again. Finally he said, 'You have a mass of blood cells on your liver which is Fibroid Adenoma. In all likelihood, it is benign.' So what can you say? You listen, ask questions and follow orders. Dr. Eckoff set up surgery a week later for June 21.

"This time it was not a 'weekend of hell,' it was a 'week of hell' waiting for the surgery and the results. We prayed for a week and friends rallied around us as they did the first time. The day came for the surgery. As before, I felt no discomfort. I was wheeled into the operating room feeling as focused as if I were on a golf course.

"There were 12 family members and friends there for me at 6 a.m. when the surgery was scheduled. It finally took place at 2 p.m. Emergencies had been placed in front of me."

David had been told that the surgery would last three or four hours. "At 8 p.m., I really felt like my faith was being tested," says David. "I cried at the end of *Father Of The Bride II* and *Turner and Hooch*. So I'm feeling anxious and a little overwhelmed by the length of the surgery.

"Finally, the doctor came out and told us that he had taken a tumor the size of a nurf football from Betty's liver. He said he had also taken 60 percent of her liver and had removed her gall bladder. He had also discovered her bile ducts were twisted, probably from birth, and extra time was required to trace them to their normal position. But the good news was that the tumor was benign. We had escaped danger again."

This time, the surgery required a 21-inch incision across Betty's stomach. The next day they had Betty sitting in a chair. Nine days later she was learning to walk again. Walking became difficult since so much movement has to do with the stomach.

Once again, the healing process was largely due to family and friends. "Sarah Patterson and her assistant, Rita Martin, arranged for meals through the athletic department for four weeks. It was a wonderful thing to receive such love when there is not a thing you can do about it but just receive it. I don't think we could have survived without it.

"I have always been a very religious person. I believe in God and pray several times a day. My faith has grown so much through it all. Also, I can truly say that this athletic department has been through a lot over the past few years and many have had serious health problems like I have. But in times of crisis and need, we look out for each other as friends. We work to prepare young people to be better adults, yet we rally around each other when there is a need."

During this rehabilitation, Betty lost 15 pounds in six weeks. It was different for Katie this time at six years of age. She spent some time in Tennessee with David's parents, but it was hard for her to see her mommy out of commission for several weeks.

David and Betty kept her life going as normal as possible.

Three months after the surgery, Betty's liver regenerated itself. Betty feels fortunate that the tumor was on the only organ that does reproduce. Doctors continue to keep a close watch on Betty's health. In April of 2000, Betty's doctors told her that she was free of cancer. She feels so strong physically again and plays hard for the church softball team.

So in seven years, Betty has survived three surgeries. "I am too mean for God to have me yet," Betty says she tells people. "He has plans for me to finish here on earth."

Yet in it all, the Book of Matthew has been comforting to Betty the most of all scripture. She says she has read through it over and over, particularly Chapter eight and verses 1-17..

"Matthew 8:16-17 has brought comfort and strength to me many times," says Betty. "When evening had come, they brought to Jesus many who were demon-possessed. And He cast out the spirits with a word, and healed all who were sick, that it might be fulfilled which was spoken by Isaiah the prophet, saying: 'He Himself took our infirmities and bore our sicknesses.'"

David and Betty turned 40 in 1999 and their marriage has remained strong through trying times. During their ten years together, they have been through a lifetime of trials for one couple. Betty counts herself blessed to have David, whose faith is like a rock.

A man of strong convictions and deep faith, David has taught the Singles Department Sunday School Class for the past two years at Calvary Baptist Church. Through his marriage with Betty, he often times finds himself at home with Katie while Betty is away for golf tournaments. She will leave on Wednesday and return on Sunday night. David always makes sure that the house is picked up, neat and clean when she returns.

Through that experience, he has learned a valuable spiritual lesson.

"When Betty leaves home for 11 tournaments a year, it is just Katie and me. When Betty returns on Sunday night, I always make sure the house is in order. It says to me that I must always keep my life in order with the Lord because you never know when He is going to return. By keeping your house and your life, in order with Him, you don't have to worry when He may come. That's the way I live my life. My house is always going to be in order."

Compared to others in the athletic department who have experienced cancer and other health setbacks, Betty says, "My scrapes with life and death have had a very happy ending. My prayer is that theirs will also. I know that Jesus Christ has an eye on David, Katie and me. I hope to think by the way we live our lives, that is our way of preaching the good news of faith and of Christ."

David says, "I am just happy to have Betty. God has been good all the time."

CHAPTER FOURTEEN

COACH DAVID PATTERSON

Y ou feel great. Life is wonderful. Yet you have cancer and you don't know it.

Such was 37-year-old David Patterson's status in August, 1996. As Assistant Head Coach of Alabama's gymnastics team, his life couldn't be happier. He couldn't have felt any better.

Life was grand. At least that's what David thought until he had a freak accident on a loading dock one afternoon.

How can a person feel so good and have cancer?

In David's case, God smiled down upon him. There was no pain of any description that led David to his discovery of a golf ball size tumor that was enclosed in one of his kidneys. When it was detected, it had to come out right away.

Everyone knows you deal with cancer immediately.

The story unfolds after Alabama had just won their third national championship in gymnastics. Winning a national title will keep you on a high everyday until your first meet of the next season.

The gymnastics team had won three NCAA titles while practicing in the National Guard Armory building on Paul Bryant Drive for the past 15 years. The University had purchased the old building, which adjoins the campus, for the gymnastic team to have its own workout facility.

Perfect timing, after the championship, was a state-of-the-art gymnastics practice facility that was added on to the back of Coleman Coliseum. It also included a huge basketball facility that several sports would utilize for practice. It was a handsome addition to the stately Coleman Coliseum.

"We were moving from the Armory to the new gym in the back of the Coliseum in August of 1996," explains David with a smile. "Everything was wonderful. We were so excited about the national title and now a brand new facility.

"We were moving some equipment off the loading dock at Central

Receiving across the campus. We backed the truck up next to the loading dock. I was carrying a big load of foam that we were going to put in our pits. I didn't realize that the loading dock wasn't hinged. You are supposed to back your truck up and then set that hinge ramp on top of it.

"I didn't do that, so I just walked out on that metal ramp, which I thought was stable and secure. When I did, it dropped and I fell four or five feet onto my back. It was painful, but we went on and finished with the moving. In fact, we kept moving for the next week or so. I was in some pain, but we just felt like we needed to complete the job.

"Then one morning, our youngest daughter Jordan, who was four at the time, crawled up into the bed with us and bumped the spot in my back that was sore. I jumped because it was still very painful.

"At that point Sarah said emphatically to me, 'You are going to the doctor!' So I went in to see (Dr.) Jimmy Robinson and he did an x-ray. He found out that the lowest rib on my left side was broken. He thought about it for a minute and said, 'Let's get an ultra sound just in case.'

"He normally would not have done that and he still doesn't know to this day why he ordered the ultra sound. Because he knew that what I did in catching the athletes in their gymnastic routines, he thought that the ultra sound would be a safe measure since that rib was so deep and so hard to break. He said, 'Let's just make sure you didn't bruise your kidney.'

"We were about to go into our practice season and I spot and catch the girls in their routines and exercises everyday. Therefore, I need to be at full strength myself. So the ultra-sound was scheduled."

David and Sarah were just pleased to find out that taking care of this broken rib could eliminate the pain. Lots of people break ribs and recover in short order. Such was the thinking here, except they were about to find out some heartwrenching news that would turn their lives upside down.

"It was Labor Day weekend on a Friday morning when I had that ultra sound," remembers David with clear recall. "We were planning on going down to the beach with two other couples. It was just painful for me to sit in the car.

"Sarah and I were actually at lunch at the Olive Garden discussing that maybe we should just stay at home. Then about that time, I got beeped. I had always carried a beeper with me so the kids could get in touch with us when they needed us.

"I didn't recognize the number that was on there. So I called it and it was Dr. Robinson's office. He got on the phone and asked what we were doing. We said, 'Well, we are eating lunch.' Then he said, 'When you are done, why don't you stop by my office, both of you.'

"I knew something was wrong then. I felt like, Oh, you have somehow damaged that kidney. When we got there he said, 'Well, y'all sit down.' Sarah said, 'No, tell us what's wrong.' Sarah didn't want to sit down. You see Jimmy is our family and team doctor so we are very close anyway. It's like talking to a friend.

'Well, you have kidney cancer,' Jimmy said, as bad as I know he dreaded to tell us.

'But......and,' before he could say anything else, Sarah fell to the floor."

Even though it was David's kidney, his body and his life, such news can be just as devastating to the spouse. For Sarah Patterson, who is known nationwide for producing some of the finest gymnastic teams in the sport's history, those were the toughest words she had ever heard. There come times when success means nothing when compared to a family member who has just been told they have cancer.

"My first reaction was my husband is going to die. I have two small kids and I have a job that I can't do without him. What am I going to do?" said Sarah who still is moved when thinking back on that moment.

"I heard the word 'cancer' and all I could think of was, 'David is going to die.' I just couldn't shake that thought and it literally made me collapse to the floor.

"David was so good in accepting the news. He kept saying, 'Sarah, Jimmy thinks I'll be okay. You are not hearing what he is saying.' But I didn't hear anything. All I heard was cancer.

"You know it's weird. David's mom had cancer. My mother had cancer. David's brother's wife had melanoma. We've known a lot of people who have had cancer in our own family and have survived. But when they are talking about your spouse, all I could think of was, 'He wasn't going to make it.' I didn't hear anything else for I don't know how long.

"I couldn't get up off the floor. I thought I was going to get sick. I thought I was going to pass out if I stood up. I just couldn't get up off the floor. David was much more calm about it than I was."

When Dr. Robinson did explain his thoughts about David's cancer, there was hope of a good outcome with surgery and time.

David explains Dr. Robinson's earliest prognosis and where they would go from there. "First of all, he told us that it wasn't even the side that he was concerned about. When they did the ultra sound, he was concerned about my left kidney. However, they did an ultra sound on both sides in order to do a comparison.

"So they actually found the cancer in the opposite kidney from where the injury was. So the left kidney where the pain was coming from was not the one with the cancer. It was the right kidney that didn't bother me at all.

"In the next few days, the tests revealed that the cancer was enclosed within the kidney. It could have been months or more than a year before I would have had symptoms and gone to see a doctor about it. By then, it would probably have been outside the kidney.

"The cancer was about the size of a golf ball they discovered later."

Dr. Robinson told David and Sarah that day in the office that he didn't think it was life threatening. Being that the cancer was enclosed, surgery to take out the right kidney would probably get all of the cancer. It had been caught early and that was a blessing.

That news was somewhat comforting and hopeful for the Pattersons. Still, there were days of anxiety and emotion ahead until the surgery would be performed ten days later.

"We ended up telling our friends that my ribs were sore and we couldn't go to the beach for the weekend," says David. "We didn't tell anybody about the cancer except our families over the weekend. I went to see Dr. Ken Aldridge the following Tuesday, since he was out of town until then.

"For Sarah and me, our reaction was let's go in tomorrow and get this out. We were very anxious and ready for the surgery as soon as possible. Recognizing our urgency, he explained it to us like this. 'Look, you are coaches and you always want to put your best team on the floor when you compete. Well, I am the same way. You see I have my best team to do surgery and you can either wait a week for the best team or go ahead with a team I can assemble.'

"When he put it that way, we naturally said we would wait a week. So that's what we did. We had the surgery the following Tuesday, a week later. However, it was a long ten days of waiting, the longest ten days of our lives.

"So much goes through your mind. You have those thoughts that maybe I won't see my children graduate from high school or go off to college and get married. All of those things in their lives I want to be a part of as a parent. Then there was the concern for Sarah. It is obviously a tough enough job to be a head coach without being a single parent at the same time."

Outside of family, David and Sarah gave the news first to the gymnastics team. It was crucial that they know before hearing it from other sources.

Word spread fast about David. He was on every prayer list in town and throughout the state and beyond in a flash. When experiencing a cancer valley, nothing soothes more than prayer support and love expressions from family and friends. David and Sarah were showered with such blessings. They were surrounded with love.

The day of the surgery came. David felt fine except for the soreness in the broken rib area. Circumstances have a way of completely reversing whatever plans we have and we can't do a thing about it. Such was David's case as he was prepared for surgery.

For people who are faced with 'sudden change' in their lives, there are sources of strength that they seek. David had his sources.

"One of the most important persons who helped us through this was our pastor, Steve Screws. We were members of St. Mark's Methodist Church at the time. One of my most vivid memories was when he said a prayer for us and was holding our hands before they wheeled me to the operating room," says David in a thankful tone.

"It was so comforting to know, while you are lying on the table looking up at everyone knowing you are about to go out, that your pastor is there saying a prayer for you. Jim and Carol Sue Jenkins, some of our closest friends, were there also. They have been an important part of our lives for years."

When David went in for surgery, the waiting room area was packed with family and friends for Sarah. "It was a long surgery, something like three hours," says Sarah. "There were never less than 15 or 20 people with me in the waiting room. Those people were so positive and I kept thinking that everything was going to be okay and he was going to be better. Phillip and Linda Jenkins, our Sunday School teachers, were there the entire time we were in the hospital.

"I remember Ray Melick (*Birmingham Post-Herald* writer), Marie Robbins, and Donna Robinson, Jimmy's wife, brought muffins she made for everyone. It was funny that when David was in the hospital, we had more surgeons around. Ken Aldridge was David's surgeon. Jimmy (Robinson) was there and Les (Fowler) came by to check on him. Julie Estin Vaughn's (former gymnast) husband, who is a doctor was there. Even David's brother, Guy, who is a doctor from Birmingham, was there. In fact, Dr. Aldridge allowed him to observe the tumor once the surgery was completed."

David's right kidney was completely removed. David did much research on the Internet about kidney cancer and found that it is one of the slowest growing cancers. David could have had the cancer for a year or so. It may have been two or three more years for it to be discovered. By then it could have been too late once the cancer had spread to the outside of the kidney.

In the all-important days of recovery, David's faith in God was assured by other sources besides his pastor and close friends.

"There were several things that helped me a lot. I would read Scripture. Then reading stories in *Guideposts*, a favorite magazine of mine, about how people's faith helped them through hard situations in their lives really helped me. Another wonderful source, which is not as faith based, was the *Chicken Soup for the Surviving Soul*. That book was wonderful also," David says remembering the days of recovery.

Through his discovering cancer, going through surgery and the healing process, David feels that he has been 'touched by an angel,' to borrow a popular expression.

Sarah has her own opinion. "I definitely feel that there was an angel that pushed David off that loading dock. I just think it was not his time yet and the good Lord was not ready for him. I told him there must be something on this earth that the good Lord wants you to do.

"Also, when you talk to Jimmy (Robinson), he would say that he could have 15 patients in there for the same problem. But then, he doesn't know why he ordered that extra test on David. Because of how active David is, he just wanted to make sure he didn't have a puncture on the kidney. Without that test, it might have been two or three years before we found out about the cancer and it could have been too late.

"Also, most people who have this cancer are in their mid-50's and 60's. David was just 37, so that would be another reason why we would never suspect kidney cancer."

Feeling fortunate and blessed of God was ever present in the hearts of David and Sarah. Every day is a healing process. It is constant on your mind. There was another means of support that encouraged them.

"People would call our home out of the blue and I had no idea who they were," Sarah says in a grateful tone. "They would tell me a really good story of an experience they had similar to ours when everything turned out real well. I would share it with David and he would be so encouraged and lifted up.

"But then there was this one call from a lady one night. I had the kids in one room and he was visiting with some coaches in another room. She was telling me all these things and then she proceeded to tell me that her husband had died.

"I said, 'Yes, we feel very fortunate. Doctors say they have gotten the cancer early and it appears that all of these things are going to be fine.' Then she said, 'Yes, that's what they told me too.' Then she told me how he died and how awful it was. Then taking it as long as I could, I hung up the phone and immediately ran out the front door of the house down the street to a neighbor's house.

"No one was there, but I sat there and bawled because I couldn't let David see me cry. When people would call he would say, 'Was that another good story?' I would say, 'Yeah, it was great.' They would tell me how a person had survived and I would share it with him. But I couldn't tell him that story.

"I could not believe that lady called and told me that story. You don't want to hear the bad things. You want to hear the good things."

But the positive far outweighed the discouraging times. "One day, Ruth Ann Stallings (wife of Coach Gene Stallings) and I were standing on University Boulevard in front of a bank downtown. We were doing the 'Apple Annie Day.' People would roll down their windows and tell me how they were praying for David. They were people I didn't even know, but how encouraging that truly was at that time."

Then with gymnastic practice for the upcoming season fast approaching, Sarah and David had to rely on newly acquired assistant coach, Bryan Raschilla to be in charge for a short while. Scott Mackall, who had just departed for a new job in Atlanta, was given a waiver by the NCAA to return and help in the gym while David was out. It was a difficult time for Sarah and David. His needs came first. The gymnastic team, as hard as it was to do, had to be placed in the hands of someone else for a short while.

"There were times when we were at home and it got to the point where David was okay and I could leave him for awhile," Sarah remembers. "But I had to go into work and he wouldn't want me to leave. I look back on that time and I think, nothing was as important as him and our children.

"I think sometimes we all become too busy. For us, I just have to think back on that period of time when things get all out of whack today. We said we would never let this experience change us back to where we were before David's cancer. Life has taken on new meaning for us and each day is a precious gift. That has been a major lesson we have learned through it all."

David slowly moved from home back to the gym for practice as the season approached. At first, David was limited to sitting in a chair and watching practice. At Christmas, the team usually gets 10 days off and that enabled David to regain added strength. Still, during the season, he would assist with the team but when practice ended at 4 p.m., David headed home to lie down and rest many days.

A month after the season ended in April, David began to feel back to his normal capacity, eight months after his surgery.

"The hardest thing for me still is the constant reminder of other people even within our department who are being treated for cancer or have regular checkups from past cancer surgeries," says David.

"I have to trust that I am still here for a reason. There are so many other wonderful people I've known like Robert (Scott, assistant basketball coach), who are not with us any longer. I think the only way to reconcile that is knowing that God has a plan and is not finished with me.

"I wonder why I am here and others aren't. I just have to believe there is a plan and we are all a part of it.

"As a coach here at Alabama and even when I was coaching in high school, I have always felt an obligation to try and set a strong example before the young people. That's something we talk to our gymnasts about also. They are in the spotlight, too.

"Over the years as we have stressed setting good examples for others, we have had very minimal problems. Sarah and I have been doing this for 22 years. Obviously in coaching, we love to win. We have won more than our share of championships... SEC, regionals and nationals as well as the dual meets.

"It is so enjoyable to win in what we perceive as the right way. We try to recruit strong student athletes who are also morally strong. I don't think the winning would be as gratifying if we didn't do it as we perceive the right way to do it."

Winning has been Sarah and David's trademark over the past 22 years. Their three incredible national championships came in 1988, 1991 and before their huge following of fans in Coleman Coliseum in 1996. Their teams have finished in the top three at the NCAA championships 12 times and sixth or better 17 times.

Individual NCAA championships have been won by 12 gymnasts, including four all-around titles. Alabama has produced 30 All-Americans who have earned over 100 honors between them.

Known for their academic achievements, Alabama gymnasts have produced a national-best total of eight NCAA Postgraduate scholarship winners and a conference-best 84 Academic All-SEC honors under Sarah and David.

With the winning came the crowds at Coleman Coliseum. In a duel meet with Georgia in 1997, the Coliseum sold out with a crowd of 15,043 which is an SEC record. The average attendance that year was 10,301 fans per home meet, a mark that is still best in the nation for gymnastics and third best for women collegiate sports.

It is most unusual to find an NCAA sport coached by a husband and wife or a wife and a husband in their case. Sarah was a recent Slippery Rock (Pa.) College graduate when she interviewed for the graduate assistant job at Alabama in 1979. The first four Alabama gymnastic teams had four different coaches. Before Sarah started as a G.A., the coach resigned and Sarah was asked if she would be the head coach. She accepted at age 22.

Sarah was interviewed by Ann Marie Lawler, associate athletic director for women, and was hired by Athletic Director Paul Bryant. Her salary was $5,000.

One summer prior, Sarah taught gymnastics as an intern at the Huntsville Athletic Club. She had lived in Huntsville from the second through the eighth grades since her father was with IBM and associated with the space program. At the same time, David, three years younger and an Eagle Scout, taught trampoline and gymnastic lessons at the Club and the two became casually acquainted.

"When Sarah got the gymnastics job, she knew I was a student at Alabama," says David looking back. "In fact, I was a diver on the Alabama team. I was a sophomore when she took the job and she needed some help. She remembered me instructing gymnastics with her in Huntsville and called me to see if I would help her out. As it turned out, I gave up diving after one year and helped Sarah with the team. I was also an Alabama cheerleader as a sophomore."

David joined Sarah and was given $500 which was an unused partial women's basketball scholarship. David, even as a student and 19, helped Sarah with the team. They held practice in Foster Auditorium, the old basketball gym, at the same time the volleyball team practiced. There were no pits and their mat was an old worn out men's wrestling mat with a big hole in it. They covered the hole with a huge 'A.' David drove the van for meets, recruited, made phone calls and got heavily involved in every aspect of the sport.

So when did the romance between the two begin? David explains. "Even though I was finishing up school, we worked together for several years. I was heavily involved with recruiting, going to meets to watch athletes, so we spent tremendous amounts of time together. Lots of times we would make phone calls to athletes until 9 or 9:30 at night. Then we would go over to The Storyville restaurant a few blocks away and eat dinner. There was a group of us really that spent a lot of time together.

"All this time, we discovered that we had common interests. That led to our engagement and to our marriage on May 8, 1982. Both of us were raised Methodists, so we got married in the Trinity United Methodist Church that adjoins the campus by Pastor Joe Estes."

Their two daughters, Jordan and Jessie, came along in 1986 and 1992. Both girls lead active and diverse lives, following their parent's example quite well in that regard. Basketball, volleyball, swimming, gymnastics, teeball and piano lessons keep them busy. They also excel academically.

Still, the one magic question has not been answered. How do a husband and wife have such a happy marriage and work together so successfully with offices side by side? Then add, how does it work for the wife to be the head coach and the husband the assistant head coach? David and Sarah provide the answers.

David fielded the question by saying, "It's not like we got married and I went to work for her. Pretty much, our relationship started by working together. It's really not like a boss-subordinate relationship, obviously. If it were that way, I don't think it would have worked that well for so long. Both of us consider it a team.

"Obviously, she is in the forefront because she is dealing with the media. She is the head coach and should be doing all of those things. She is the disciplinarian of the team in most cases. There are some times when Brian and I have to step in and do some things, but she sets the tone for that.

"Other than that, we three have our own responsibilities with the team and go about doing them. Very rarely have there been times over the years where she has had to say, 'Well, no, even if you guys think this way, I think differently.' We always come to a decision as a group.

"I guess part of it is that we rarely disagree. There is rarely any conflict because we are so much in agreement. When we are not, it is easy to sit down and resolve it. It is never a situation where she says, 'Well, I'm the boss. We are doing what I say.'

"What I tell people is that I married Sarah for job security," David says with a big laugh. "What better way to have job security than to marry the boss. I'm the father of her children. I think my job's safe now."

David admits that a lot of people have said to him that there are not many husbands and wives that can work well together in a job situation. However, their marriage and work relationship is a shining example for the student/athletes and those who know them.

From Sarah's standpoint, their relationship has always been very compatible and a major reason for their success. "The biggest thing is that we are in a job where we do different things. I think if David was one of these people who had a huge macho male ego, it would never work.

"We've always said that he does not enjoy speaking to the press and being in the limelight. On the other hand, I enjoy that. We both do things we like to do. I think his strengths are my weaknesses, and my weaknesses are his strengths. I think we compliment each other really well.

"Of the two of us, he is much more balanced than I am. He is the one that puts the balance in our home life. He will say, 'You have been gone too much. You have had this many speaking engagements.' Then he will look at the week's calendar and say, 'Well, it's time to be home with the kids. We have been out two nights and we have to say no to that.'

"Whereas I would go, go, go and try to please everyone at the expense of myself, him and our children. I don't have to worry about being so balanced because I think he does it for us.

"The only time in our marriage when it has been really hard, when we both knew that we didn't want to do this without the other one, was in my first pregnancy. I was confined to the bed for four months. David had to take the team on the road and leave me at home. I was bedridden and that was a long four months.

"Then when he was sick and out of work and I had to do it myself, neither one of us liked that. We always said, 'When we are done we are done together.' "

Through all of the healing process for David, his youngest brother Barry was a source of compassion and inspiration. After the surgery, David had to sleep in his recliner for several weeks. Barry came and spent many nights and would sleep on the sofa so Sarah could rest better.

"Barry wanted me to set a goal that was really different. He knew I had started fly-fishing and traveled a lot. So our conversation evolved into finally deciding that I would try and catch a fish on a fly rod in all 50 states. So much of the time while traveling on recruiting, I'm not scheduled to see someone until six in the evening, so sometimes I have the opportunity to fish. I also take trips on my own. So by the end of the summer (2000), I should be up to 35 states or so," says David.

"It has been most enjoyable. I have my brother to thank for such a neat idea in always staying on the positive side and having things to keep my spirit on the highest level possible.

"Also, through it all, Sarah has been so wonderful and so support-ive. You can't measure the support of a wife like Sarah." Today, his health is wonderful again and he sees his doctor for a checkup every six months.

Sarah and David have always given themselves to numerous com-munity projects and charities. In the past three years, they have involved themselves with cancer projects such as Relay For Life and the Help and Hope Barbecue. The barbecue project raises $50,000 each year to pay for pain medication and treatment for people who cannot pay for it.

"In terms of support and prayer that the community gave to us, these projects have been a means of trying to give something in return. We have been involved in a number of community projects, but these have been very dear to us and have taken on a sense of urgency to help other people in need," says Sarah who is so willing to lend her influence and energy where needed.

In summation, Sarah states well the reality of cancer. "It doesn't matter how nice you are, how healthy you are, how good of a person you are, how good of a Christian you are, or what a great father you are, cancer does not discriminate. You look at kidney cancer and it is supposed to be people who smoke and drink and David doesn't do either of those things. Besides, he is much younger than those who nor-mally have this cancer."

The Pattersons believe that angels have watched over them, even the one that gave David a push off of a loading dock. God has shown his mercy and they continue to show their praise and gratitude as a cou-ple who loves each other very much and works so successfully together.

Greater days lie ahead for David and Sarah, thanks to a loving God.

CHAPTER FIFTEEN

RYAN PFLUGNER

Twenty-four hours before Ryan Pflugner missed the overtime extra point that gave the Orange Bowl game to Michigan 35-34, Ryan was praying.

Ryan was thanking God for the privilege of playing football for Alabama and the role he had received as a Christian leader on the team.

All season long, players had piled into Ryan's motel or hotel room 30 minutes before curfew the night before each game. It was a volunteer team function called Prayer Time. It had started the season before as an idea from Assistant Head Football Coach Ronnie Cottrell. That first year, players gathered in John David Phillips' room.

FCA advisor Wayne Atcheson would meet with the players. As many as 32 players had piled into a double bed room for Prayer Time. Prior to the season, players were assigned Bible readings and a brief explanation of what the scripture meant. Prayer requests followed before everyone joined hands. Two players were selected to pray and on some occasions any one could offer a brief prayer before Atcheson closed in prayer.

In Room 628 of the Wyndham Miami Beach Resort Hotel the night before the Orange Bowl game, it would be Ryan's last Prayer Time with the team, since he was a senior.

Five days before, Ryan and Shaun Alexander had spoken with Coach Mike DuBose at the Greater Miami FCA Orange Bowl Breakfast. Ryan had stood before some 2,000 people to give witness of his faith in Jesus Christ and what a blessing it was to serve Christ on such a high pedestal as a college football player at Alabama.

In Ryan's prayer that night, he thanked God for the awesome privilege of being an Alabama football player. He was grateful for the opportunity to be a leader for Christ on the team. He was grateful for the many opportunities granted him to speak to youth all over the state. He prayed for those players who would be returning next year asking God to bless their Prayer Time, their chapel services, and their involvement in the Fellowship of Christian Athletes.

Ryan's prayer came deep from his heart. He was deeply sincere. These times had meant so much to him and his prayer reflected that he would miss such times together. In a way, it was a happy time, but a sad one as well.

Of course at that time, Ryan would never have fathomed what would happen in the game the next night, only 24 hours later.

Fifth ranked Alabama had made it to the elite Orange Bowl to play another team with great history, the Michigan Wolverines. It was Alabama's first trip to the Orange Bowl in 25 years. It was the only bowl game on TV that evening. The entire nation was watching two great football powers, Alabama vs. Michigan.

Alabama jumped to a 14-0 lead in the second quarter on two Alexander touchdowns and two of Ryan's extra points. In the third quarter, Freddie Milons dashed 62 yards with a punt return and Alabama was in command of the game 28-14 with 8:29 left in the quarter.

Things looked good for Alabama. A prized victory was in sight. However, Michigan staged two drives within the quarter to make it 28-28 at the end of the third quarter. In the fourth quarter, Alabama stopped the Wolverines with a goal line stand at the one-yard line. On the final play of regulation, lanky Tide linebacker Phillips Weeks leaped high to block a field goal attempt to send the game into overtime.

So the game ended at 28-28. Ryan had made all four extra point attempts. He had not even attempted a field goal. Ryan had made every kick when called on.

There were other individual breakdowns in the game that could have made the difference for an Alabama win. After dominating most of the game, Alabama was now fortunate to be in overtime.

Alabama won the overtime toss and put the pressure on Michigan to score. That they did on the very first play, a 25-yard touchdown toss with the extra point tacked on. It was now 35-28, Michigan in a flash.

Alabama answered immediately. Alexander gained four yards. Then quarterback Andrew Zow executed a nifty fake and found split end Antonio Carter in the end zone for a 21-yard touchdown. The scoreboard lights showed 35-34 and it appears that this action packed game was headed into a second overtime.

"When we go for one point, Coach DuBose holds up one finger. At that point, Brad (Ledbetter, the snapper), Patrick (Morgan, the holder) and I run onto the field. I had already warmed up between regulation and the overtime. Everything went so fast because there were only three plays in the overtime," recalls Ryan.

"However, I was ready for the kick. Everything was like normal. We lined up just as we always do. There was no need to rush. The snap was good. The hold was good and I hit it solid. It didn't feel any different than any other kick. Usually I can tell if it is going in one direction or another before I even look, by just how the kick feels.

"I knew it was going in but when I looked up, it was complete shock. My first look at the ball was when it was almost even with the upright. That's when I knew the ball did not go through."

The ball went wide by the length of a football. It was to be Ryan's last extra point attempt in his college career. Prior to the kick, he had made 57 of 63 extra point attempts in his career at Alabama.

"After the kick, the first thing I remember was that I was lying on my back. I don't know how I got there, whether one of their guys or one of ours had hit me. I remember lying on my back thinking, 'Oh my gosh, I have just lost the game,' says Ryan.

"Truthfully, God's spirit just spoke to me and said, 'Get up Ryan and prove who you really are. Get up and congratulate Michigan. Get up and show people that this isn't the end of the world for you.' "I felt such a burden on me, but I wanted to react in the way a Christian should.

"Dustin (McClintock) picked me up and we started walking to the center of the field. He pushed a couple of cameras away. I shook some Michigan players hands and that's when Shaun grabbed me to try to console me. Then we had a prayer on the field and Shaun and I walked to the dressing room together. He had his arm around my shoulder trying to console me. I was in a daze.

"It was real quiet in the dressing room. Everyone was in a state of shock. We had dominated the first half and everyone just felt that we should have won, but we just let it get away.

"Coach DuBose said some comforting words to me. He told the team that we had a lot to be thankful for and that we were SEC champions and had played above everyone's expectations except ours."

Ryan made quite an impression upon the large thong of media covering the game when he was the first player to walk into the interview room. Facing the media in that situation is rather difficult, but Ryan's spiritual maturity gave him the courage to face the questions and cameras in a tough and trying situation. After all, the entire nation just saw you make a mistake that will forever be in the record books.

It was after midnight when the game was over. When Ryan reached his room around 2:00 a.m., his phone rang. Ryan picked it up and the caller only said one word… "Terrible."

The next morning, Ryan drove to his home in Sarasota, just four and a half-hours north of Miami. Two days later, he was back in the classroom at the Alabama campus for his final semester.

Reaction to Ryan's missed extra point was rather surprising to Ryan. "I received so much mail. In fact, I had never received mail like this even when my kicks won games. Most all of it was from fans writing to console me and telling me how much they felt for me. I really appreciated it and it helped a great deal," says Ryan.

Interviews followed as well. On January 6, Ryan told Tommy Deas of The *Tuscaloosa News,* "I got one bad phone call the night of the game at the hotel and that was it. I got a stack of letters and they all have return addresses, so I'm guessing they're positive. I guess the people of Alabama are very forgiving and very supportive. All the feedback my parents have gotten has been positive."

Calls for speaking engagements in churches and to youth groups came to Ryan several times a day. For two years as an FCA leader Ryan had already been sharing his faith and loved doing it.

Now Ryan had some new material. We all have missed extra points in life, but there is always victory in Jesus.

A week after the game, Ryan's interview with Victor Lee at Crosswalk.com Network was surprising to Lee coming from a 22-year-old young man. When Lee first called, he sought information on Shaun Alexander. Then he hesitantly inquired, "Does Ryan Pflugner happen to be a Christian?" Victor gave an audible sigh of relief over the phone and asked if it might be possible to talk with him.

Victor was delighted when Ryan told him, "I think it (missed kick) will have a long-lasting effect, but it will be a positive effect. It will be a reminder that God is in control of what is going on in my life that he is always looking to give me opportunities to point to him. This isn't the way I wanted to get an opportunity, but that's what it is."

Lee wrote in his Internet story, "The source of strength to pick yourself up off the dirt and get on with life for Ryan Pflugner is Jesus Christ."

Two weeks after the game, Ryan received a large brown envelope that simply had a return address of "The White House." It was a full-page hand written letter from President Bill Clinton who was watching the game and wanted to write him a letter of encouragement. The letter said the following:

THE WHITE HOUSE

Washington

1-8-2000

Dear Ryan,

   I watched as an avid football guru, the Alabama bowl game. I know how hurt and disappointed you were when you missed the kick.

   I wanted to write you this note of encouragement. You made a lot of kicks that contributed to Alabama's great season. Life has many ups and downs, many of them unexpected and sometimes heartbreaking.

   The important thing is to be grateful for the good breaks we get and to learn, as we go along, how to live with pressure better. I have found it a lifelong task. You have real talent and have been able to use it to help your team. Hold your head high and keep pursuing your dreams. I wish you well.

Sincerely, Bill Clinton

Ryan received many letters, but it was quite an honor to receive one from the President of the United States.

Since Ryan and Shaun had been sharing the leadership role for FCA meetings in the fall semester each Wednesday night at nine, Ryan was the sole leader for the spring semester. Shaun had graduated.

The Orange Bowl game was played on Monday night and Ryan led the FCA meeting two nights later. A tragic disappointment was not to wreck Ryan's life. Ryan also hit the speaking trail immediately.

One never knows what turns and bends are in the road ahead. While growing up in Sarasota, Ryan played soccer almost from the time he could walk. He didn't start playing football until he was a junior in high school. He played wide receiver and defensive back and was honorable mention all-state as a kicker.

His dad Jeff had played college football at Davidson College in North Carolina. His head coach was Homer Smith, who would later become an offensive wizard for the Crimson Tide. A tape on Ryan was sent to Coach Smith who gave it to recruiting coordinator Randy Ross.

Ryan's first two years (1995-96) at Alabama were pure survival as an unknown walk-on. In Coach Mike DuBose debut and opening game with Houston in Birmingham in 1997, Ryan Pflugner was first team place kicker and kick off man. On his first kickoff, Ryan made the tackle also. In fact he made two tackles that day. "I got hit a lot that day and was baptized into college football real quick," Ryan remembers. He also kicked four of five extra points and had no field goal attempts.

That game would be Ryan's last for the 1997 season. The following Tuesday in practice, he tore all of the muscles in his kicking leg.

After several medical opinions, Dr. William Clancey in Birmingham told Ryan that he had what's called a "sports hernia." He recommended the only doctor he knew that does this kind of surgery. So on February 13, 1998 Ryan underwent surgery at the University of Massachusetts Hospital in Worchester, Mass. Ryan felt immediate relief.

Three months of kicking rehabilitation went on into July because when he kicked, there was always pain. "At this point, I was struggling with God a lot. Why did he bring me here? I was doubting my purpose here. Every time I went out to kick, my leg hurt," Ryan recalls. "On Friday of this weekend in July, I kicked and was getting frustrated. I just said to God, 'If you want me to play football here, I'll just kick this ball and I know there won't be any pain because I know you can heal my leg.' I kicked the ball and there was just horrible pain.

"I stood there and God just seemed to say, 'Just be quiet. I'm going to do it my way.' I was distraught. So I was led to just spend the entire weekend in my apartment alone with God praying and reading the scripture. I just got close to God.

"I came back out on the field Monday. From the very first kick, I felt no pain whatsoever after five months of kicking with pain. So right there on the practice field, I knew God had given me a miracle. I realized then that I had been trying to do things my way instead of letting go and letting God have control of my life. It was at that point that I knew God had healed me."

During that 1998 season that followed, Ryan converted 28 of 28 extra point attempts and made 11 of 22 field goal tries. His second career field goal of 55 yards against Arkansas was the second-longest in Tide history and the longest without a kicking tee.

"There was a five-yard penalty before that 55-yard kick, a delay of game or something," remembers Ryan. "I didn't even realize how far it was when I kicked it. Someone on the sideline came up to me and asked how far it was and I had to count before I knew it was 55 yards."

Does Ryan ever count off the yards for a field goal attempt? "No, I just run out on the field and find the ball. The only thing I count is the seven and a half yards behind the ball. Then I take three steps back and two to the left. Then I just line up and kick it," says Ryan.

"I've got a strong enough leg that I can kick 60 yards. I kick every kick with the same strength including extra points. So I don't ever worry about distance."

In the season opener with Brigham Young in newly renovated Bryant-Denny Stadium, Ryan kicked five extra points after Shaun Alexander's school record five touchdowns in a 38-31 victory. He also had a 34-yard field goal. Later in the year, Ryan kicked a 22-yard field goal in overtime to defeat Ole Miss 20-17. Ryan ended his junior year with 60 points. He contributed well as a walk-on kicker.

Two weeks before his senior season in 1999 during two-a-day practices, Ryan had an unforgettable three days.

On Monday, he was elected team co-captain. On Tuesday, Coach DuBose called him into his office and awarded him a scholarship. On Wednesday, Ryan joined Shaun as co-leader of the FCA.

After such a good junior season, Ryan was confidently poised for his final Alabama year. Ryan's performance in the first two games was a repeat of 1998. He was off to a great start. However, warming up for the third game against Louisiana Tech in Birmingham, Ryan pulled a quad muscle in his leg. Disappointingly, Ryan sat out that game and the next two against Arkansas and Florida.

Junior Chris Kemp from Jacksonville, FL filled in well as the Tide won all three. Co-Captain Ryan even missed the 40-39 overtime thriller over Florida in The Swamp.

Ryan healed up in time for the Ole Miss game in Oxford, MS and finished the season injury free. It was amazing how Ryan and Shaun, the two Fellowship of Christian Athletes leaders, scored most of the points in early season games. They combined to score 22 of 28 points in the first game against Vanderbilt and 26 of 37 against Houston in the second game. In Ryan's return for the Ole Miss game, he and Shaun scored all 30 points in a 30-24 victory.

In Ryan's first three games after the injury, his kicking was perfect in nailing five of five field goal attempts and seven of seven extra points.

Late in the year against Auburn on the Plains, Ryan gave Alabama a 6-0 lead with 33 and 41-yard field goals that started a 28-17 win. Two weeks later in the Southeastern Conference game against his home state Florida Gators, Ryan had a big night.

In the awesome 34-7 shocker, Ryan kicked field goals of 29, 48 and 49 yards, the latter an SEC championship game record. He was two for two on extra point tries. How sweet to now come home to Sarasota with two victories over Florida in one season.

Also, what a high for Ryan to play his last game in the Orange Bowl which was close to home. Ryan's kicking stayed true with four of four extra points against Michigan and no field goal opportunities until disaster struck with the narrow miss in the overtime.

Ryan discovered more at Alabama than just a fun opportunity to kick before 83,000 fans on Saturday. His faith in Jesus Christ reached a new level.

"I grew up in the church. My parents and grandparents always took me to church. I had faith in Jesus but didn't have a relationship with him. I had not heard that word 'relationship' until I got to Alabama.

"I attended FCA meetings as a freshman and slowly my faith life took on a new dimension. I began to have a relationship with Jesus Christ, and by the start of my sophomore year, I felt like I had a true relationship. Teammates Chad Goss and Mickey Conn helped me to know Christ in a greater dimension."

"Friends like Chad, Mickey, John David Phillips, Ross Gunnells and others allowed me to feed off them, and to learn what Christianity is all about. Too, the FCA meetings were always a boost for me. Some times you get burned out with classes and studying. The FCA meetings just became an energy boost for me for the rest of the week.

"So I discovered a true personal relationship with Christ as a freshman and sophomore and in my last semester, I was the leader of the FCA group. How special is that."

On April 14, the day before A-Day 2000, Ryan had the thrill of placing his hand prints and cleat marks in cement at the Walk of Fame at Denny Chimes. He joined Shaun Alexander, Chris Samuels, Cornelius Griffin and Miguel Merritt for the high and special Crimson Tide honor for those selected as football captains.

On May 13, Ryan donned his cap and gown and graduated with a degree in biology. Ryan plans to go on to graduate school in the fall at Alabama and is thinking of possibly studying medicine. Someday he could be Dr. Ryan Pflugner.

From walking on, getting to start, earning a scholarship, being selected as co-captain and being a leader of the FCA, Ryan summarizes it all well. "It almost seems like a dream."

Not in Ryan's case. It actually happened.

CHAPTER SIXTEEN

ANDY PHILLIPS

A ndy Phillips finished his collegiate baseball career at Alabama as the most celebrated baseball player in school history.

He was a hit with everybody. Not only was he the home run king for Alabama and holder of most hitting records, he was the boy you wanted to come knocking at your door to see your daughter.

Andy could not only swing a bat for game winners, he won big in his life as a champion for Christ. In his four years at Alabama from 1996-1999, he walked with the Lord daily among his teammates. The huge crowds at Bama games loved him because they knew in his heart he was a person that made God his all in all.

Andy Phillips represents apple pie, vanilla ice cream, strawberry shortcake and all that's good about being a role model All-American boy.

After a year of minor league baseball with the New York Yankees, Andy reflected on what was the most satisfying aspect of his storied baseball career at Alabama.

"So many opportunities came my way to share what God has done in my life," says Andy of his four years at Alabama. "I was blessed to be a part of three World Series teams and SEC championship teams and even state championship teams in high school. Those things are great.

"However, what I have realized is that all those things are going to pass away. It's gone. Somebody could take your rings. The trophies get dusty. But there is no greater feeling than to have a Mom walk up to you as you are walking off the baseball field and say, 'I just want you to know that my son prayed to receive Christ last Sunday.' Or to have someone walk up to you and say there was something you said or something you shared in our church last week that really spoke to me and God has blessed my life through that.

"There are just countless stories that would be worth it all if I never stepped in the batter's box again. My opportunities with the pedestal I had at Alabama mean everything in the world to me.

"One of these days when I stand before God, he is not going to ask me how many home runs I hit or how many trophies I won. The simple question is going to be, 'What did you do with my Son?'

"Part of my life shamefully is going to be that I didn't do enough. But my deepest desire is to experience everything that God has planned for my life."

Andy's life began with godly parents, Larry and Linda Phillips in Demopolis, AL. Andy was blessed with a home where prayer, Bible reading and faith in God were the main ingredients. Larry and Linda also loved music and Andy was singing soon after he began to talk. Sister Erin came three years after Andy. The family would even sing at church and where opportunities were presented. Andy developed just as great a love for singing as playing baseball, basketball and football.

Larry and Linda rarely missed a game Andy played in from the time he started playing ball. God had blessed Andy with athletic ability. It was evident. The talent was there. His parents were always there for Andy also.

Life at the Phillips home consisted of Sunday School and church on Sunday morning and back to church on Wednesday night for prayer meeting. The rest consisted of work for the parents and school for the children during the week, plus the ball games, of course. It was through that agenda that the Phillips family bonded and became as close as honey on bread.

Andy attended Demopolis Academy which was a small, Christian school with grades 1-12. He was an outstanding quarterback for the football team, excelled in basketball and led the team to three state baseball titles. He was even drafted by the Milwaukee Brewers in the forty-second round as a high school senior.

Alabama was always Andy's team. He also was enamored with Jay Barker and the Fellowship of Christian Athletes group at Alabama. So in the tenth grade, Andy's youth director, Grant Willett at Fairhaven Baptist Church, brought him and a few other athletes and students to an Alabama FCA meeting.

That was an hour's drive for a meeting that started at 9:00 p.m. on Wednesday, a school night to boot. However, that was the beginning of Andy attending several FCA meetings at Alabama as a high school student for three years. He loved meeting Jay and the other Christian athletes and enjoyed the outstanding speakers and programs.

When Andy was a high school senior, he sang at one of the Alabama FCA meetings. With his confidence and love for singing,

Andy appeared not the least bit intimidated by the college audience. If he was nervous, he didn't show it. The students were blessed. They were impressed. They loved Andy.

FCA was making quite an impression on Andy as well.

"After I started going to the FCA meetings, I always just thought, man what an awesome thing it would be to come here and be a part of FCA," remembers Andy. "Being in high school, I was just awestruck by being around athletes like Jay Barker and others like him and to know that one day you could be a part and take on a leadership role in it. I wanted to be a part of special group as a college student."

Of course, Andy would attend Alabama baseball games as he could. Many colleges were seeking his services in baseball especially. His recruiting visit to Alabama couldn't have been better. For Andy, God's presence and leading were all over his visit.

"My official visit came on the weekend of the Alabama-Georgia football game in 1994 when Alabama won 29-28 and Jay Barker had such a great game. That was the time when Jay made his profound statement after the game acknowledging Jesus Christ, and that He would lift you up in due time if you would just humble yourself before Him. That, of course, was what led to his book, *In Due Time,* which inspired me so much.

"I went in the next morning after the game to talk to Coach Jim Wells about my recruiting trip," Andy fondly recalls . "I remember he had been at Alabama only one year. He just looked me straight in the eye and said, 'What I want from you is that you come in here and be the Jay Barker of this baseball team.'

"So I knew then that God was calling me to Alabama. I knew that I was not to come in and lead this team necessarily to national championships, but more importantly to be a godly influence. If I had those priorities straight, I knew that God would bless.

"When Coach Wells said that, I was ready to sign that day. But I had to wait until signing day."

The road to three College World Series appearances in the next four years for Andy was not always easy. There were struggles, ups and downs, but still mostly highs. His first year was a growing up season, however.

"My freshman year was a struggle from the get-go. It was a struggle because I had let pride slip in. I was going to start getting attention from people athletically and from others who said I would have an influence on others. I took my eyes off God and put them on myself.

199

"God has a way of humbling you and that's exactly what he did for a year," says Andy. "I don't regret it at all because it humbled me and really made me appreciate God for who He is and the sport that I play. It was a miserable year but God used it to help me grow up."

On the field, Andy's talent got him into 46 games, 27 as a starting third baseman. He batted .238 against the powers in the Southeastern Conference and throughout the playoffs to the College World Series in Omaha.

The next season in 1997, Andy had more than a banner year as a sophomore. His season was more like a career.

Andy set career highs in most every statistical category. Andy was the only player to play in all 70 games. He ended the season with 560 consecutive innings at third base. His batting average was a remarkable .366 (102-279) with 15 home runs and 65 RBI. He got his 100th career hit in his 100th career game against LSU on May 12. He was named to the SEC All-Tournament team, leading Alabama to three straight post-season titles.

In NCAA post-season play, he was named to both the NCAA South II Regional and College World Series All-Tournament teams. He was a major factor in Alabama's reaching the final game of the World Series before losing to LSU 13-6. In six CWS games against Mississippi State, Miami and LSU, Andy batted .308 (8-26), with three extra-base hits and five RBI. His infield play was outstanding.

Looking to improve himself as a baseball player, Andy chose to play in the Jayhawk League, a summer league in Kansas and Missouri for college players before both his sophomore and junior seasons.

"It was a wooden bat league and I really enjoyed it. I played with great players and made many good friends from across the country. After my freshman year, it was a great time to get away from everybody in Alabama and do some soul-searching and to spend time with God. It gave me time to get my focus back on God and get my eyes off of myself," Andy recalls.

"I was assigned to the team out of Liberal, Kansas and all of us stayed with host families. Mine were James and Sara Odom who were from Alabama. They were the greatest people and they were one of the main reasons I went back before my junior season. I gained so much confidence in my game and the experience in the Jayhawk League was so good for me."

Andy would follow his sensational sophomore year with another as a junior. Alabama would miss the College World Series by one game.

However, Andy was the only player to start all 64 games. He started 36 at shortstop and 28 at third base. He batted .351 (93-265) and hit 21 home runs and had 82 RBI.

One of the joys of Andy's junior year was playing with his first cousin Paul Phillips, who transferred in from Meridian (Mississippi) Junior College. Paul was primarily a catcher who played other positions. He had such a good season that he signed with the Kansas City Royals and is a prospect for the big leagues. Paul also displayed a close walk with the Lord and his presence was a blessing for the team and his friends if only for a year.

Many felt that Andy would get drafted and could pass up his senior season. When the draft came, to everyone's amazement, Andy was not drafted. For many, it was a joy to know that Andy would be in an Alabama uniform for one more season.

"As the draft approached, I prayed to God for clarity. I was willing to do whatever. Lord, just show me what I am supposed to do," says Andy.

"I didn't even get a phone call. So it was pretty obvious that God wanted me to stay."

Was Andy disappointed? "I was disappointed for about 30 minutes," Andy is quick to point out. "How can you be disappointed in playing another year at Alabama? It was a blessing. Truly my heart wanted to play another year at Alabama.

"I realized in 30 minutes that my prayer had been answered. God had clarified everything for me. It was a blessing for Paul to be drafted and a blessing for me not to be drafted."

Three months later, God helped Andy to see some of the reason why he should stay at Alabama.

"In August just before school started, my best friend Jason Cox (first baseman) called me up and was really down. Usually Jason is so happy all the time. A minute into the conversation, he just broke down in tears. He said, 'My life is a mess. I'm miserable. I realize for the first time what people know me as and my life is not what it is supposed to be.'

"The next day," says Andy, "I came to Tuscaloosa and he and I went into our baseball locker room. It is a place where so many times I had gotten dressed for games, had celebrated some great wins and agonized through the worst losses.

"But I never knew it would be the place where I would get to lead my best friend to pray to receive Christ. If nothing else, if I didn't get to play another day of baseball, that one day was worth it all.

"I just took my Bible and pointed out scriptures that said that we are all sinners and we all fall short of what God expects. Then I told him that Jesus Christ died on a cross to pay the penalty for his sins. All he had to do was to ask for forgiveness of his sins and invite Him into his life to live as Lord and Savior of his life. Then God would forgive him of his sins and give him a peace that brings relief from his misery. Plus, there is the extra reward of having eternal life and the assurance of going to Heaven when you die.

"Well right there in the locker room, Jason bowed his head as I led him in the sinner's prayer. He quietly asked Jesus to come into his heart.

"Jason's life has never been the same since that day. You could see an immediate difference in his life. His speech, his attitude and his heart had changed. He became a regular at FCA, entered in prayer times and Bible studies, and has gotten involved in the church. I'm so proud of Jason."

Andy's Christian witness at Alabama was up front and out in the open. Indeed, he was a fixture at FCA meetings each Wednesday night at 9 p.m. He touched students like none other when he got up to sing a song.

Student-athletes would sit in awe as Andy would belt out moving songs about Christ's sacrifice for our sins, his dying on the cross and how he loves you and me. Andy would sing with greet feeling. He would shut his eyes and sing as only to God alone.

Everyone got excited when Andy was to sing. They knew something out of the ordinary was about to happen. His anointed voice and witness never failed to bless hearts. Too, Andy joined the praise team that led the group in choruses and it was a blessing to see Andy sing with such reverence and joy unto the Lord.

Throughout his years at Alabama, Andy loved going to many churches and youth gatherings to sing and give witness of his faith. Before his senior year, Andy sang one of his favorite songs, "The Sparrow," at Squad Sunday at the Calvary Baptist Church. All the teams and coaches were invited. Members of the church were still talking about Andy and his song for months afterwards and how thrilling it was to hear him offer such a blessing in song.

As a senior in 1999, Andy made first team All-American and rewrote the Alabama record book. He became Alabama's all-time leader in games started (224), at-bats (904), runs scored (222), hits (322), home runs (61), RBI (226) and total bases (590). He was second in career doubles (63) and triples (11).

His numbers are more than remarkable! Even his 36-game hitting streak established a Southeastern Conference record.

As a team, Alabama was SEC tournament champions, NCAA Regional and NCAA Super Regional champions and finished third at the College World Series. Andy was the MVP in the NCAA Regional.

Andy's feats and accomplishments in an Alabama uniform would require a lengthy term paper. He was a key contributor to a combined four-year won-loss record of 205-67 (75.6), the best four years by far in Tide history. Alabama won 50 or more games in three of Andy's years, the only 50-win seasons at the Capstone.

Near the end of his senior season on May 1, Andy counted it a joy to share his faith at the West Alabama Festival with Franklin Graham in Coleman Coliseum on campus. All eyes were on Andy with a sparkling senior season going in baseball. Now 20,000 people listened as he spoke about a matter that meant even more to him than baseball.

"A lot of people know me as an athlete who has had some success here at Alabama in baseball. But what I want people to know me as is a guy who is a Christian who just happens to be a baseball player. God has given me some ability and I want to use that ability to speak His message.

"That message to me is that God is in the life-changing business. He changed my life when I was seven years old. I have had up and down times but in the last few years God has shown me so much spiritually.

"When I got here at the University, I had these plans of coming in and being a success on the baseball field and seeing people's lives changed through me. But what I had to realize is that God had to change me first. I spent so much time worrying about everybody else and what God could do in my life to see others' lives changed. When I got my life in tune with His, He began to use me.

"God is a life-changing God and He is a God of hope. I don't know what my future holds, but I do know that my hope and my strength abides in Him. God is going to bless me no matter what he chooses in my life.

"In just a few moments, Franklin is going to come and he is going to share with you this same life-changing message that changed me many years ago. My prayer is that you will pay close attention and you will answer as to what God wants to do in your life. Don't leave tonight without accepting Christ and without accepting what His future plan is for you."

A few days later, Andy was off with his team to Omaha for the

College World Series. While there, he was drafted by the world champion New York Yankees. Andy was assigned to the Staten Island Yankees in the New York-Penn League which is a "short season Class A ball," says Andy.

In no time, Andy found himself in New York in a completely different world. Certainly, it was not Demopolis, Tuscaloosa or Liberal. His welcome to professional baseball was far different than expected.

"Coming from a small town and moving straight into New York required quite an adjustment on my part," Andy recalls. "The fast pace up there was a unique experience. I didn't have transportation. I roomed with a couple of teammates in a small apartment. Even it was really expensive. We didn't have TV. I really had a lot of time for prayer and reading the scripture. God just wanted to take my life to the next level spiritually.

"It was an awesome experience just to wake up everyday because it was just me and God. It was an earthshaking venture but I enjoyed the baseball."

Andy played third base and led the team in hitting and RBI. He received high praise from his coach and blended in well with other outstanding baseball talent hoping for the majors one day.

His season highlight came near the end when he smacked back to back grand slam home runs in one game.

One of his happy memories in New York was being asked to speak at a men's prayer breakfast at a church one Saturday morning. "It was two weeks before we left and I got to share my testimony and sing a song. Todd Mitchell, our second baseman from Illinois State, decided to go with me. He had not been asked to speak, but he got up and shared about his life. He was not much of a church goer.

"When he got up to speak, he shared about his life and how he had left school early for the draft. He said he had spent a lot of time wondering if he had made the right decision. Then he said, 'I now know why I made the right decision.' He pointed to me and told the people that my Christian influence on his life was the reason. I was so surprised but thrilled that perhaps he had seen Jesus in my life. I had a chance to share with him more about the faith in those last two weeks."

Andy returned to Alabama in the fall of 1999 to work on his graduation requirements. He will complete his degree in the fall of 2000 and graduate with a major in Sports Fitness Management.

For the 2000 baseball season, Andy reported to the Yankees and was assigned to the Tampa Yankees, which is their Class Advanced A team.

In the second half of the season, Andy was the team's leading hitter with a .318 average. "I'm finally swinging the bat like I did at the University," Andy says.

Ironically, his roommate is David Walling who played his collegiate baseball at Arkansas. David is a pitcher and it was off him that Andy tied the school record for home runs while at Alabama.

Alabama fans will never forget Andy Phillips. They will never forget Public Address announcer Barry Allen's booming voice saying, "And now, batting fourth is Number 2, third baseman Andy Phillips," as the musical theme of *The Andy Griffin Show* played over the speakers for Andy.

Andy left a legacy that young men in other years will be told to emulate. Andy Phillips fulfilled his purpose and dream at Alabama and beyond. He never lost his focus. He will always be known for his Christian stand and impact he made as a role model in the highest fashion.

Coach Jim Wells had a special love and appreciation for his star infielder.

Said Coach Wells, "Andy Phillips is different because not only is he an outstanding baseball player, but he is a tremendous person. He has made himself a great player because of his work ethic.

"There will be no finer person ever to come through the University of Alabama than Andy Phillips. He is the best leader a team can have."

Andy has a heart for God and lots of people know God better because of Andy Phillips.

CHAPTER SEVENTEEN

JOHN DAVID PHILLIPS

When Coach Paul "Bear" Bryant died, John David Phillips cried his heart out.

So did thousands of others, but in John David's case, he was only seven years old and in the second grade.

For two years, John David had already begun to dream of the day that he would play football for the great Bear Bryant. "We were going to church one Sunday and I can remember leaning over from the back-seat and asking my parents if I was going to get to play for Bear Bryant?" says John David smiling about such a remark made when he was six years old.

"At that time, I couldn't tell you about any person who played for Alabama. I couldn't tell you about anybody at Alabama. Bear was all I knew about and all I cared about. I just wanted to play college football for the Bear," indicating the mind and clear focus and purpose in life that John David has always possessed.

Even at six and seven years old, John David had a deep appreciation for the kind of man Coach Bryant was. "I always admired Coach Bryant and I can't pinpoint any reason why I thought that way then. He had that way about him. You wanted to play for somebody like that.

"You could say I was too young to understand it, but I just respected him so much at my young age. I admired the kind of person he was, hard-nosed and tough, but showing class. They were the things he lived by.

"My dad, even though he was an Auburn fan, always talked about Coach Bryant and had great respect for him," says John David.

The Auburn persuasion didn't last long for John David. His parents took him to Tuscaloosa to visit relatives when he had just turned six. John David had on an Auburn jacket which the relative replaced with an Alabama jacket. He told John David he couldn't wear that Auburn jacket in Tuscaloosa. He's been an Alabama fan ever since and his parents eventually changed loyalties to the Crimson Tide.

Then that fateful day of January 26, 1983 came when Coach Bryant suddenly passed away. "My mom was teaching in the same elementary school that I was attending," remembers John David as if it was last week.

"She came into my classroom and took me to the office to break the news to me early that afternoon. When she told me that Coach Bryant had just passed away, I placed my head in my hands, started crying and dropped to my knees. I remember saying through my tears, 'I'm not going to get to play for the Bear! I'm not going to get to play for the Bear!'

"It crushed me. It was probably the hardest news I had to take at my young age," says John David who continued to follow Alabama and still dreamed of the day he could play football for the Crimson Tide.

That opportunity came for John David 11 years later. Alabama wanted John David as bad as John David ever wanted to play for the Tide.

His role as an Alabama football player would become one of the most unusual stories in Alabama history. His story about adversity and big dreams that slipped away may be the finest story of spiritual maturity ever demonstrated in an Alabama uniform.

As the son of David and Glenda Phillips, John David was born on October 15, 1975 in Anniston, AL. The town of some 27,000 people is one and a half hours east of Birmingham on the Atlanta highway 20 interstate. John David lived at 1208 Robertson Road from the time he was born until he left for college.

His dad was in marketing for the Alabama Power Co. His sister Leigh Ann was four years older. The Phillips family was your model family, active in church, hardworkers, and together as a family to the core. Grandparents were part of the package.

Growing up, John David fell for athletics. Football, basketball, baseball and swimming provided the young man year-around activity. Football, however, was his first love.

As a sophomore at Anniston High, a Class 6A school in the top division, John David played a lot of football. He was a starter at defensive back, was back-up quarterback, the long snapper for punts and played on all specialty teams. "I just enjoyed playing the game. I didn't care what position or role they had me playing. As a junior, I kept playing the same positions with the addition of some linebacking duties," says John David.

So when did he get noticed at quarterback? It came in the final game of his junior season. Anniston, No. 19 in the nation, traveled to Crampton Bowl in Montgomery to meet the Robert E. Lee Generals, ranked No. 2 in the *USA Today* poll.

"I had been playing defensive back all year. We fell behind early and because we were a running team, we felt like we needed to pick it up a little," says John David. "Our coach, Rodney Bevins, put me in at quarterback at the end of the second quarter. We went down the field and it was one of those nights when you just felt good throwing the ball and everything just clicked. You just felt like you were unstoppable.

"We kicked a field goal to get on the board just before halftime. Then I played the entire second half at quarterback and threw for good yardage. With a minute left in the game, we went 80 yards passing the ball down the field to make it 17-15. We almost connected on the two-point play but time had expired. But that game propelled me as a quarterback. As a senior, I played nothing but quarterback. We had an average season with a young team, but colleges got interested in me."

John David came out of his senior season as the top quarterback prospect in Alabama. He had thrown for 887 yards and had eight TD passes. He narrowed his choices to Alabama, Tennessee and Georgia. They liked his 6-4, 195-pound frame as well.

Tennessee intrigued John David because he liked their quarterback Heath Shuler. He had one season left, was up for the Heisman Trophy and John David felt it would be good to spend a year learning from him.

On the Sunday night return from their official Tennessee visit in January, John David got one of those dozens of phone calls a top recruit gets. "It was Randy Ross, Alabama's recruiting coordinator. He said, 'Coach (Gene) Stallings has gone out west to talk with Coach Homer Smith about the offensive coordinator and quarterback coaching job.' It had been a rumor, but Coach Ross told me he was going to hire Coach Smith. Of course, we knew of his great success with Gary Hollingsworth in 1989 and winning an SEC championship. Everybody knew Coach Smith as an offensive genius.

"We found out the next morning that Coach Smith was already in Tuscaloosa. My dad and I decided that we would just take off for Tuscaloosa and meet Coach Smith and see how things were. We met him at lunch in Bryant Hall and he showed great interest in having me come there. We talked with other coaches that day also.

"I was so impressed with the way Alabama recruited anyway. They didn't talk about other schools. There was not one time that Coach Stallings said anything bad about Tennessee or Georgia or Auburn or any other school. He just talked about Alabama and what he thought about Alabama. Other schools would say things about Alabama comparing their school to Alabama. So I thought, hey, why go to other schools trying to be like Alabama when I could be at Alabama? So I just decided that Alabama was all I had thought it to be growing up and made the decision."

When John David entered Alabama in 1994, Jay Barker was the senior quarterback. Other quarterbacks were junior Brian Burgdorf and sophomore Freddie Kitchens. With all that talent at quarterback and with John David's talent and the team's shortage of defensive backs, it was the logical choice for this brand new freshman. In the first game against Chattanooga in Birmingham, John David played quite a bit at defensive back in the second half.

The next week he moved into the specialty teams lineup. On the opening kickoff against Vanderbilt in Bryant-Denny Stadium, John David went down field and made the tackle.

"What a thrill to make a tackle on your very first play in Bryant-Denny Stadium.

"When I heard all those thousands of fans yelling and screaming, I was hooked that day of the thrill of being an Alabama football player," says John David. He went on to play in all 12 games as a true freshman and was estactic to see so much action.

Next season would be a completely different story. Vying for a first or second team defensive back position, the coaches decided to move John David to offense as a quarterback or receiver. In the A-Day game, John David found himself playing wide receiver. That summer he ran routes and threw passes while thinking which will it be, quarterback or receiver?

In two-a-day practices, John David worked himself into rotation as a receiver. Things were going well on specialty teams also. Then John David made a decision. He made an appointment with Coach Stallings on Wednesday before the first game with Vanderbilt.

"I had been praying, unable to sleep at night and didn't have peace in my heart about my role on the team. So I ducked my head into Coach's office and I said, 'Coach Stallings, I know this is the week of the Vanderbilt game. I know I'm traveling this week, but I've just got to play quarterback. I just feel that's what God wants me to do.

"Then he said, 'You know what this means don't you? It means you will be redshirted this year. You understand that don't you?' And I said, 'Yes sir, I realize that.' Then he said, 'Well, I think that's a smart move.

Thanks for telling me before tomorrow when we post the travel list because you were on it.'

"The funny thing is I'm walking out of the football complex to get into my car and Tony Johnson, a tight end and devoted Christian, is walking by. It is amazing how God gives validity in decisions that you have made and prayed over. I was walking out thinking, 'God, I hope I just made the right decision. I just hope that is what you wanted me to do. I need some affirmation.'

"Sure enough, Tony walks up and says, 'John David, I need to talk to you about something.' I said, 'What's that?' Then he said, 'You may find this odd, but I just feel like God wants you to play quarterback. I don't know why I'm telling you this. I was just praying last night and reading my Bible. I just feel I needed to share that with you.'

"I said, 'Tony, that's funny. I've just talked with Coach Stallings about moving back to quarterback. Tony didn't think anything about it I guess. He just said, 'That's great,' and walked off. I thought that was pretty amazing how God used Tony, a godly teammate, to affirm my decision."

So John David sat out his second year at Alabama. However, he became the Scout Team quarterback, a tough job going up against the first team defense every week in practice. His quarterback skills were severely tested but what an opportunity to take snaps from center once again! Meanwhile, that Scout Team consisted of redshirt freshmen Shaun Alexander (running back), Reggie Grimes (fullback), Chris Samuels (tackle), Michael Vaughn and Shamari Buchanan (receivers) and others who would have starting careers.

Off the field, John David had fully established himself in the Fellowship of Christian Athletes meetings each Wednesday night. He also attended Sunday School and worship twice on Sunday at Calvary Baptist Church, one block from the stadium. As a freshman, John David admired senior Jay Barker as a true Christian leader on the team. While he once had thoughts of playing behind Heath Shuler, a Heisman candidate at Tennessee, he now had Jay, a role model of the best kind. Jay made All-American himself and placed fifth in the Heisman.

In the Spring of 1996, Coach Woody McCorvey replaced Coach Homer Smith as offensive coordinator. John David would battle Freddie Kitchens and Lance Tucker for playing time. On the Scout Team, John David ran the opposing teams offense. Now he was in an altogether different role. He was rusty and unpolished while trying to play quarterback in his own team's offense for the first time since high school.

As a sophomore, John David had his best season on specialty teams. He occasionally played quarterback but did not throw a pass. He was often sent in for the final play or two to mop up victories. Friends kidded him on Sunday that John David hurt his kneecap on the sprinkler cap when he took the snap while taking a knee on the last play of the game.

When the 1997 season rolled around, Coach Stallings had retired and Coach Mike DuBose was the new head coach. Kitchens was a senior and John David was in a backup role. Coaches took him off of specialty work. As backup quarterback, he had a season-high 10 plays in the first game against Houston. For the year, he would complete only one of three passes for four yards and rush nine times for seven yards.

That one completion was one to remember, however. It was a four-yard touchdown slant pass to Quincy Jackson against the mighty Tennessee Vols in Birmingham with :42 seconds left in the game. It was relief role work for John David in a game far out of reach. The Tide lost 38-21.

"We got beat, but it was still rewarding that my first career touchdown pass came against a team like Tennessee. When I got to Alabama, I dreamed every night about playing against Tennessee," remembers John David. What followed after the game was priceless.

"I came walking out of the locker room and all the players are hurt, upset and disappointed. It was that typical post-game loss feeling. It was just quiet you know. You don't hear anything.

"Then you hear Glenda Phillips just come out of the crowd screaming her head off because her son just threw a touchdown pass. She was screaming my name, 'John David! John David! John David!' I had to calm her down and remind her that we had just lost the ball game. I had to tell her that it didn't look right for the others to see her cheering as we walked from the stadium." Such refreshing moments in athletics are among the best. Mothers can have different perspectives on winning and losing when it comes to their sons.

So John David's only completion of the season was a touchdown pass against Tennessee. "I'll take it," says John David, who made the throw in the 80th Tide-Vols meeting before 83,091 spectators and an ESPN audience.

Alabama finished 4-7 that season after winning the first three of four games. Then the season ended with that fateful 18-17 loss at Auburn in the last few seconds when it seemed that Alabama had the game won before a screen pass fumble led to Auburn's winning field goal.

John David now entered Spring Training as a senior. He was now locked into a battle with redshirt freshman Andrew Zow for the starting job. At Union County High in Lake Butler, FL., Andrew had directed his team to two state titles and a 40-game winning streak at quarterback. At the end of the spring, John David was ahead and looking forward to his senior season.

Even though he had not been a mainline player, his teammates voted him the Charlie Compton Award recipient ten days before the season for displaying the most outstanding Christian leadership on the team. John David's family and grandparents were present at the Calvary Baptist Church service, along with teammates, on Squad Sunday to see John David receive the award given since 1964. Outstanding speakers are always brought to the pulpit each year. This year, John David and Shaun Alexander shared the sermon time and Andy Phillips sang. It was an anointed hour of worship.

Also that week, John David was voted by his teammates a team Captain for the season. It was a fitting honor and a valued dream for the young man who cried at age seven when Bear Bryant died.

Moments of glory lay ahead as the first game with Brigham Young approached. John David won the job. A newly constructed east side upper deck and 81 skyboxes were in place, raising Bryant-Denny Stadium from 70,000 to 83,818 capacity. Also, the largest scoreboard on a college campus was in place with a giant Jumbotron and instant replay screen.

The setting was perfect. Game time was 6 p.m. Starting in the late afternoon sunshine on September 5, the game would later be under the lights. A nationwide ESPN audience awaited. It would turn out to be one of the most memorable games in Bryant-Denny Stadium ever. The atmosphere was electric. It was a beautiful sight to behold for Alabama fans.

"From the second I put my foot on the grass that night…it is difficult for me to put into words," recalls John David proudly. "You have put all you have into something, have prayed for something, and it just culminated that night. It had all come together and it just felt right.

"I can remember not only am I starting but I am a captain. I walk out on the field and the first thing I hear is Coach Bryant's voice on the Jumbotron. By the time I get to midfield to meet the BYU captains, I am just crying. I've got tears running down my face. Try to look tough when you are crying. It's not easy."

John David did his job and Alabama jumped to a 24-14 lead at halftime. He would hand off to Shaun Alexander for five rushing touchdowns, a school record as Alabama won 38-31. John David's FCA buddies, Shaun and Ryan Pflugner scored all 38 points. John David passed for 187 yards on 17 of 29 passes in his starting debut wearing Number 12 on his uniform.

"It was the highlight of my career by far. It was an incredible night all the way around, not just the game but the atmosphere present. All the lessons football ever taught me were brought together that night. It was so neat. It was just an awesome gift from God."

John David had passed the test in his first start. He was now more settled and confident for the next game against Vanderbilt in Birmingham. In the second quarter, he threw a 31-yard touchdown pass to Quincy Jackson and Alabama clipped Vandy impressively 32-7. John David was 19 of 30 for 179 yards passing.

With a 2-0 start, disaster struck the next week at Fayetteville against Arkansas. Behind 14-6 at the half, Alabama went on to lose 42-6. John David and the offense struggled against an aggressive Razorback defense. The Tide defense gave up 445 yards. The team was penalized 13 times, for 104 yards, tying a school record. A Shaun Alexander fumble gave Arkansas the ball on the 3-yard line and John David had a pass intercepted on the 17 that led to two easy Arkansas touchdowns. It was one of those games where nothing went right for the entire team.

Next up was Coach Steve Spurrier and highly ranked Florida in Tuscaloosa. It was a golden opportunity for the Tide to redeem themselves. John David was pumped and ready to lead his team to victory. Instead, it would turn out to be the most painful day of his life.

A swarming Gator defense dropped John David time after time early in the game. Their pressure defense was dominant. To give John David some relief and try a different strategy, Andrew Zow was sent in to run the offense on the last series of both the first and second quarters. Alabama trailed 13-3 at the half.

Zow quarterbacked the entire second half completing 12 of 26 passes for 185 yards. The Tide defense played much better, causing the Gators to lose two fumbles inside the Tide's 5-yard line and to miss another late scoring opportunity. Florida won 16-10.

The Alabama team rebounded respectfully from the Arkansas game, but for John David, it was the most humiliating day of his life. Wanting to play well, the worst case scenario awaited.

As a fifth-year senior quarterback, he had lost his job and would not play a down for the next seven games.

"I look at the Florida game a lot differently now," as John David reflects. "At that time, it was very painful. In fact, it was the worst I have ever felt in my life emotionally and not even physically, even though I got killed.

"I look at it as more of a blessing now. I learned more on that day and in that game than in any other experience in my life. It was one of those divine intervention things.

"Beginning in the August three-a-day practices, my roommate Chad McGehee (walk-on safety, specialty team player) and I committed to just prayer and scripture everyday between and after practices. There was no TV, no nothing but prayer and scripture reading together, take a nap and back to practice. Our prayers were that God would make us spiritual leaders on and beyond the football team and that he would show us how he wanted to make us that way. We wanted to reach others for Christ. It was sort of like a fast, not a food fast, but a commitment we made for three or four weeks.

"Then there was a quote that I got from a man named Samuel Brengle on Spiritual Leadership that meant so much to me.

"The quote said, *'Spiritual Leadership is not won by promotion, but by many prayers and tears. It is attained by confession of sin and much heart searching and humbling before God, by self-surrender, a courageous sacrifice of every idol, a bold uncomplaining embrace of the cross, and by an eternal, unfaltering, looking unto Jesus crucified. It is not gained by seeking great things for ourselves, but like Paul, by counting those things that are gain or loss for Christ. This is a great price, but it must be paid by the leader who would not be merely a nominal but a real spiritual leader whose power is recognized and felt in heaven, on earth, and in hell.'*

"I took that and pinned it to my wall and my prayer every day was, 'God make me this kind of spiritual leader.' I wasn't thinking of the repercussions of it or how God would make me into that person. Then we go through the season. BYU, great game. Vanderbilt, great game. Arkansas, terrible. Florida, worst for me personally.

"After the Florida game, I came into the locker room. Of course, they have the starting quarterback locker sitting aside from everyone else. It is right there by itself. I remember looking at that locker and thinking, 'There it goes. It's over. I've lost it.'

"I remember sitting at that locker and they call out the names of those the media wants to talk to. My name is called. I'm sitting here praying to God, 'How am I going to stand in front of these people and not be bitter? How am I going to show Christ in all of this?'

"I couldn't do it at that time. So I sat inside that locker and continued to pray until I thought I could make it. By God's grace and power, he enabled me to do that. It was the only way I could face people who were hungry to know what was going on. People who would try to work it out of me about how I felt. God got me through the interviews. It wasn't easy. I was hurting, just dying inside.

"Then I finally got dressed. I walked out among all the families who were waiting on their sons. I still have my tough face on. I still have my media face on. My dad takes my bag from me like he does every game. He sat it down on the ground and hugged me. As soon as he touched me, I just lost it. I was just hurt and couldn't stand up. I fell to my knees hurting.

"I just remember thinking, 'I'm not going to get through this. This is too much. You feel so much humiliation. You feel that this goal has just slipped out of your hands, and there was nothing you could do about it.

"Then we went back to my apartment. I'm sitting there talking to my sister. She's kind of got her arm around me talking to me. I said, 'Leigh Ann, I just don't understand. I just can't understand this. What's God doing in my life?' About that time, I glance over and see that little quote by Samuel Brengle that I had pinned to my wall.

"At that moment, I went from despair to a little smile that cracked on my face. I was still hurting, don't get me wrong. But I go, 'Wow, I see what God is doing now. God is taking his molding material. He is chipping away at me now. He's chipping away pride, chipping away this and chipping away that. He's making me that spiritual leader that I had prayed so hard for. That's when I first started my journey of allowing God to mold me into His likeness.

"Your normal reaction is to fight it and be bitter and angry. But as soon as I saw that quote, I felt a little bit better. I pointed it out to my sister and said, 'That's why all of this has happened.'

"That's pretty much been my testimony from the whole experience ever since. I still have a hard time with it. But I have learned that through such a blow in your life, a relationship with God is not always having to constantly work and work at it. It is more of a letting go. There is such a freedom in that. There is such a beauty in that. God says, 'I don't want you to bust your rear end for me. That will come out of love for me. I just want you to let go and fall into my arms. And when you see just how much I love you, you will do that because it is fun.'

"It is a daily thing. Everyday when I get up, I just put it into God's hands and commit it to him, everything good, bad and indifferent. Then I go through the day knowing that I am in His mercy and His grace is perfect."

John David had lost his starting role. For the next seven games against Mississippi, East Carolina, Tennessee, Southern Mississippi, LSU, Mississippi State and Auburn, John David did not take a snap or set foot on the playing field. His spiritual maturity kept him from crumbling from the humiliation and embarrassment of losing the job he had dreamed about and it was slipping away week after week.

Each Saturday, John David would walk to the center of the field with the other co-captains for the coin toss. Each Wednesday night, he continued to lead the Fellowship of Christian Athletes meetings before 225 student/athletes. Each Friday night, as many as 30 teammates would gather in his room for Prayer Time before the game the next day. John David was admired for his strength and faith in Christ.

His roommate on the road was Andrew Zow, who had taken his place at quarterback. Many times Zow was hit hard and went down but managed to stay in the game. "Everytime, Drew went down, my chinstrap was buckled. I was ready to go. I love Andrew Zow to death. I told him that. We roomed together on the road and in his first start against Mississippi, I told him in the room, 'Andrew, I realize that the only way I am going to get to play is if you do bad or if you get hurt. I want you to know, I don't want you to do bad and I don't want you to get hurt. I love you to death. If I am going back on that field, I want to do it because I am better than you are. That's the only reason I want to be out there.' I told him I was his biggest fan. I wanted to help any way I knew how. I told him if he had any questions, ask. I reminded him of that every now and then.

"Each time he went down or was a little slow getting up, I think that was a little test of me. It was really hard because I was dying to get back out there. I was wanting to so badly. I remember in the Mississippi State game, he went down once and we were behind. I started warming up as he was limping around. I kept thinking I was going in and we were going to win this thing. Once again, I leave the game a little down and all the rest that way, but I just took those games as, 'Let it go. God is at work in my life.'

"The hardest thing was looking past my own needs and looking toward the greater cause of Alabama football, most importantly, these guys' spiritual lives. That was difficult for me. But I got through that simply because of Jesus Christ. You see, I'm a fighter. It is like me to fight and be a competitor. But God just kept me in the right frame of mind and I knew that was how He wanted me to be. I constantly stayed in tune with the Lord and he was faithful in keeping me that way."

So John David's last play at quarterback came in the second quarter of the Florida game, the fourth game of the season. Then Alabama had a 7-4 record going into the Music City Bowl in Nashville on December 29. John David saw action at wide receiver and on all the specialty teams throughout the game.

Since John David had graduated the previous August in public relations and marketing, he spent from February through October of 1999 accepting speaking engagements throughout Alabama and other parts of the southeast. His talks to youth and adults about adversity were powerful witnesses for the Lord he loved and served so faithfully. To be so young, God has blessed John David with wisdom far beyond his years and has gifted him as a speaker. Today, he is a pharmaceutical representative and lives in Tuscaloosa.

Perhaps the last high moment for John David as an Alabama football player came in Nashville during the Music City Bowl week. It came wearing a suit and not in a football uniform. He represented Alabama's team for a brief testimonial at the Fellowship of Christian Athletes Breakfast attended by 500 people in the downtown Renaissance Nashville Hotel.

For a young man who had faced adversity, had started the first four games and had not played for seven games, his talk was a masterpiece. As he stood before men and women, high school athletes and coaches, and players and coaches from the Alabama and Virginia Tech teams, this is the message he delivered from his heart and only from an outline:

"Ladies and gentlemen, athletes and coaches, I want to read from Philippians 3:10. To give you a little background on this verse, my teammates have heard me talk so much about Paul and how much I admire him. First of all, Paul is in jail. To me, this verse is his creed and what he lived by and because it is his creed, it is something we should live by. Because as Paul says, 'Follow me as I follow Christ.'

"Philippians 3:10 says, 'I want to know Christ and the power of his resurrection. And the fellowship of sharing his suffering and becoming like him in his death.' About two years ago, God laid this verse on my heart and it has stuck with me ever since. I have always found Paul interesting as I have said before, but there is something about this verse that just hits me funny.

"From this verse, there are three things that I have pulled from it. There are three things that Paul says he wanted to know. The first one of these is that Paul says he wanted to know Christ. I think because Paul wanted to know Christ, we should want to know Christ. The reason for that is the power and the strength that is in Christ. Paul knew it first hand because of how Christ had affected his life. Christ had changed his life. If you don't know, Paul was a guy who had persecuted Christians.

"And yet Christ came to him and showed his love to him and it changed Paul's life forever. I think the reason we love God, the reason we love Jesus Christ is because Christ first came to us. He said he loved us by dying on the cross to save us from our sins. The more we learn about God and his son Jesus Christ, the more we grow to love him. That's a tremendous thing.

"The second thing that Paul says he wants to know is the power of the resurrection. And Ladies and Gentlemen, that's the reason I stand before you today. It's the power of the resurrection. It's everything. It is the reason we are here today. It is simply this. You and I are sinners and there is nothing we can do about it. We were born sinners. We are going to die sinners. We have a void in our lives that wants to know God. The thing is, God knows no sin. He is perfection. He wants to destroy sin. He can't stand sin.

"So you can see the problem there. We are sinners. We want a relationship with God. But God loved us enough that he sent his only son in Jesus Christ to be the living sacrifice, the ultimate sacrifice. He took our sins to the cross with him when he died. The third day when he arose, he defeated those sins so that when we confess our sins and believe on him, we become Christians. God now sees us as perfection and we can have a relationship with him. He sees us as his children. That's amazing to me.

"That's power that my sins tomorrow, my sins today, my sins from yesterday were forgiven because of Jesus Christ. That is the power of the resurrection. It is very powerful. You will know no greater power than the power of the resurrection. You will know no greater love than the love of Jesus Christ.

"And the third thing that Paul says he wants to know, is the fellowship of sharing in his suffering. That is Christ's suffering, becoming like him in his death. A year ago, I remember sitting down and just asking God, 'What do you mean by that? The fellowship of shar-ing in his suffering becoming like Christ in his death?'

"And I think it is this. Paul caught a hold of something. He real-ized that through his adversity and through his suffering, that it was one of the greatest ways he was able to show Christ. Let me tell you something, if you are living and breathing, you are going to face adversity. You are going to suffer. It is just a part of life. You can either sulk about it. You can be upset about it, or you can say it is an opportunity to glorify God. And that's how Paul saw it.

"I look throughout the whole Bible and there are not many peo-ple who didn't face adversity. In fact, Moses led his people out of the Promised Land and was constantly persecuted and people tried to kill him. The book of Job talks about all he went through, and yet he persevered and was able to glorify God in it all. You look at Paul's whole life. They tried to kill him. He was put in jail. There was noth-ing you could do to Paul to upset him because through suffering, Jesus Christ could be glorified.

"It's an amazing thing for a Christian to say, 'Through my good times I can glorify God. Through my bad times I can glorify God.' There's nothing in this world that can do that for you. If things are going good, they are good. If they are not, they are not. In Jesus Christ, through the good and bad times, you can still glorify God. You are still meeting your goal. And that's all God asks of us.

"In closing, I want to read Philippians 3:12-14. It says this, 'Not that I have already obtained all of this, or have already been made perfect, but I press on to take hold of that which Christ Jesus has taken hold of me. Brothers I do not consider myself as taken hold of it, but one thing I do, forgetting what is behind and straining toward what is ahead, I press on toward the goal to win the prize for which God has called me heavenward in Christ Jesus.'

"God doesn't ask us to do much. He just asks us to keep mov-ing. I believe it is Paul's creed and it should be our creed, that we should want to know Christ, and that we should want to know the power of his resurrection, and some times when things don't go the way we think they should, we should understand that there is fel-lowship in suffering. There is fellowship with Jesus Christ, our Lord and Savior.

"I close to tell you this. Press on. Keep going. Because God can use you."

AMEN.....John David!!

CHAPTER EIGHTEEN

COACH ROBERT SCOTT

This story was composed after interviewing Cynthia Scott,
the loving wife of Robert Scott, three weeks after Robert passed away.

God gave Robert Scott 42 years upon this earth and he lived every year like he was in a full court press.

When the final buzzer sounded on his life on May 9, 2000, Rah Rah Scott had played the entire game for his entire life with total purpose. He had given his all. He had given to the world all he had—a life fully lived for others.

Raised in the Birmingham inner city, Robert was blessed with maturity beyond his years and a no-nonsense demeanor even as an elementary school student.

His basketball coach detected in Robert at that age a hint that proved to be Robert's destiny. One day in a championship elementary game, Robert suddenly called Time Out to the surprise and astonishment of his coach.

"Coach, we are getting killed in this zone defense. If we don't go to a man defense, we don't have a chance and it's going to get worse," exclaimed young Robert to his coach. "We have got to put the pressure on them!" The coach looked down at Robert and said, "Okay, Robert, if you think that's what we should do, we'll go to the man defense."

Robert was right. By switching to the man to man defense, his team won the game. His coach thought right then that this young man could be a basketball coach someday.

No doubt, the seeds were already sown. Robert Scott was indeed going to be a basketball coach.

The youngest of four children, Robert grew up in the Titusville community near downtown Birmingham. His daddy worked in a foundry while his mother took care of the home front. His dad was an outstanding baseball player but never had the opportunity to pursue it as a career.

Robert acquired his famous nickname "Rah Rah" as a toddler from his oldest sister. With a career in athletics, one would suspect that his enthusiastic play earned him that name along the way. Not so, the name came long before any athletic activity. Robert's dad was named Robert and was called "RB." When young Robert came along, the sister didn't want to call him "Rob...bert," so she called him "Rah" and then started saying "Rah Rah."

When he was born on December 9, 1957, Robert was not given a middle name. However, he was called Rah Rah so much that later on his name became Robert "Rah Rah" Scott, III.

It was a God sent nickname for what He had planned for this man who would touch thousands of people through the sport of basketball.

Robert learned his basketball skills in the neighborhood gyms. As he passed through junior and senior high school at Parker High, he played every sport with a passion. He lettered four years in basketball, football, baseball and track.

He excelled at a high level in basketball and was coached by the legendary high school coach, Cap Brown. Rah Rah earned many MVP honors at Parker and carried an impressive academic average along with his other accolades. Then he made the Alabama Crimson Tide his collegiate choice under Coach C.M. Newton.

Perhaps the most important score of his life came in the 11th grade when he met a pretty young lady named Cynthia Clark. Cynthia was a majorette, a very good student and came from a fine Christian home.

"At first we were just friends and I liked it that way because my daddy wasn't ready for me to start dating," says Cynthia with a broad smile. "He would call me on the phone and we talked. That went on for a semester until one day he said he was going to stop calling me as a friend. He said he wanted me to be his girl friend.

"I told him I couldn't do it and just wanted to be friends. I respected my daddy so much and his wishes that I not date yet. Rah would ignore me in class and not say anything. He was playing games with me and I got to where I missed talking to him. So I agreed to be his girlfriend."

When Rah Rah was being recruited, Cynthia didn't interfere with his decision. "I wanted to go to either Alabama or Alabama A&M," says Cynthia in reflection. "I never told him what I was thinking. It needed to be his decision. When he decided on Alabama, I chose A&M. I just didn't think we needed to be on a big college campus together at that young of an age until we got some growth and maturity. So I went to A&M and he to Alabama and we still dated.

"The next year, I transferred to Alabama and went on and got my degree in Home Economics while he played basketball and got his degree in Health, Physical Education and Recreation."

Robert had four outstanding years of basketball with the Crimson Tide. He made an impression even as a freshman when he scored 20 points in a game against Florida. Alabama went 25-6 that year and ended the season in the National Invitational Tournament in New York City.

During Robert's four years of college basketball, the NCAA tournament had a much smaller number of teams in the tourney. Alabama was third in the SEC three of Robert's four years. They were fourth when he was a sophomore but Robert played in three NIT tournaments against some of the nation's best teams.

Robert made All-Southeastern Conference as a senior in 1980. In January of that season, he was selected National Player of the Week by *Sports Illustrated.*

As a junior and senior, Robert was team captain, which speaks volumes about his leadership qualities, his maturity and character. As a 6-2 guard wearing No. 10, score sheets would reveal what an asset he was to the team. At game's end, Robert would have scored points, dished out assists, rebounded and contributed all over the court as an all-around solid competitor.

His final two seasons were also the last for Coach Newton, whom he drew close to in later years when basketball was over at Alabama.

Drafted by the Golden State Warriors in the fourth round, Robert didn't make the final cut but opted instead to play basketball for the next six years overseas. It was a good experience for Robert as he traveled extensively throughout the world.

"I played six years overseas and got to experience being a coach a little bit while I was there," Robert said years after his return home. "The traveling helped me to develop a thirst to coach. I had been in sports for so long that it seemed like the best thing for me to do. I was offered a coaching position for a professional team overseas but family considerations caused me to return home and pursue coaching here."

Two years after college, he and Cynthia married on August 11, 1982. Rah Rah played in Qatar near Saudi Arabia in the Middle East and one of his former teammates, Ricky Brown was on the same team. Ricky's wife and Cynthia found themselves as the only women at the games. A year later, Robert Rahmun was born, so Cynthia stayed in the states with their newborn.

Robert would be overseas for seven months. Upon returning home, he got involved with coaching night league teams and assisted Coach Cap Brown in many ways in Birmingham.

Hayes High School offered Robert his first coaching job as an assistant coach in 1985. The next year, the team won the 4A state championship. West End High School principal Alfred Cottrell was impressed with the young Hayes assistant and approached him at the tournament.

"Do you want to be a head coach?" he asked Rah Rah at the tournament. Robert was delighted with his request but first he had to make a phone call. "Every time Rah had a decision to make, he would call Coach C.M. Newton and asked for his opinion," says Cynthia in no uncertain terms. The call was made and West End had themselves a new head basketball coach.

"When Rah took the job, he said to Mr. Cottrell, 'I am going to build you a basketball program over here. I am going to build you a program where people will look up to this side of town instead of looking down at it. As long as you are behind me, I am going to build you a program that the West End community will be proud of.'

"And he did," Cynthia recalls with a proud heart for her man's strong will, sense of purpose and determination

"Rah knew the community and how it needed a lift. He took it on as a challenge. He went to families who had sent their kids to private schools and told them that if they came back to West End, he would take care of them and make sure they got their education."

True to his word, Coach Scott instilled pride and respect back into West End High with basketball teams over the next 11 years that compiled an amazing record of 234 wins and 64 losses. His last team in 1996 went undefeated and won the Class 6A state championship.

Everything at the Scott household was going so well. While coaching at West End, Robert and Cynthia had Daniel Rahkeith in 1988 and Rahshaé Evanna in 1991. All three children had the name Rah and for a reason: "Only because Robert wanted it to be that way," says Cynthia. It was a good decision by Robert and perhaps a divine purpose for the children to hold their beloved father dear for the rest of their lives.

Robert's success reached yet another plateau after the championship. Murry Bartow, the UAB head coach, offered Robert a job as assistant coach. "Robert considered it a very big achievement and an honor when he was offered the job. Once again, he called Coach Newton and then he accepted the job. He was ready for the college level. It was a perfect situation for Rah. In fact, he grew up three or four minutes from the campus," says Cynthia.

"He loved his two years at UAB. He bonded well with the coaches. He drew close to the players. They would hang out in his office almost like it was Daddy's office. When Coach (Mark) Gottfried offered him the opportunity to come to Alabama, it was not easy for him to leave. He was reluctant. Still, it was his alma mater this time. So once again, he called Coach Newton before he accepted the job.

"Once he made the decision and it was announced to the media, he came home and I remember him saying, 'Oh, I feel like a ton of weight is off of my shoulders.'

"It was hard to let go but at the same time he was so excited about going back to Alabama. It took him back 20 years and it was a good feeling. He didn't know the staff, but he would tell me that they pulled him in and treated him like they had known each other for years. He thanked God for that and he knew he could do some wonderful things at Alabama."

Robert joined the staff in April, 1998. He thrust himself into recruiting. It was one of his strong suits. He was a tenacious recruiter.

October came and practice began. Alabama's fans welcomed Mark and his staff with exuberance and excitement. The first year saw the team compile a 17-15 record and reach the NIT tournament. They won games that were surprising to the experts.

Robert recruited with a passion. Birmingham's Rod Grizzard and Uniontown's Erwin Dudley committed to Alabama. Both were prize recruits. Terrance Meade from Scottsboro, D.J. Towns of Pleasant Grove and Kenny Walker of Jacksonville, FL gave Alabama one of the nation's top recruiting classes. Schea Cotton transferred from Long Beach City College (CA) to also strengthen the class.

"After a year at Alabama, we were living better than any other time in our lives," says Cynthia in deep thought. "Financially everything was better. I was teaching Special Education at Lloyd Wood Junior High School and Rah dearly loved his work. He was so happy and felt so good walking out the door as an Alabama basketball coach. The kids were happy. His mother had been sick and now she was doing well once again. Everything was just nice.

"It was early in the summer of 1999. On this particular night, I said my prayers and got into bed. Out of the clear blue, I said, 'Rah, do you believe that everything happens for a reason?' He said, 'Naw, go to sleep.' I didn't pursue the conversation because I didn't feel he wanted to get into that deep of a subject at that time. I just thought to myself, 'Well,' and I went off to sleep.

"The whole deal was, I was just looking at our lives and how good things were going. It wasn't that things were perfect, but it was okay. It was nice. We got to a point where we could breathe a little bit. His mother had been sick and whenever she needed anything we could do it for her. We had never known a time when things were this good for our family."

The Scott family was blessed to have a godly mother and wife in Cynthia. She radiates the love of Jesus in her life and Robert, too, had a deep and abiding faith in the Lord. Robert would appear to be a quiet person until you got to know him. Cynthia could strike up a conversation with anyone in a minute and her spirituality came through clearly. She had a love in her heart for people. Special Education was her profession, which explains her caring concern for others. The children were well mannered, respectful and polite. You couldn't find better people than the Scott family.

Then early in the summer, the trial for Robert gradually began.

"Rah would say, 'I'm not feeling real good.' He would go to the doctor and they would give him some kind of medication and he would be back on the road again," says Cynthia. "Then in August, he got severely ill and he went to the Kirklin Clinic in Birmingham. They ran tests and at first detected fluid in his abdomen.

"At that time, I started feeling kind of leery. I have always been a person who read medical books. I love to read and with three kids, I always wanted to be on top of things medically so that I could have a better knowledge of health and illnesses. In fact, he saw a good medical book at Kirklin and told the doctor he wanted to get that book for me. He would sometimes ask me, 'Why didn't you become a doctor because you love to read those medical books?'

"So when he told me about the fluid on his stomach, I had read about that but didn't say anything. I was concerned for him then. Two weeks later, he went back to Kirklin for another test. I put it in the back of my mind that it wouldn't be the word 'cancer.'

"Anyway, he called me on his car phone on his way back home and told me they said it was some form of cancer. When he got home, I didn't show any sign of weakness. I didn't even talk to him about it. I just asked him, 'When is your next appointment?' He gave me the appointment date.

"The next day, I called Robert's doctor unknowing to him. Robert told me that he didn't need me to go to the doctor with him. That is why I called his doctor and he told me I should come. It was the most devastating news I've ever had since my father and a younger brother were killed within six months of each other several years earlier.

"Now I found myself needing to be strong for Robert. I prayed and asked God to give me strength when we went to see Dr. Robert Centar, Rah's doctor. I didn't want Robert to feel down or even feel my sadness. That wasn't what he needed at that time. God gave me strength. I sat there and I listened and didn't shed a tear."

It was the first week of September and the next step was a biopsy. The results were malignant cancer in Robert's stomach. It was shocking news, but Robert remained calm and Cynthia remained solid in her faith in God. Robert was referred to the cancer center in Kirklin and Dr. James Posey became his doctor.

"When we met with Dr. Posey, he told us it was a tough form of cancer," Cynthia remembers. "So we asked, 'Okay, what are our options?' We didn't ask the big question that is obvious. We didn't ask how long does Robert have to live? In fact, we never asked that question.

"We never questioned Robert's illness. Robert never sat back. He kept doing the things he would normally do. He kept going until he just couldn't go any more. He was a warrior through all the treatment and that's what kept me strong. I never allowed myself to mope around and show any sadness.

"We lived each day as if it was a common cold and it was going to go away.

"I knew if we lived every day like it was cancer, we would have lived the last year emotionally humiliated. It was like, I take this medicine, I take that medicine, I go to the doctor and treat this as if he was going to be well again. We did what we could to not allow this crucial disease to tear down our last year together."

"When Robert went to the Radiation Clinic for his treatments, he always carried a Bible," Cynthia recalls. "Robert would read the Twenty-Third Psalms aloud and when he finished he would say to me, 'Your husband is going to be okay.'"

Through the treatments, everyone who knew Robert and hundreds that didn't had him on their prayer lists. Robert carried on his coaching duties in practice and for games when they began in November, as his strength would allow. His condition weakened, however, as each month passed. Rah Rah even endured the loss of his mother to heart failure in November. That added to the heartbreak and trials he was already experiencing.

Robert was determined to make every game of the season from the outset of his illness. As January and February games were played, Robert came to the bench dressed neatly in his suit after some games were already in progress. It was always inspiring to the players and coaches. They knew he had mustered all the strength he had to get there. There were days when he walked into practice after the session had begun. He would instruct or sit on the side court and observe.

Vanderbilt came to Tuscaloosa on February 12 for a Saturday four o'clock game. It was televised by the Fox Sports Network. "Robert was dressed and ready to go to the game, but he got real sick," Cynthia recalls. "He said, 'I can't make it.' So he lay down on the bed and watched the game on TV. At halftime, Darron Boatright (director of basketball operations) called him and asked him what he saw and what they should be doing against Vanderbilt, even though Alabama was leading.

"Robert responded by saying, 'Darron, y'all need to get so and so in there,' and he proceeded to list several adjustments that might be helpful for the team. He told Darron that he was real sick and that he might not make it for this game.

"A few minutes later he looked at me and said, 'We're going.' I said, 'Rah, you can miss this one. Mark will understand.' Then he said, 'Just get the kids. Let's go.'

"When we got to the game, there were about four minutes left to play. The kids went on out and sat in their seats. I went to the player's lounge with him where the game was on television. Then he insisted that I go to my seat and I said, "I don't want to leave you back here by yourself. You are not feeling good. No one knows you are in here.' He said, 'Just go watch the game, please!' I said, 'okay.'

"With two minutes and a few seconds left to play, I saw him walking and coming out on the floor to sit on the bench. Then I knew, that's why he wanted me to leave. He thought I wouldn't let him go out there because I knew how sick he was. He was determined to go out to that floor."

Robert's appearance that night caught the attention of the media. It was evident to everyone that Robert was very sick. Yet, his strong will to persevere despite his sickness was inspiring.

The following Monday, was Valentine's Day. Robert went back to the Kirklin Clinic in Birmingham for another chemotherapy treatment. Such treatments brought such excruciating pain that Robert couldn't get out of bed some mornings.

"I had told Robert not to get me anything for Valentine's Day because he always did. I knew he was sick and I didn't want him using that energy to get me something. I told him the best Valentine's present he could get me was for him to be well.

"Because he knew he couldn't get me the best Valentine's present that I wanted, he got me what he could get me. He got me a big beautiful basket through his friend Matthew Lewis. We went to Matthew's house and there was the basket in the backseat of his car. It had flowers, candy, soaps, stuffed animals and even a big doll because he knew I always loved dolls.

"I think he was realizing now that he was coming pretty close to being with God. It was like he was saying to me, 'I know I'm not going to get well, not on this side anyway. Not until I cross over will I be healed of it all.'"

On Wednesday, February 16, *The Birmingham News* ran a front page story on Robert with the headline, 'Battle of a Lifetime.' Steve Kirk did the interview and wrote, "His 6-foot-1 frame is now a shell of his former self and often at practice he pauses to lie down on top of the scorer's table."

In the story, he quoted Robert: "Mentally, I'm in pretty good shape. I feel like the Lord has been very good to me. He's blessed me with a wife and beautiful kids. He's blessed me with being able to coach in high school to UAB to here. He's just done so much for me.

"I just feel it would be shallow of me to look out there and say, 'Why me, Lord? Why me?' I know things are out of my hands. I've just got to battle and stay positive. Because, if you don't try to stay positive and battle, there's nothing but pain and pity to live on every day. And you can't live like that.

"Everybody wants to live a long time and live forever. Some of us unfortunately can't. I hope that I can live to be 100 years old, but I really don't know.

"If they told me I've got two weeks to live, I'd never question (God). I'd just try to live my days out the best I can."

What a testimony for a dying man. What a remarkable attitude. Robert's faith in God was his greatest strength.

On that same Wednesday, Alabama played at Kentucky and it was the first game Robert missed all season. He was too weak to make the trip and it was disappointing for two reasons for Robert. He would miss the game, of course, and then he would miss seeing his former coach, C.M. Newton, Kentucky's athletic director.

Alabama had a game at South Carolina the following Saturday. Cynthia and daughter Rahshaé were to join Robert on the trip. "When I got home from work, he said, 'We're not going to South Carolina.' I said, 'We're not?' He said, 'We have got to go to York. Do you feel like traveling to York?' I said, 'Why?' He said, 'Gerald Wallace is playing in York.'

"He felt it was more important to go to York and recruit Gerald Wallace than to make the trip to South Carolina. He told Mark he needed to go see Gerald play in the big match-up game with him and Mario Austin (another national cage prospect)."

Wallace was considered by most as the No. 1 basketball prospect in the nation and had already committed to Alabama. Robert had a powerful influence in Gerald's decision. Robert felt his presence was important because if Gerald's Childersburg High team had lost, his season would be over. Besides, he didn't want Gerald to declare for the NBA either. He needed to be there.

Even in his weak condition, Robert was there. Cynthia had given him earlier a special chair he could take with him to games that was more comfortable than the bleachers. The gym was packed so Robert was placed on the side court. Childersburg won on a last second dramatic shot by Gerald. Robert missed the South Carolina game, but he was where Alabama needed him the most that night.

March came and Robert was getting weaker. One day he made it to practice and Coach Gottfried called for a standup session with his players at center court. Robert walked out to the players and a manager got him a chair to sit in to hear the coach's remarks. A few minutes later, Robert gained the strength to get under the basket and give the centers and forwards some coaching for only a couple of minutes. Every player and coach gave their full attention to Rah Rah. It was probably more of an emotional moment than it was for taking instructions.

Robert didn't make the SEC tournament in Atlanta. His condition was getting progressively worse. On April 4, the basketball team reception was held at the Bryant Conference Center to honor the team. Robert was unable to attend. On April 12, the players and coaches drove to the UAB Hospital in Birmingham to visit Robert. They watched the season highlight film together in his room which had been shown at the reception. Rah Rah took the opportunity to admonish the players on their off-season workouts and training.

On April 28, Robert was admitted to the DCH Hospital in Tuscaloosa after spending two weeks at home. Prayers for Robert escalated. A children's Sunday School class at St. Mark's Methodist Church had sent prayergrams every week. Before Cynthia took Robert to the hospital, Robert signed six of his pictures for them upon Cynthia's request. He signed them 'Coach Scott,' and they would be his last autographs given. Cynthia kept one of them.

Robert was moved to the Critical Care unit on Saturday, May 6. That week during final exams, basketball team members would come by and see Robert as they finished their exams and returned home. The end was now near for Rah Rah.

On Tuesday morning, May 9, Robert was moved to the Intensive Care unit.

"I didn't tell my children that Robert had gone to Intensive Care that morning," says Cynthia thinking back on the final hours. "I wanted them to go to school and have a good day. But I asked God to spare Rah until they got out of school and could get up there to see him.

"At 9:30, I received a call in the Intensive Care ward from Daniel's principal at Englewood Middle School. He said, 'Mrs. Scott, Daniel is in the office. He is having a very hard time. He says his Mom wants him to be at school but he thinks he needs to be at the hospital with his Dad.' I said, 'Dr. (Steve) Lamon, did somebody call there?' He said, 'No, he's just having a hard time this morning.'

"I felt then that all three should be at the hospital and he took it upon himself to contact the other children and get them to the hospital.

"It was a blessing. God had shown Daniel that his Dad was leaving. God was also showing me that it was better that they be there while their Dad was conscious. He could still hear them and respond to them, but if we had waited until school was out, Robert wouldn't have been conscious enough to hear them.

"So I let each one of the children go in with their Dad individually. They talked to him and said what they wanted to say and I know he understood what they were saying. Robert was still moving his arms and responded with his eyes. Those were tender moments and I thank God that he sent that message to Daniel. It was glorified. Otherwise, I would have made a mistake by sending them to school all day. It would have been too late that afternoon. Robert had slipped into unconsciousness by then.

"I went in and had my time with Robert after the children. I told him that I thanked God for the life I had with him. I told him he had been a wonderful husband, a wonderful father and a wonderful person.

He had touched a lot of lives in a positive way. I told him I was going to miss him, but I knew I had to let him go. I told him I loved him and I knew he loved me. Still, I have to let go and I'm going to be okay. I know he heard me. He couldn't say anything.

"When I did that, I think I gave him some relief. I let him know that I was going to take care of the kids and everything was going to be okay. I think at that point, he felt okay. I could see peace in his face and it was like he finally realized he couldn't stay here. I think Robert had time to absorb what I said because he had a few more hours."

Robert fell asleep at 9:28 p.m. that evening and woke up in heaven. He had died of metastatic cancer of the stomach. By his side were Cynthia, Robert Rahmun, Daniel, Rahshaé, Cynthia's mother, Dr. Jimmy Robinson, the team doctor, and other family members. The basketball coaches and support staff were notified and they came immediately to comfort Robert's family and to express their love and support.

"Robert died knowing how much he was loved," Cynthia said tenderly three weeks after he had passed away. "Over the months and in his last days, the outpouring of love was indescribable. We received hundreds of meals, cards, phone calls, and so many kind gestures. The prayers were felt from untold numbers of people.

"Rah and I were always close but you really become one in a situation like this. We prayed together every night. We'd pray the Lord's Prayer together and a healing prayer together. Robert's faith in God never wavered.

"Never did we ask the one big question. We never asked how long Robert had to live. We just trusted God for the outcome and prayed for His will to be done. Rah was healed, but it was on the other side," says Cynthia, a woman of strong faith whose life rests on the sure foundation of Jesus Christ.

Two memorial services were conducted for Robert. The following Saturday on May 13, the first was held at The Bill Harris Arena at Fairpark in Birmingham.

Coleman Coliseum was the place for Robert's second service on Sunday afternoon. Graduation had taken place the previous day, and the same stage setup with the floral arrangements were left in place for Robert's funeral service.

A memorial service program was given to each person as they arrived in the coliseum lobby. Also the gospel tract titled, *More Than Winning* was handed out explaining the basics of receiving salvation in Jesus Christ.

Robert's casket was positioned in almost the exact spot of the basketball goal on the west end of the playing court. A basketball was placed on the back corner of each side of the casket. Flanking the bronze casket was Robert's No. 10 Alabama jersey in a glass frame and a painting of him as an All-SEC performer. Robert was buried in a beautiful brown suit with a yellowish-brown tie with a speck of crimson in it. A lapel pin had the moving words of "No. 1 Dad" on it. A crimson Alabama cap was placed beside Robert.

It was a moving sight to watch the basketball team members slowly file in from the same entrance they take the court for a game. Players walked reverently by the casket in a solemn mood before taking their seats on the front row. The team served as Pallbearers including Myron Ransom and LeAndrew Bass of UAB and Gerald Wallace, an Alabama 2000 signee.

Coaches, support staff, doctors and spouses sat behind the players. The family sat in the middle section and filled several rows. Game event ushers wore their crimson jackets just as they do at basketball games. The video screen was used prior to the service with highlights from past games, focusing in on Robert's coaching years.

The service began at 3 p.m. about the time practice usually began. Rod Asberry, a member of the athletic academic staff, sang a stirring rendition of "His Eye Is On The Sparrow." Pastor Bill Overstreet of the Church of Tuscaloosa and team chaplain began with a brief message. He described Robert as "a man who left a testimony and not titles." After his prayer, five men were selected to share memories of Robert.

Athletic Director Mal Moore: "We talk about the qualities we want from our student/athletes, the ones that will make them successful whether on the court, in the classroom or in life. But words ring hollow compared to Rah Rah's action. He showed us courage, sacrifice and fortitude. He did so with dignity, grace and a lot of class. With his faith, he won a race by running straight ahead where others would stumble. Rah Rah, with his abbreviated life, made something of himself and the world around him. We will kindle his spirit inside us through our words, thoughts and deeds. We will always remember him."

Former teammate T.R. Dunn: "I was a senior at West End High while Robert was a freshman at Parker High. Then when I became a senior at Alabama, Robert was a freshman. My wife and I had an apartment off campus and Rah would constantly be there and constantly be in our refrigerator. I would joke with him and ask him how could he eat as much as he did and stay as thin as he was. He still had that baby face.

"Over the past months, we talked quite often. He would have good days and bad ones, but he never talked about those. Next to the last conversation we had a month ago, he said to me, 'Well, T, I know you are thinking about me. I really appreciate that and I'm going to be okay.'

"Well, I would just like to say, 'Rah, we are all still thinking about you. We love you and we will always remember you.' "

Former Assistant Coach John Bostick: "T.R. mentioned that Rah Rah was baby faced and small. But he was a tough, hard-nosed competitor as a player. He was smart. He was our coach on the floor. He was a great person to have on your basketball team.

"I was away when he did most of his coaching, but I know this from comments I've heard from his players that he loved his players. That's the greatest thing that a coach can do is to love his players. I also know that they loved him back and had great respect for him.

"The thing I will remember most about Rah Rah, and I just found it out recently, is how much he loved Cynthia, Rahmun (16), Daniel (12) and Rahshaé (8). Cynthia was a trooper. She could not have done more for Rah. Along toward the end, he didn't respond to anybody much, but he responded to Cynthia because there was so much love.

"He loved his children. Rahshaé... I remember he had an Easter basket for her this past Easter. Sick as he was, he had gone out and bought an Easter basket for his girl and hid it in the closet until Easter.

"Daniel...When Rah was home, he would go into his room and say, 'I love you Dad.'

"Rahmun...When he got his ACT test score while Rah was in the hospital for the last time, he went up to his room and told his Dad what his test score was. And his Dad held out his arms and hugged him.

"Cynthia, Rahmun, Daniel and Rahshaé, when I think of Rah, I will always think of you. May God bless you and strengthen you always. We love you and we loved Rah Rah."

Alabama player Rod Grizzard: "I would like to say that I am thankful to be around a man like Coach Scott. He taught me a lot while he was here. He encouraged me all the time. Even when I was going through a lot making the transition from high school and Coach Gottfried and I had our differences, he would say, 'Hang in there. I know where you are coming from.' Everything turned out good after I went to him. All the things he told me I'll never forget. I just want to tell him that I love him and thank him for everything."

Coach Mark Gottfried: "Coach Scott...Robert...was my friend, co-worker and over the past two years was probably teacher to me.

Before we came out today, we had a few minutes with our team in the locker room and reflected there about Coach Scott. Rah Rah cared about people and individuals about as much as anybody I've ever been around. He wasn't different from anybody because of color, money or status. He was a genuine loving person.

"He loved to work. He worked hard. Many, many nights he was up in that office working late, calling guys on the phone. He did what needed to be done. One of the first things I noticed after I hired him was how hard he worked and how much passion he had for people.

"He taught our players this year through his illness what it means to have courage. I don't know if our players will ever see courage defined any better than they saw it in him this year.

"Our first game together he and I walked out in that hallway there (pointing to the area). He grabbed my hand and thanked me for letting him come back to the University of Alabama. After he was hired, Cynthia knows how proud he was to put that crimson shirt on and wear Alabama across his chest. When we went into young men's homes and we saw somebody who was coming to Alabama, you could tell he had a passion for the University of Alabama. Even this year when he started to lose his hair, he wanted to make sure he had an Alabama cap on all the time.

"Many times this year he had just enough strength to get to practice. I would see him come through that door down there at about three o'clock. Some days he would have to sit on the scorer's table and he would fall asleep.

"Never did he complain to me one time. He loved Cynthia. He called her often wherever we were.

"He was a man I truly loved and I thank God for the times we had together. He made quite an impact in Birmingham, UAB and here at Alabama. We must never forget what an unbelievable human being he really was."

Grown men used their handkerchiefs to wipe tears as they spoke. There were many pauses before they could continue their remarks because they were filled with emotion.

After their sharing, a sentimental video of Robert's playing and coaching career to the song, *There's a Hero,* was shown on the scoreboard video screen. Cynthia had chosen the song. Tom Roberts of Crimson Tide Sports Marketing and Gary Shores of the Paul Bryant Museum had produced the video which included remarks made by Robert in talks he gave over the past year, which had been recorded.

Then the players came forward and moved Robert's casket to the southwest tunnel of the coliseum where a shiny blue hearse was waiting to take Robert to Birmingham for burial in the Elmwood Cemetery. It was a gripping scene to watch the hearse roll slowly in a possession of cars from the side road of Coleman Coliseum and drive down the front lane to Paul Bryant Drive. The cars turned left and drove for the Interstate to Birmingham.

As it turned out, Robert spent part of his last hours on earth in the place where life had given him some of his most cherished memories, on the Coleman Coliseum floor, home of the Crimson Tide.

One week later, the City of Birmingham declared "Robert Scott Day" on May 20 at the Memorial Recreation Center. There was basketball competition of course. The crowd grew silent when the announcer said, "The winner of the 3-point shooting contest is Robert Scott." Rahmun had won the contest.

Three weeks after Rah Rah's service in Coleman Coliseum, Rahmun played in the AAU Challenge tournament with the Tuscaloosa Roadrunners on the same floor where his dad's service had taken place.

Several weeks before Robert died, Coach Gottfried formed The Robert Scott Foundation. Many men in the Alabama family gave enough money to ensure that all three Scott children would have their college education fully financed. Robert had insisted that money would also be used to support other members of the state's basketball community. Particularly, he wanted to help families battling illness such as cancer who were in financial need.

On February 26, 2000, Robert was home in bed and not feeling well. Cynthia came into their room and starting writing on notebook paper a creed for Rah Rah. When she finished, she read it to him and he smiled and said, "That's so good, Cynthia."

RAH RAH'S COACH'S CREED

Pardon me, but may I talk to your child about the powers of God? May I teach him self control? May I teach him the importance of life? May I stress the importance of an education? May I teach him to never be selfish, to help somebody? May I comfort him when needed? May I demand that he surrounds himself with good people? May I influence him to be a good person? May I be a father figure for him? May I talk to him about my "Game of Life" and lastly, may I teach him the game of basketball?

CHAPTER NINETEEN

COACH DICK SPYBEY

I n most every man or woman's life, there is a day that represents a turning point. Life has never been the same since that day.

Such a day befell Dick Spybey, 39-year-old Alabama men's golf coach.

"Since April 4, 1999, this has easily been the best part of my life," says Dick with joy and a smile.

"I was sitting in a motel room in Augusta, GA one night. Our team was there for a golf tournament at Augusta College. I had gotten to the point where I was really lonely, really bad, and just miserable," remembers Dick when times were not so good.

"About three o'clock on that Sunday morning, April 4, 1999, and that's something I will never forget, I woke up. I was lonely and in tears. Right on the lamp table, the first thing I saw was a Gideon Bible.

"It was like God lifted me up out of that bed and put the light right on that Bible. I figured it out. That's what I was missing. That's why I knew I was feeling so bad. That's why the low points were killing me.

"That morning, I got up and showered and made sure my team was ready to go for the tournament. Then I went down the street to a Baptist church that I had passed earlier that week.

"So I walked in for the early service and I sat there and I prayed for God to take me back. I'd had enough of the misery that was in my life for the past several months and even years.

"Since the day that I walked into that church and emptied myself to God in prayer, I have been on fire for the Word and my walk with the Lord ever since."

Dick's drifting from the Lord began several years before. In 1992, his golf team finished eleventh in the nation and was selected the most improved team. After the first two days in that NCAA tournament the team was fifth, but an eleventh place finish was still the second best in school history. What's more, Dick was selected national "Coach of the Year."

"We had also won the Southeastern Conference and District III tournaments. After being named national, Southeastern Conference and District III Coach of the Year, I'm thinking, 'I'm a hot shot.' I was feeling at the top of my life as a golf coach.

"From that point until April of 1999, I just did a lot of drifting from the church and in my faith life. It got to the point in the last two years prior to this April that church was not a part of our family's life. Sunday School was not a part of our lives like it had been," recalls Dick sadly.

Low points were still ahead which would soon get Dick back on track with the Lord.

"I was having a really rough year in 1997-98. It was a bad one for us and my teams had really never failed much. The 1998-99 year wasn't going a whole lot better. I began pursuing the after dinner drinks again. I got to the point where I just felt really lonely."

It was at that point that Dick found himself miserable in that motel room in Augusta. At the lowest point in his life, he was on the verge of being at the highest point. Dick's life was about to experience a happiness and joy that he had never known could be possible.

"That day in Augusta when I got out of that church, I called my wife Mary. I was very emotional. I told her, 'Honey, I am sorry for not being the person I should have been. I think I have figured out why and I want you to help me with my growth in getting back in touch with God.'

"Through these years of drifting, she would say, 'Let's go to church. Let's get up and go today. I had dedicated my son Rick to the church. Many times I would say, 'No you go on ahead and take Rick.' I would go on to the golf course and she would take him to church.

"We wanted that atmosphere to be there for our son, but it wasn't for me, you know. So I told Mary on the telephone at Augusta that day that I needed some help.

"I got back home and I told her that alcohol was a problem. I certainly wasn't an alcoholic, but was a social drinker. From now on I told her, I don't want this in my life. I don't want it in the house. I knew it was a bad influence on my son, Rick. I didn't want it around people I was with, either.

"I wanted back into the church and I wanted to find our Sunday School class again. So we started going back to church again at the First Baptist Church downtown.

"Right at that same time, what a gift from God that the Franklin Graham Festival was coming to Tuscaloosa," says Dick. On April 30-May 2, Billy Graham's son, Franklin, led the West Alabama Festival in

Coleman Coliseum on campus. It was the only Festival Franklin had in the United States in 1999. All others were abroad in other countries.

"Mary and I wanted to go. So instead of going by ourselves, we talked some other people into going with us. We had a group of six or eight plus our kids. So we went to the Sunday night Festival service which was the only service we attended of the three.

"What a wonderful time we had. Franklin spoke and made the call for people to come forward. One of the couples that was with us went down to accept Jesus into their lives.

"I didn't know whether I should go down or not because I had already made a re-commitment of my life a few weeks before. Franklin had ended his call for people to come to Christ and the floor was packed with people who came forward. Franklin led those people in a prayer of repentance.

"Then I looked over at my son Rick, who is 10 years old. There were just huge tears streaming down his face. I hugged him and I said, 'What is it buddy?' I knew he wanted to go down there, but I felt strongly that he needed to say to me, 'I want to do this.' I guess he didn't have the courage to say he wanted to go down that night.

"But the next morning he said, 'Dad, I should have gone down there last night at the service. Can I commit my life to Christ?' I said, 'Yes you can.' Then we prayed, and he invited Christ into his life right then. What a sweet experience for Mary and me."

There was a new joy that entered into the lives of the Spybey's and their home simply because Dad had renewed his faith in the Lord. The following Sunday would prove to be one of their finest days together as a family.

"That week, we went down to the church at First Baptist and talked with interim pastor Ricky Michael. We talked and set up baptism for Rick two Sundays later.

"But on that Sunday after the Graham Festival, our family walked down the aisle when the invitation call was given. It was one of the most electrifying times of my life. They introduced us and said, 'Most of you know Coach Spybey and he is here to rededicate his life with his wife Mary. Their son Rick wants to be baptized because he has accepted Jesus Christ into his heart as his Savior.

"And I looked at my wife and there was so much relief. There was so much emotion, so many tears that were falling. My wife is not very emotional especially in crowds. It was right then, on that Sunday, that I knew what I had been missing. I knew what she had been wanting me to do. Her mother, who had been such a godly influence on me, wanted me to do this also. Most of all, it was what God wanted me to do.

"It has been such a wonderful, peaceful time since. Our marriage is better. Our son's life is better and our relationship as a family is better. Mary and I have joined Tommy Ford's Adult Sunday School Department and Rich Wingo (former Alabama star linebacker) is our teacher. We love that and look forward to it every Sunday morning."

The Graham Festival and the church family had been a blessing. Still, there was another source of strength awaiting Dick in his new-found joy and peace in Christ.

"Another gift to me has been our 7 a.m. Tuesday morning Bible Study in Mark Gottfried's coaches conference room," says Dick. When Coach Mark Gottfried became head basketball coach two years ago, he suggested that a Bible Study be organized for men in the athletic department.

"The Bible Study each Tuesday has done so much for me. You know when you are a relatively new believer, it can be intimidating to be around a bunch of believers," Dick is quick to point out. "You don't know what the Bible says. You don't want to say the wrong thing and be embarrassed.

"I have never been short on words and am not afraid to speak, so the study and the fellowship with other believers has been great for me. This and the Sunday School class have helped me grow so much. When others do not share in the Sunday School, Rich knows I will share."

The change in Dick's life caused him to share his love for Christ with others. God placed a burning desire to share Christ with his team, with opposing coaches and opposing team players.

"When we go on the road, there are so many temptations. That's what got me into trouble in the first place. So I kept thinking if there was just somebody like Tommy Ford or a Rick Moody who could talk to these guys.

"Then I got to thinking, there is an organization called College Golf Fellowship that is run by Rick Massengale, who is a believer and a Senior PGA tour member. He would come at periodic times to tournaments and speak and pay for a dinner. He would speak or have someone else speak and he would say, 'Guys, I once did this, this and this, but now God leads me. You are going to either heaven or hell. You need to understand this. It is hard for you to think about it maybe as college students, but you need to think about it.'

"Well, I started thinking, 'Man what if we did this every week? What if we just did this every week in an informal setting?' So everytime the College Golf Fellowship is not there, I just have a session in my room for any player or coach who is interested from our team and the other teams in that tournament. I started this in the fall of 1999.

"We've had as few as three and as many as eleven. I never press the issue. I lead a Bible Study and just talk about the problems they may have in life. I tell them, 'You may have those temptations, but you don't have to go down those kinds of roads'.

"You know when you are not a believer, Christians are sometimes portrayed as weirdos. They are a different kind of people when you are out there in the material, secular world. So you are apprehensive sometimes to find out who those people, the Christians, are. Then when you find out that we have so many dynamic people in the world who are strong Christians, it just makes you feel better.

"It is amazing, when you come to accept the Christian life, how God just brings these people out and into your life. That's exactly what happened to me. Once I got back to God, there were so many people and opportunities waiting to help me grow and experience my new found faith in Christ."

Dick was excited about the volunteer Bible Study in his room. There was yet another group where Dick was to share his faith that broke down walls for the first time among a group of coaches. It happened in Orlando in January, 2000 at the Golf Coaches Association of America Convention. Dick was prominent in the Association because he had just served as president for two years.

"I felt that we should have a time of fellowship, sharing and Bible Study among any of the coaches who wanted to get together. So one of the fellow officers, Mark Simpson from the Unversity of Colorado who is now president, liked the idea also. I found out the previous summer that he is a believer. We have been sharing ever since.

"Anyway, we just put up an announcement that a Christian fellowship was going to be in a room at a certain time. We sat there and waited and all of a sudden, nine coaches showed up. So there were 11 of us in that room.

"I can't tell you the look on a couple of those coaches faces when they saw me in there. They didn't know who organized this because we didn't announce who organized it. We just had it posted.

"I gave my testimony there. How neat it was to discover other coaches who were believers. You just look at people differently. You know how they feel when they have Christ in their hearts and lives like you do. So when we see each other now, we are strength to each other. You look forward to seeing them. The old ways have been replaced with the love of God and the happiness and joy that only He can put there in your life."

In November, 1999, the shocking death of PGA golfer Payne Stewart gave Dick even more opportunity to share his testimony and love for Christ with others. Payne's new life in Christ two years prior to his death in the plane crash had been well documented. His two-hour memorial service from the First Baptist Church of Orlando was televised worldwide on CNN.

"When Payne Stewart died, he was wearing the W.W.J.D. (What Would Jesus Do) bracelet. At the funeral, Payne's pastor, Jim Henry, talked about that and he also said, 'Remember GOLF can be spelled two ways. It can mean God Offers Life Forever and it can also mean Go Out Lost Forever.'

"That's why I wear my G.O.L.F. bracelet everywhere I go as a witness. I wear it not only to remind myself, but to give testimony and witness to these golfers that you can go out lost forever and you don't want to do that. You don't want to do that."

Dick acquired a videotape of Payne's Memorial Service and has shared it many times with his team and in Bible studies. It has been most effective in helping many to see that everyone needs Christ and will be lost forever without Him.

Discovering Christ in Dick Spybey's life became a reality only after joining the coaching staff at Alabama in 1984 when he was 24 years old.

Growing up in Columbus, Ohio, Dick's mom and dad were hard working people. His dad was not raised in a Christian home but his mother was. His dad ran bar and restaurant establishments in Columbus. After late Saturday nights at work, Dick's dad would sleep in on Sunday morning, but his mother would take Dick and his younger sister and brother to church.

"My dad made sure that the three of us got involved in sports and other activities. He kept us busy and made many sacrifices for us to be active and involved," says Dick.

While Dick would go on to a prestigious coaching profession, his sister Dina would become an actress. She has appeared in several motion pictures including roles as the young Goldie Hahn in "First Wives Club" and one with Demi Moore. She is currently in a reoccurring role in NBC's "Stark, Raving Mad" TV show. Dick's brother Danny is the Food and Beverage Manager for the Lakewood Golf Club at the

Marriott-Grand Hotel in Point Clear, AL. "My dad is one of the proudest men you'll ever meet," says Dick.

At Centennial High School, Dick excelled in basketball, baseball and golf. At the time, golf was his third interest. Being a good student, Dick got an academic scholarship to Ohio Wesleyan and lettered four years in golf and two in basketball.

"I always wanted to be a coach early on," says Dick. "You had to be 18 years old to coach Little League, but I told them I was 18 when I was only 16. So I got to coach Little League at 16. As a senior in college, the local middle school needed a basketball coach, so I got to coach that team and it was so much fun.

"When I graduated, I sent out resumes looking for a basketball or golf opportunity in coaching. My most appealing call came from Coach Conrad Rehling of the University of Alabama. I was 24 years old and I will never forget the conversation.

"He called my house and said, 'Hey, boy. This is Coach Rehling from Alabama. I got your resume.' I said very excitedly, 'Yes, sir.' He said, 'Do you need a job?' I said, 'Yes, sir, I'm looking.' This was like on a Monday. He said, 'Well, I need you Saturday.' Then I said, 'You mean this coming Saturday?' He said, 'I need you now. I need you to help with camps.'

"To make a long story short, I called him back two days later and said I would take it, sight unseen. I had an old Pinto with three tires the same size and one another size. That Saturday morning at 6:30, I had all of my belongings packed in that Pinto and said goodbye to my parents. We all cried.

"They were very supportive. Even though we had grown up around Ohio State, we had a great respect for Coach Paul Bryant and the Alabama tradition. Dad even told me that I couldn't pass up this opportunity. So on July 3, 1984 I drove to Tuscaloosa and arrived late that day.

"I got into town to McFarland and fifteenth street and got a little lost. I stopped at two or three places and asked, 'Do you know where the University Golf Course is and they said, 'No, I have no idea.' I thought, 'What have I got myself into. Is this really for sure?'

"Finally, I got to the golf course before dark. I spent my first two nights in the clubhouse. I had $200, which was all the money I had and couldn't afford a motel room. I met Coach Rehling on Monday and I've been here ever since."

Dick first came as an assistant professional and in January, 1985,

Dick was named by Athletic Director Ray Perkins and Assistant Athletic Director Ann Marie Lawler as Head Women's Golf Coach. In 1987, his team finished ninth in the nation and Dick was named South Region and SEC Coach of the Year.

When Coach Rehling retired in June, 1988, Athletic Director Steve Sloan named Dick as Head Coach of the men's golf team the next month. Since then, Dick has had six teams to participate in the NCAA golf tournament.

Two special honors have come Dick's way as well. He was National President of the Golf Coaches Association of America in 1996-99. Dick became the youngest president of the group. Then in 1997, Dick was Manager of the 1997 United States Palmer Cup Team, named after Arnold Palmer.

The Palmer Cup competition is similar to the Ryder Cup in professional golf. The best United States collegiate players play the best from Great Britain and Ireland. The first tournament was held at Orlando's Bay Hill Golf Club owned by Palmer. The second was at the famous St. Andrews course in Scotland.

However, his biggest prize was Mary Holderfield, who was Pro Shop Manager for Coach Rehling at the University course when Dick arrived. "We liked each other from the get-go. It was one of those love at first sight things and we married on July 19, 1986. One of the great blessings of my life came with Mary. Her mother, Marie Holderfield, is one of the strongest and neatest Christian ladies I know."

Mary plays a most important role in the athletic department, in football rather than golf. She is administrative assistant in football recruiting.

"It was through Rick (head women's basketball coach) and Sandra Moody that Mary and I got involved in worship and then Sunday School at the First Baptist Church. I saw how important Christ was in their lives and shortly after our son was born on September 24, 1989, I went down the aisle at the First Baptist Church to accept Christ and was baptized by Pastor Rick Lance. Then after 1992, I began to drift away from the church until April of 1999. My life in Christ hasn't been the same since.

"We have even moved out to Lake Tuscaloosa and our next door neighbors are Rick and Sandra Moody.

"God is good and the great thing about it is, He can do in anyone's life the same thing that He's done for me.

"I'm overjoyed that He took me back."

CHAPTER TWENTY

KEVIN STEPHEN

The remarkable story of Kevin Stephen is a human spirit classic. Lost dreams, disappointments, trials, loneliness, sickness, bicycle transportation, lack of money and being 3000 miles away from home could not break his will or spirit.

The three-year wait for a kidney transplant was a terrific struggle. Yet not even his closest friends could detect the hardship that Kevin endured. He was busy being a blessing to everyone he met.

The word "complain" was not in Kevin's vocabulary, even though he had studied English, Spanish and French.

Kevin came to Alabama on a track scholarship from Trinidad in the fall of 1993. He was a decathlon man. Decathlon athletes compete in ten events. The Olympic champion in the decathlon is considered the finest athlete in the world.

Trinidad is a country of two islands located in the West Indies. It lies in the Caribbean Sea, near the northeast coast of South America. It is six miles east of Venezuela. English is the official language and 95 percent of the people can read and write. The average annual temperature is 78 degrees.

Kevin is the youngest of six children. His father is an aircraft mechanic and his mother is a nurse. They live in the small town of D'Abavie.

His high school was Queen's Royal College. Most of the better high schools in Trinidad are called colleges. There are 13 grades instead of 12. Three years of Spanish and French are required.

Like all boys in Trinidad, Kevin grew up playing soccer. He added basketball, field hockey and track to his soccer playing in high school. A talented athlete, Kevin loved sports and the competition.

"Soccer was my passion," says Kevin. "However, track was the sport I had the most ability in on a national scale and eventually on an international scale. I started as a sprinter and was third nationally in the junior meets. Then I started throwing the javelin, discus and shot put and was ranked No. 1 in some of those.

"At track meets, I would complete my two or three events, go sit in the stands and get bored wishing I had more events to compete in. Then I met a coach who introduced me to the decathlon and that was it for me. I fell in the love with the decathlon. It was something I could do to take advantage of my all around skills. It was a lot of fun. It was hard, but I enjoyed working hard."

So, how does a high school athlete from Trinidad get to the University of Alabama?

In 1992, Kevin was competing in the Carista Games in the Bahamas. Coach Ed Whitt, assistant track coach at Alabama, was there on a search for future Crimson Tide track athletes. He liked what he saw as Kevin competed in five events.

Whitt spoke to Kevin's coach and then to Kevin, who had never heard of the University of Alabama. Phone calls led to a recruiting visit for Kevin who was to also visit LSU, Grambling and Southern California. Kevin's first and last stop was the University of Alabama. He fell in love with Alabama and didn't visit the other schools.

Kevin moved into Burke Hall East in the fall of 1993 with three other track athletes. He loved everything about Alabama but the water. There was something about the taste of the water that he had to adjust to. We all have our peculiarities.

Kevin was on a full track scholarship. The scholarship was a must. He was the first in his family to attend college. His parents were supportive and pleased for him.

Remarkably, a major event occurred in Kevin's life the second week of school that had nothing to do with track.

At an orientation meeting for freshmen athletes, Kevin heard a short announcement about the Fellowship of Christian Athletes meetings each Wednesday night at nine. The meetings were held in Bryant Hall, in the very room that Kevin was sitting in.

"I never considered attending the FCA meetings at that time. However, I met a couple of girls that I was interested in. One of them told me the next week that she was going to the FCA meeting and invited me along. The only reason I went was to go with her.

"When I got there, I saw a bunch of other athletes I had met in the short period that I was at Alabama. I felt so comfortable being there. During the course of the evening, I just felt that the message was being directed to me.

"I felt that the speaker was speaking to me and no one else. What he said made me feel a little bit strange. But I did feel that everything he said had to do with me. I was on his every word. I was struck that it came so close to home.

"Finally, at the end of the message when he asked, "Do you know where you are going to be for eternity?' I realized that I didn't know.

"I had always gone to church every Sunday with my mom," says Kevin. "Our family worshiped at The Church of England Anglican Church. Mother read us all the Bible stories when we were kids. I knew all about God. But there was nothing personal about it. In my mind, God had no direct impact on me.

"She said one thing when we grew up that always stuck with me. We had frequent power outages and they would last a day or two. It would merely rain and the power would go out. One day, I worried that the food would go bad and we wouldn't have anything to eat. My mom said, 'Don't worry, God will always take care of us. He will always provide.' Inside of two hours after she said that, the power came back on. She said very confidently that God will always take care of us and that has always made God real to me."

Then the FCA meeting speaker gave Kevin another prospective about his faith. "When I listened to the speaker, it was like God was speaking and saying, 'It's time. You know about me; you have heard all these stories, but it is time for you to get a little deeper and develop a relationship with me.'

"So when he made the call, there was nothing for me to do but to respond. I was a little shocked, though. We had our eyes closed and I raised my hand. Then after the prayer, he asked Toby Shields (the center on the football team who had also raised his hand) and me to come up front.

"In my mind, I was hesitant about going up front. But the commitment was made and I didn't care what others thought about me. I felt it was something I had to do. It was a special time as several of the athletes came forward and prayed with us. Jay Barker was one of them and he was also thrilled that his center on the football team had asked Christ into his life."

For Kevin, it was the beginning of a close personal relationship with Jesus Christ that would develop during his years at Alabama. He was a fixture in FCA. He rarely missed a meeting and only because of sickness or academics.

One early friendship that transpired through FCA was with Chad Goss, who had arrived at the same time as Kevin as a football walk-on. "Chad would invite me to attend church with him on Sunday morning.

I would usually study all day on Saturday and stay out late, so I was always tired on Sunday morning.

"One Sunday morning, he knocked on my door all dressed for church and said, 'Get dressed. You have ten minutes.' So I got dressed and we ended up at the Trinity United Methodist Church with Brother Dan Kilgore up there preaching. Trinity was less than 200 yards away from my dorm on Paul Bryant Drive. I loved the people. Brother Dan and I met and got acquainted. He had me in his home for socials and that was how I found my church home in Tuscaloosa during my Alabama career."

For Kevin, it also marked the beginning point of a very close and important relationship he developed with Dan and Glenda Kilgore, who would become his parents away from home.

Meanwhile out on the oval track, the 6-foot-4, 210 pound freshman decathlete was eager and ready to go. "Everything started off really well. I was feeling great and was in really good shape. I got to know the athletes. Workouts were going well," Kevin remembers with the excitement still fresh in his mind.

As a decathlon athlete, Kevin worked with all three coaches. They were head coach Doug Williamson and his assistants Ed Whitt and Wayne Williams.

Then one day in October at practice while running, Kevin felt a sharp pain in his left knee. In no time, he had trouble walking, much less running. Dr. Jimmy Robinson, the team doctor, told Kevin he had an OCD, which means the blood supply had stopped in his knee. Without surgery, he could not run again.

Kevin's mother encouraged him to rely upon God and that God could heal the knee. Kevin decided to pray for healing even though doctors had ruled out running again without surgery. In late November, Kevin was jogging again and started running workouts.

"That summer (1994) when I went home, I had the best track and field period of my life. I ran in the nationals. I took almost a second off of my hurdles time. I increased by two and a half feet in the pole vault. I was running faster than ever before and jumping higher than ever. There was no doubt that God had healed me."

Further complications set in for Kevin, however. Before he left for home that summer, it was discovered that his blood pressure was extremely high. Kevin went to see Dr. J.D. Askew, a nephrologist, or kidney specialist, and was told that he may have kidney problems. Kevin was to check his blood pressure periodically and be careful.

"Still, I had that great summer of competition in my country and I came back that fall in the best aerobic shape of my life," says Kevin. "When I came back for the fall, I had a kidney biopsy and it was discovered that I had only 10 to 11 percent kidney function. They told me it was just a matter of time until my kidneys would fail.

"After talking to my coaches and doctors and trainers, they decided that I should not compete anymore. That was a pretty huge blow. At that time, I felt that I was developing a pretty good relationship with God. At the same time, track was like a god to me. It was what I dreamed about at night. It was something I woke up thinking about at night. It was probably the thing that dominated my life the most. Even though I was making good grades, track still dominated my thoughts.

"Track was so much a part of me that I felt there was nothing else left to do. Coach Williamson offered me counseling. The athletic department gave me a medical hardship, which would pay for my education. As far as track went, my career was done that day."

It was harsh and devastating news for Kevin who dearly loved his sport and had the highest aspirations as a decathlete. A couple of weeks went by as Kevin relied heavily upon his faith and began to size up the situation that seemed bleak at the time.

Yet, even with this disappointing news, Kevin's greatest trial was yet to come.

There was still an important place for Kevin with the track team. Coach Jeff Sparks came in and had so many athletes to work with that he asked Kevin to help him as a student coach. So for the next three years (1995-97), Kevin was a student assistant coach and was a real inspiration to Bama's tracksters.

When Kevin came to Alabama he had a passionate goal of competing for Trinidad in the 1996 Olympic Games in the decathlon. It was a realistic dream. So when he developed kidney problems, that high goal was over. Yet God would provide another way for Kevin to participate in the Olympic Games.

"In October of 1994 when I got the knee injury, I met Anthony Brown of Athletes In Action, which is part of Campus Crusade for Christ," says Kevin. "I was in a stage in my life where I had become a Christian, I was saved, but I wasn't doing much else. I had crossed the first hurdle but when I met Anthony, he started helping me develop my relationship with Christ.

"He taught me how to read the Bible and how to start expressing my faith. He was a Christian guy that I hung out with quite a bit. He made Christianity an everyday thing for me as well as Brother Dan, his wife Glenda, Chad and several others through FCA. I realized that Christianity was a lifestyle and not something you do on Sunday. I learned that the goal is to become more like Christ in everyday life."

Through his relationship with Anthony and AIA, Kevin later learned of Project Atlanta, a Christian ministry to the athletes at the '96 Olympic Games in Atlanta. The idea was to go to the Olympic athletes and share with them that there is more to life than winning the gold medal. The theme of the project was "More Than Gold."

Kevin needed $1100 to be involved and was allowed to share his mission and need before the Trinity church congregation one Sunday morning. He needed $500 the next day. A $500 check was handed Kevin that Monday and the rest followed from the church. Kevin was indeed learning that God does provide needs.

In Atlanta at the Games, Kevin was one of 165 AIA athletes from 33 countries representing scores of languages that would witness to the Olympic athletes and coaches. He wasn't there to compete like he once dreamed of, but to share the Good News of Jesus Christ to those he might have competed against.

"We had a system in place where we would stand outside the Olympic Village. When they came out, we had spotters who would look at their tags and figure out what language they spoke. Then we would signal to a person in our group who could speak that language. So by the time our athlete got to them, he would have a pamphlet and a JESUS film to hand them in their language. He or she would speak to them and share the gospel.

"When we first arrived, we were overwhelmed with the stacks of boxes that contained the JESUS film videos. We thought there was no way we could distribute all of these. But after four days, we ran out of videos and had to scramble to get more. Some people from Cuba came and got them by the bag full. Athletes from Russia took hundreds of them in their language. That project was a huge success."

It also did wonders for Kevin and his faith. "I just felt so close to God that summer. I felt like my life was going in the right direction," Kevin recollects with great joy about his Olympic opportunity.

Even though Kevin had experienced a fantastic time at the Olympics, serious health problems were just around the corner. Kevin went home from Atlanta for the rest of the summer. It was good to visit his family again. One night while having dinner with a couple of friends, Kevin felt pains in his stomach. When he told his mother, she started crying. She told Kevin that stomach pains were the beginning of his brother's kidney disease that led to his death one year before when he was only 25.

As it turned out, Kevin's mother was right. Kevin soon discovered that he had the same disease from which his brother had died.

When Kevin returned to Tuscaloosa, his condition got worse. He was cramping up all over his body. He couldn't walk very well and had trouble standing up and sitting down. Kevin got to Dr. Robinson's office and was given two IV's and a blood sample was taken.

"Dr. Robinson called me the very next morning and he was panicked," Kevin recalls. "He was emphatic. 'Go to the hospital and go right now! Call 911 now!' So I did and went to the hospital. They did all their tests and I overheard a doctor or nurse say the next day that 'someone with my test results should not be alive because my kidneys had failed probably a week before.' By then, my blood was so toxic that there was no way I should be alive."

Intensive care treatment followed for Kevin at DCH Hospital and kidney dialysis followed. Kevin never felt sad or angry. FCA and Campus Crusade friends plus Brother Dan and Glenda were a constant support. Besides, the setback came when Kevin was at his highest spiritually.

Kevin maintained such an upbeat spirit that doctors and nurses hung out in his room during breaks for the lifts they received. Rarely had they found a patient like Kevin.

"They couldn't get over how cheerful and happy I was, but I just told them that it was God who was here in this room taking care of me along with their help," says Kevin.

Kevin had many options, but decided on the peritoneal dialysis. Every day he would place a tube in his mid-section into his peritoneal cavity. It was hooked up to a machine called a "cycler." A fluid was pumped by the cycler into Kevin's body over the course of nine hours every night. The fluid would make four cycles a night through the machine and into Kevin's body. Kevin would be fine during the daytime hours.

Incredibly, Kevin did this procedure for three years! Kevin says the *good* thing about the machine was that you could take it anywhere you wanted to go. The cycler was twice the size of an average brief case. Kevin would take it on track road trips and even when he spent the summer of 1997 in Spain studying Spanish.

Right from the start of Kevin's severe kidney diagnosis in 1996, Dr.

Askew told Kevin that he was a good candidate for a kidney transplant. Kevin's name was placed on a transplant waiting list, but Dr. Askew and the doctors in Birmingham who gave him a transplant evaluation told him to also see if he could find a relative that would donate a kidney.

Because of family illnesses and age considerations, no one in Kevin's family was available as a donor candidate at the time. But Kevin never lost hope. It was always, *when* and not *if I* get my kidney. He trusted God and patiently survived with the cycler.

Three years later, his sister Pat, a nurse from London, called Kevin and expressed her desire to give him a kidney. She was concerned that her brother's name had not moved up much on the transplant list. It was the beginning of the summer of 1999. What a happy day for Kevin.

"By this time, my sister had her second child, all that she wanted to have. I could tell she was most sincere. I told her to talk to my mom about it and we would all pray about this decision. She kept telling me it was something she wanted to do. She was sure.

"I knew I wanted to do it. I just wanted her to make sure she understood everything and knew what she was getting into. She did. So we called the doctors and they were really excited.

"She flew over from London and the doctors at UAB Hospital in Birmingham did an evaluation on her. It was a perfect match. She matched up in every category. Less than a week later, we scheduled a transplant.

"My mom was really nervous because my sister was the oldest child and I was the youngest. So two of her children were under the knife at the same time. No other family members were there for the surgery.

"Anyway, we were prepared and waiting for the next morning to come. We woke up that morning and everything felt right. The day was Wednesday, August 11, 1999. We went ahead with the surgeries," says Kevin. Generally the donor suffers worse than the recipient in transplants. Pat's incision was made from the middle of her back around to her naval area. Kevin's was a lone incision in his stomach area. Dr. Mark Deierhoi performed the surgery.

"When I woke up, I really expected to be in a lot of pain, perhaps a difficult surgery and something that would take a long time to recover from," Kevin recollects. "When I woke up, I wondered if something went wrong and they couldn't do the operation. I didn't feel any pain or discomfort. So I felt down in my abdominal area to see if there was a bandage there. That was how I realized they had done the surgery.

"I spent the first night in intensive care and went back in my room.

The very next day, my sister comes walking into my room. Two days later, she is walking around. Three days later, I start walking around my room. Four days after the surgery, I was walking around the hospital. Six days later I walked two miles.

"One of the medications they gave me excelerated my appetite. So in walking those two miles on the streets surrounding the hospital, I was searching for a restaurant. Up until this time, I had been a vegetarian but now I had this craving for chicken. Later, I found out that a donor recipient could take on the same cravings that the donor has. My sister loves chicken and eats it all the time. So I found some chicken and have eaten it regularly ever since," Kevin says with an amusing smile.

Since the transplant, Kevin has experienced no complications. He has not taken pain pills or any other medication. The transplant surgery worked perfectly for Kevin and his sister has had no problems as the donor. A person of strong faith herself, Pat had virtually given her brother new life.

Kevin was 25 when he received the transplant, the same age his brother had died of kidney failure. Kevin was in graduate school completing a master's degree in Human Resource Management. He had received his undergraduate degree in December of 1997 with a major in Spanish and a minor in International Business. He graduated with a 3.0 GPA, which would have been higher without his sickness.

Prior to the transplant surgery, Kevin was offered a track graduate assistant job at the University of Southern Mississippi by his former coach Wayne Williams, now head coach at USM. After much prayer, Kevin took the job in September 1999 to see if coaching was a possibility for the future. Also, he is currently working on a master's in Business Administration.

At USM, Kevin is assigned to the decathlon. Amazingly, his first meet was on March 24-26, 2000 at the Alabama Relays on the University of Alabama campus. Kevin's entry in the decathlon, Jason Wilson of Theodore, AL, who had spent two years of his life at John Croyle's Big Oak Ranch, won the decathlon event over 23 other competitors. What a start for Coach Stephen!

The long journey from Trinidad to Alabama to Mississippi has been an eventful seven years. Kevin came to develop a strong personal relationship with Jesus Christ. He overcame many hardships physically. Everywhere he went was on a bicycle, which is still his mode of transportation today. He would borrow an automobile occasionally but his bicycle was literally his wheels.

Still, Kevin got the best medical attention and treatment in his journey with sickness. Also God blessed him with a sister whose supreme and compassionate love restored his life with a kidney transplant.

Through his years at Alabama, he gained a multitude of friends and was a great friend to many. You always found an ever-cheerful Kevin regardless of where you met him or regardless of how sick he might have been.

While being away from his family and homeland for seven years, Kevin has only been able to return five times. Yet, God provided him with parents away from home in Dan and Glenda Kilgore.

Kevin became like a son to the Kilgore's. It was at their home that he spent spring breaks, Thanksgiving, Christmas, weekends and the sick times. Brother Dan was his go-to man when he needed a ride to the hospital many times in the middle of the night.

Even when he came back for the Alabama Relays as a coach, Kevin and Jason stayed with the Kilgore's. An e-mail of thanks was sent to Dan and Glenda a day later with the closing, "It's so great to have parents like you."

Says Brother Dan with smiles, "We would do it all over again in a minute."

Kevin is living proof of God's grace and power. God never allows more than a human soul can bear. Kevin has endured far more than his share.

Yet, he stands on top of the podium with a gold medal around his neck for courage, the will to overcome insurmountable trials and a faith in God that conquers all.

The world is a much better place because of rare people like Kevin Stephen, a classic human spirit story.

CHAPTER TWENTY-ONE

COACH JIM WELLS

People know Crimson Tide baseball coach Jim Wells as a 'miracle worker' in resurrecting Bama baseball to one of the nation's best programs.

During his six years as head coach, the superlatives are truly remarkable.

Most all coaches would consider his helm at Alabama as a career in just six short years. For starters, Alabama has averaged 48 wins per year since Jim took over in 1995.

His teams have played in the College World Series in his second, third and fifth seasons. His 1997 squad sailed to the final game of the World Series with LSU. *Baseball America* honored Jim as National Coach of the Year that season.

In the SEC, considered the best collegiate baseball league in America, Alabama is the only Southeastern Conference team to reach the NCAA Regional championship game in each of the last six years. Jim's teams have won an unprecedented FOUR SEC tournament championships in 1995, 1996, 1997 and 1999.

To cap these and many more superlatives off, Alabama's 2000 home attendance of 211,331 was second best in the nation behind LSU.

Jim's magical six-year run at Alabama is indeed one of the most successful sports stories in America. People have discovered Jim Wells to be some sort of a baseball genius.

What most people don't know about Jim is that he was an only child, his father was a prominent attorney in Louisiana, he NEVER played a collegiate sport including baseball, and he is a Roman Catholic in a predominantly Protestant state.

Jim was born in Shreveport on March 21, 1955 to the parents of James and Bettye Wells. He lived from birth through his high school years in Bossier City, a small town at that time across the Red River from Shreveport in northwest Louisiana.

Jim's parents divorced when he was 14 and he then lived with his mother and grandmother. His father was a very successful attorney until he died of a heart attack in 1988. He was a World War II and Korean War veteran and eventually got his law degree from LSU. Jim's mother was a homemaker and still lives in Bossier City.

"It was my mother who got me involved in sports," says Jim. "Back then, kids played neighborhood and sandlot ball. I remember one day when my mother came in and said, 'You are going to be on this team. You are going to play on a team instead of neighborhood ball.'

"I just always loved sports. My father was into boxing. He wasn't into football, basketball or baseball. My wife Lisa and I talk about it even now. We don't know where he acquired his interest in boxing. I don't know where my love for sports came from, but I had friends and we collected baseball cards, played Little League and every sport.

"I would cut out articles on Terry Bradshaw when he was at Woodlawn High School and my parents would tell me that I needed to study more. I was keeping scrapbooks of all the best players in town. I had a great childhood."

Jim was educated in Roman Catholic schools from the first grade through his senior year in high school. "From grades one through eight I was taught by nuns and nine through 12, I was taught by priests. That was probably the last era where there were enough priests and nuns to teach.

"I attended Jesuit High School in Shreveport. It was an all-boys school. I wore a uniform my entire life until I went to college. It was black pants and a white shirt. It was the greatest thing in the world. Then in high school, you wore a blazer, a tie and gray pants. The only choice you had was a shirt and tie.

"When I look back, I am proud of the education I received and the discipline. Especially, when I started teaching myself. My parents did allow me to get a good education and I didn't know that at the time. There was tremendous discipline. That's an era gone by now.

"If you didn't make your grades, you couldn't play sports. If you had an 'F' on your report card, you couldn't go back to school. You were gone. If you were a great player and had an 'F', you had to transfer to another school. There was such a demand for entrance in the school.

"The priests didn't take any wages so it was affordable for Catholic families. It just wasn't Catholics who attended either. Back when I went, all the Catholics went there and discipline problem kids were sent there. Parents sent kids for the priests to get them into shape. Even a lot of Jewish people sent their children there. Still, you didn't know who was Catholic, Jewish or whatever. It didn't matter and it still doesn't matter."

At Jesuit High, Jim played third base on the baseball squad and was a safety on the football team. "I loved football. It came easier for me. Playing safety, you didn't have to be as skilled. As someone said, 'You just had to have courage.' There was a position for everybody on the football field, at least there was then if you had courage. I really liked football maybe because I was a little bit better in it than the others."

It is quite interesting to hear Jim reflect on his thoughts for his future coming out of such a fine high school with a top education. His plans for himself were already shaping up in his mind and against the grain of his friends and even against his father's goals for him.

"I remember one of my friends saying, 'I am going to be a dentist. When I'm 40, I won't have to work but three days a week.' Others had their sights on being doctors, dentists and lawyers, a lot of those. None of us thought about athletics, even playing in college. Everyone seemed to concentrate on a professional career. At that time, I had no idea what my career was.

"My father wanted to send me to Harvard. Buddy Roemer, from Bossier City who later became governor, was a Harvard graduate and a close friend of my dad. I was so naïve. I didn't know where Harvard was. My only question to Mr. Roemer was, "Would I be able to try out for the football team?' I felt like I was good enough to play at Harvard. But I ended up going to Northwestern State University in Natchitoches, 75 miles away. I wasn't going to go too far from home."

When Jim went to Northwestern State, he still didn't think he would be a baseball coach one day. So it wasn't necessary to be on the baseball team or on any other team for experience that would lead to coaching. Jim was simply a student majoring in physical education. It was while he was in college that Jim got his first exposure to coaching.

"I worked for the recreation department in Bossier and I was a lifeguard each summer. I worked on the athletic fields and I had different jobs there. A man named Bill Howell came to me and asked if I would coach one of the teams. A local lawyer had too much business so he needed someone to coach his team. So I started coaching this 13-14 year old team in Dixie Boys ball when I was 20 years old.

"It could very easily have been soccer, football or basketball. It just happened to be baseball. I liked baseball and I wanted to do well. I knew a little bit about it, having played in high school and because I followed baseball. I also wanted to do well because it was fun. That's when I started to thinking after a couple of years, 'Wouldn't this be a neat way to make a living?'

"I was always drawn to coaches. People who were big in my life were coaches. Coach Carl Hardy was a coach at Jesuit and I always thought that being a coach would be the neatest thing. I really never gave it serious consideration earlier because I was supposed to go to law school and be a lawyer. From my father, that was just supposed to happen.

"But I got my first chance to coach in Bossier and a guy named Joe St. Andre encouraged me. But no one encouraged me like my mother. When there would be weak moments and my father would tell me I couldn't make a living coaching, she always encouraged me to follow that and I did.

"Mine is a very odd story. It is amazing that I didn't play college baseball. It is not the typical deal where the real good athlete gets into coaching. I was just a regular guy. I would go to school for nine months and go home and coach my team. I put a lot of energy into it, and sometimes more than any other job.

"I had found something that really excited me. I had friends who knew at 15 and 16 what they were going to do. Now at 20, I said this is what I can do. But from the school I came from at Jesuit, coaching was not kosher."

In 1979, Jim graduated from Northwestern State with his sights on coaching high school baseball. He soon learned that football coaches were the only ones being hired, to his disappointment. So for four months, he worked in Louisiana and Texas selling portable signs. Then Jim got a call asking him if he could take the Princeton Junior High baseball job in a country school a few miles from Bossier. The coach had been in a serious auto accident, would be on sick leave and they could pay Jim $25 a day.

Jim stayed there two years coaching all the sports. He was given a salary his second year. He loved every day of it.

"At that time, I felt like there was a plan for my life. Doors kept opening. It was from my summer league times that my next job came. There were some young boys I coached who had gone on to Jesuit High School, which is now Loyola High School. They called me and said the coach was leaving. They wanted me to apply and I did and got the job. So I was at Loyola for four years. As was the case at Princeton, I loved it. I had good talent. We played for the state championship a couple of times.

"Then I started to think, wouldn't it be great to try it on a college level. So my goal was to be a college graduate assistant. I looked at all the area schools and saw that every G.A. was going back into high school coaching. Well, I already had a great high school job.

"I knew nothing about Louisiana State University. I remember opening up the paper and saw the All-City team in 1984. There in the corner it said, "LSU NAMES NEW COACH, SKIP BERTMAN FROM MIAMI." And I wrote him about a G.A. job. He wrote me back and said, 'Thanks, but I have a guy. Keep in touch.'

"The next year I wrote him and he said, 'Thanks, come down and interview.' I interviewed with another coach. The other guy got it. The third year, I wrote him again and I got the position after three years.

"I really knew what I wanted. I had a plan. I wish everything else in life was that easy. There was a narrow focus there. I had no backup plan. I could stay where I was, but I was really driven to pursue this."

Now Jim was an LSU Bengal Tiger grad assistant under highly respected college coach, Skip Bertman. He had been a great success at Miami and had already won a national championship when Jim arrived. With no rules on time limits with the players, Jim found the long hours year round to be testing times as a coach. Jim stuck it out and the next year got better. The third year was a pleasure. No G.A. had stayed for over two years, but Coach Bertman asked Jim to stay for a third year. He was 31 years old his last year, which is old for a G.A. as Jim admits. Jim also picked up a master's degree in education administration.

The experience was invaluable. Jim's education was paid for, and his salary, $300 a month, was extra good.

Jim learned much from Coach Bertman. "I saw attention to detail. He was not only a great coach, but I had never been around a coach like him.

"I saw how he coached the games, how he conducted practice, how he dealt with the public, how he got people to come to the games and got the community involved. Back then, all we wanted to do was coach. He showed us that there was more to it. At that time Alex Box Stadium wasn't very much. He would say, 'One day there will be stands all the way down to here and there will be stands here.' He had a list of goals and dreams and he would read it to the team.

"He had vision. He would say, 'One day we will win the World Series. One day there will be 8,000 people in here. At that time, no one came to the games. Capacity was at 1,000 and 500 people would come to the games. He said, 'We're going to enclose this press box. There will be a state of the art scoreboard. It's all going to happen.' He worked very hard and he demanded a lot.

"I just really enjoyed his company. He was a very funny guy. He was just a real smart man who happened to be a coach. Thanks to him, I learned everything. Having stayed there three years (1987-89), coaching was engrained in me, as it has been for other guys who have gone from there and have done well."

Jim's next stop was as head coach at his alma mater, Northwestern State. His success as a high school coach and his three years at LSU gave him outstanding credentials. The offer had been extended prior to his going to LSU, but Jim felt the opportunity in Baton Rouge was too valuable to pass up.

He had five years of winning at Northwestern State from 1990-94. The Demons won three Southland Conference Championships (1991, 1993 & 1994) and made two NCAA Regional appearances (1991 and 1994). Jim compiled a 192-89 (.683) record.

If Jim had any questions about being a coach, they had all been answered by now. He was successful and he loved what he was doing. God's plan for Jim was to be a baseball coach. With success in sports, there are usually other opportunities. Alabama and the tough Southeastern Conference were Jim's next destination.

"To this day, I have no idea how my name came up for this job at Alabama," says Jim in his deliberate manner of speaking. "I did not apply. I remember Mike Bianco, an assistant coach at LSU and now head coach at Ole Miss, called me and said the Alabama job was coming open. I said, 'Mike, I can't get that job. Nobody knows who I am.' Then he said, 'Coach, you ought to try, and if you get it, I'd like to go with you.' I called Coach Bertman. I said, 'Coach, the job at Alabama, do you think I should apply?' He said, 'Let me find out about it.'

"He called back two days later and said, 'Chip Baker from Florida State is getting that job. Don't worry about it.' So I didn't. I can remember being on the road playing Sam Houston State and seeing that Alabama named Sammy Dunn, legendary high school coach, for the job. I didn't think anything of it. Oh, I thought, 'That's who got the job.'

"A few days later, I was sitting at my desk. We had just won the league championship and we were hosting a tournament at our field. The phone rang and they said, 'Steve Townsend from the University of Alabama is on the phone.' I thought, 'Why would they be calling. They already have a coach.'

"Gees, yeah, I'll take the call. Hello, Mr. Townsend. He said, 'No, this is Hootie Ingram.'" Steve served as Associate Athletic Director for Hootie, Alabama's Athletic Director at the time.

"He said, 'How are you doing there?' I said, 'We are in a tournament.' He said, 'You think you are going to a regional?' I said, 'I don't know. We need to win some games.' He informed me about the job and said, 'I'll call you every day to keep updated.' He called every day. He said, 'If you don't get to a regional, can you come in on a Tuesday?' I said, 'Yes, sir.'

"We got to the regional. We were in Stillwater, OK. I'd come into the motel room anticipating that red light (on the telephone). I'd call back. 'We lost today.' He'd say, 'Well, if you lose tomorrow, can you come?' The next day I said, 'We lost today.' He said, 'Okay.'

"Then he flew Lisa and me into Tuscaloosa. He said, 'How big is the airport there?' I said, 'Oh, the Shreveport airport is big.' He said, 'No, Natchitoches.' I said, 'Oh, it's just about like a paved road.' He said, 'Go check it out.' He flew into Natchitoches, the first jet I think that has ever flown in and out of that little strip. Lisa and I got on the University plane and Coach Ingram and I talked the whole time.

"He took us out to eat that night. Lisa was six months pregnant. We sat and talked for a while, and finally we got up from the table. I said, 'Are you going to ask me any questions on how I would run the team?' He said, 'No, I know enough. I have talked to some people.'

"We stayed here that night. We hadn't been home in several days. We came directly to Tuscaloosa from Stillwater. We thought, 'We are not getting this job.' Lisa was pregnant. We were tired. It's been a nice, fun ride. It's time to go home.

"We had planned to have breakfast at eight the next morning, but Coach Ingram said, 'Instead of having breakfast, let's go directly to the office.' So we did and he offered us the job at 8:30."

So at 39 years of age, Jim had landed a job in baseball far beyond his expectations so soon in his career. "Wow," was a true response. The Western Division of the SEC was as good as it gets in college baseball. It was a big order, but Jim was ready for the challenge.

The press conference was a comical display for Jim and a different one for the media as he recalls. "The questions I got were, 'What pro organization did you play for?' I said, 'Uh, I didn't.' 'What college did you play for?' I said, 'Uh, I didn't.' Those guys were looking at each other and I'm sure they were going, 'Who in the world have they brought in here?'

"I didn't know anybody. I had only been here two days. Thank God I didn't turn on the TV and hear their comments after the sports shows. I thought there would just be a couple of people there. I had never been in a press conference, except in a regional at Northwestern. We were always the last seed and no one ever asked us any questions.

"Then all the media wanted to talk about was LSU. I said, 'You know, we have been at this place called Northwestern State for five years.' They still had no questions except, 'What was it like working for Skip?' I said, 'Well, that was five years ago. It was really good.' So I think I baffled the media with my credentials right at the start," Jim says, still laughing about how surprised the media were about his qualifications.

Jim remembers well his thoughts as he took over the baseball reins at Alabama. "We're confident that we can coach, but we didn't know what was going to happen. I brought with me Mitch Gaspard who was on my staff at Northwestern State and Todd Butler, an assistant coach from McNeese State. We didn't know anyone. I remember some people said it would take three to five years to turn it around. By the time you do, you won't have a job there any more. So there were some uneasy times. But once that fall started, we got with the team and we had a great staff. We worked well together.

"The miracle of the first year was what turned it around. Those guys were not supposed to be any good. Everyone told us how bad we were. We won over 40 games and won the SEC tournament. It was like a miracle. I remember when we beat Coach Bertman in the SEC championship game, he came up to me and said, 'You need to enjoy this. You may never have another team like this.'

"There have been great moments here, but that was the highlight. It was more so than the College World Series and even playing for the national championship in 1997. That first team in 1995 came from behind in four consecutive games in the SEC tournament when we were picked dead last.

"The last three weeks of the season were so satisfying as a coach. It's not whether you win the championship or not, but whatever you do the best that you can do? That group, not saying that others didn't, they maxed out. When you know that you maxed out and everyone cared and did the best they could and played together, it doesn't matter. It still gives me chills.

"Usually it is the teams that are a little undermanned that are like that. If you can get a team that has a little bit more talent to play like that, then you've got something. Later we were recruiting somewhere and a pitcher from Auburn stopped me and said, 'You know, I never could understand it. Those were the same guys that won four SEC games the year before and were beat before they walked on the field.'

"Those guys were pretty good. They just didn't play well that year. (Joe) Caruso ended up being a great player. I thought Brett Taft was the best shortstop I had ever been around. Chris Moller and Dax Norris, that the other staff had recruited, and a guy like Neal Lamb, who had never played, had a good year. Lamb, a pitcher, got the win in three of the four SEC tournament games.

"The thing is, they believed in themselves. They believed in the coaching staff. They were hungry to be led. They wanted to win and be successful.

"The foundation of everything that has happened in my years here was that team."

Jim still looks back on the SEC tournament that year with awe. "It is still unheard of what this team did by being behind in four straight games by multiple runs. Being behind like 8-4 in the last inning with one out and nobody on base and pulling out a 9-8 victory in the championship game was unbelievable." Alabama scored five runs in the bottom of the ninth to defeat the defending champions LSU.

"We were an upstart group that was playing good going against Coach Bertman and the powerhouse team. It wasn't so much about playing LSU. Our group of 25 people could have been playing Saskatchewan because it was all about us. When we lost to Clemson in the regional, and they had a very good team, I've never seen a team so devastated. They didn't care about the draft. They were just a team and it was an awesome group and an awesome feeling. They were having so much fun winning."

The next season, a couple of players who were drafted came back and Alabama went on to play in the World Series. In fact, in three of the next four years (1996, 1997 & 1999), Jim had the Crimson Tide in the World Series. In 1997, Alabama played in the championship game, losing to LSU.

Jim's 1996 team set or tied 30-plus school records and became the first Bama team to win 50 or more games. Going into the World Series, Alabama was ranked No. 1 by *Baseball America and Collegiate Baseball,* a first-ever No. 1 ranking for the Tide. After the 1997 World Series, Jim was honored by *Baseball America* as National Coach of the Year after leading the team to a remarkable 56-14 record.

In the 2000 season, the team struggled early on but came back to capture third place in the SEC tournament and was sent to the Palo Alto (CA) Regional to face No. 2 ranked Stanford on its home field. The teams battled on Sunday as Alabama took the first game 14-9 and dropped the final region game 16-6. It was ironic that the College World Series championship game came down to Stanford playing Alabama's nemesis, LSU. The Tigers won its last 13 straight to win the College World Series. Its last defeat was to Alabama 18-12 in the SEC tournament. Five days earlier, Alabama clobbered LSU 14-0 in a Sunday afternoon game at Baton Rouge.

Looking back over his life and his coaching career of 20 years, Jim fully believes that God ordained his steps for a coaching career. "I believe that. It wasn't anything that I was brought up in. A good example where I knew the Lord was involved was when I was ready to get to a bigger school. I wanted to play for a national championship. I was restless all the time. Then I let go of it. Then out of the blue…Alabama, which I would have never fathomed.

"I didn't worry about other places anymore. I was content to stay where I was at Northwestern. It was like I came here from obscurity. This thing is a monster now. We have gone from winning to now thinking about winning a national championship.

"So much has happened so fast. I think the key to it all is being able to sustain it. That is the tough part. The easy part was getting it going. The tough part is keeping it going."

Incorporating a spiritual dimension to his ball club has been an ingredient that Jim has encouraged since he became the head coach. In his first year (1995) while recruiting Andy Phillips, a strong Christian young man from Demopolis, Jim saw the value of Andy's Christian example. He told Andy that he wanted him to come and be the Jay Barker of the baseball team.

"I didn't know Jay well, but I knew his value as a Christian leader on the football team. He seemed like the real deal. So I challenged Andy to come and give us that kind of leadership. He did and I've never been around a player who was more of an inspiration to me and the team than Andy. He lived by his principles and never wavered."

It was a wise approach to recruit Andy, who not only gave the team outstanding Christian leadership for four years, but also became the most decorated player in Alabama history with his play.

Jim brought with him from Northwestern to Alabama an infielder named Nate Duncan who was deeply committed in his Christian faith. Nate and Andy began to kneel and have prayer along the third base line before every game. Two and three other players joined in until it wasn't long until the entire team joined for prayer a few minutes before the game began. The pre-game prayer has continued as a ritual.

Soon after Jim came, Shayne Kelley, who worked with Navigators on campus, was chosen by the players and Jim to lead in a Team Chapel for 15-20 minutes each Sunday. Shayne later joined the baseball staff as strength coach. At that time, Wayne Waddell moved to Tuscaloosa as the Director for Athletes In Action on campus. Wayne had been at LSU for years in the same capacity, but was an Alabama graduate. For the past three years, Wayne has served as Team Chaplain for the Bama baseball team.

"We always have Chapel when the other team is taking batting practice," says Wayne. "When we are at home, we go to the Coliseum and the players like to have Chapel in the locker room. We could meet in the President's Lounge upstairs which has ample room. But we did that one time and we lost the game, so it's been the locker room ever since," says Wayne smiling about the players being superstitious even about Chapel. "On the road, we usually have Chapel in the motel before boarding the bus. The coaches go over the opposing teams and the starting pitcher, then we have Chapel. It's voluntary but the whole team always attends. They don't miss and seem to enjoy it.

"The team always prays after every practice. They also pray after every game. Jim does an evaluation of the game in the dugout and at the end of that, he will call on one of the players to pray. We join hands and pray in the dugout. It was interesting in our last game at Stanford, Jim called on Darren Wood, a senior, to pray. There were a lot of people crying in that huddle. It was a great prayer by Darren, knowing it was his last game and last prayer. It was a highly emotional moment for the team."

Two years ago, Wayne was standing in the office hallway and Jim saw him and said, "Come into my office, I want to ask you something,' Wayne remembers. "I had no idea why Jim wanted to see me. The first thing he said was, 'I wonder if we could meet one on one in Bible study. I'd like to know Christ better.' He knew I had individual Bible studies with several players. So since that time, we have met year around in Bible Study. On the road, there is a lot of free time and we meet in a motel room. At home, we will meet in his office.

"One of the first studies we did was from the book, *The Bible That Jesus Read,* by Phillip Yancey. Jim is a very intelligent man and is well read. I think he realized that there is more to the Bible than the simplicity of the New Testament. He was drawn to the Old Testament. So we did an overview of the Old Testament together.

"This past spring we studied the book of Acts. He is pretty diligent.

He read the book of Acts in one sitting and has gone back through it a couple of times. He even inspired me. I read it through one day just because he had done it.

"Jim calls on his faith in Christ all the time as he manages to keep the team winning on a high level. He prays for guidance and strength in coaching his players and making the right decisions when the team is struggling."

Wayne considers Jim a close friend and respects him greatly. "Jim has an intellect that is probably above most of us. A coach or player may pick up a tendency or an angle that may help us beat a team, and before they bring it up, he'll mention it. He's usually two or three steps ahead of everybody making observations. Coaches keep a lot of charts, but Jim doesn't need them. He has great ability to recall hitters tendencies and weaknesses in not being able to hit a certain pitch in a specific situation. He remembers those a year or two later.

"A lot of people don't realize that Jim calls every pitch from the dugout. When (Jeremy) Vaughn or (Pete) Fisher throw a slider ahead of the count 1-2, and get a ground ball double play out of it, it's not just the pitch, but the right call that Jim sent to the catcher in that situation. That's why he's so good. He has the ability to recall what hitters are going to do or can't do in a certain situation. Jim is amazing. As soon as the pitch is thrown, the catcher looks over for the next pitch and Jim has it ready for him.

"Jim has a brilliant mind. He's a very intelligent man who happens to be a baseball coach. I read a book and enjoy it. He reads a book and remembers it," says Wayne, who admires his friend so much.

With all of Jim's success, his greatest support comes from his loving wife, Lisa at home. They met as students at Northwestern State in Natchitoches, which is Lisa's hometown. "We dated some in college as we dated other people," says Lisa whose father is still a reputable physician in town. My mother would tease me and say, "Lisa, who would ever marry that guy?'

When Jim was coaching at Princeton Junior High, he called Lisa, who was working at a hunting lodge in New Mexico. They renewed their friendship and married on September 21, 1985 while Jim was coaching at Loyola High. Jim was 30.

When Jim got the Northwestern State job in 1990, it was a treat for Lisa to move back to her hometown. "Jim and my dad would laugh at this because my dad would say, 'You know, Jim, the only reason you got this job was because of Lisa Breazeale.'" Jim had not established himself in baseball, so the family connection to the well known Breazeale family came into play.

Jim and Lisa's first child, Lauren, was born in 1989 in Baton Rouge. Melissa was born in 1994 shortly after the move to Alabama. Drew came in September of 1999 and the Wells family and their faith means everything to Jim and Lisa.

"I feel strongly that being a mother and a helpmate to Jim is my mission in life," says Lisa. "I did not set out to be a mother at all. However, with each child that God has given us, I have absolutely become greedy. I love what I do.

"I love supporting Jim. I think the best thing I can do for him right now is pray for him. I pray for him when he goes to work and I know he is going to face a stressful day. Sometimes he may face some upset parents and I ask God to give him the right words to say to them. I ask God to give him energy to get through the day.

"Yes, this is very much my career. I have just realized that since we moved here. We didn't know that God was going to bless Jim's teaching and coaching as He has. We didn't know he was going to be so successful.

"One of the things I admire so much about Jim is his humility. He's dedicated to what he does, but is not driven to baseball totally anymore. He has realized that life is more than baseball.

"He's not interested in glory or honors for himself. I have to have people call me and say, 'Did you know your husband got Coach of the Year?' He just won't tell me those things. I admire that so much about him. I feel so blessed now. We aren't people who say, 'We are going to amass this fortune or to have this career. We are just simple people.

"I love it that Jim still drives that 1990 F 150. I have fans who come up to me and say, 'Did I see Coach Wells in that black Ford truck?' It's just another thing I like about my husband. He's so unpretentious."

Church involvement is most important to Lisa, Jim and their family. While Jim grew up as a Roman Catholic, Lisa is a Methodist, as is her mother.

"My father is Catholic," says Lisa. "I guess that was one of the neat things I liked about Jim when we married. I suppose a lot of times daughters look for a husband who is like their dad. I had a cherished relationship with my father and for some reason Jim was like my dad.

"Jim worships with me at First Wesleyan Church quite a lot and I still encourage him to attend Mass at St. Francis because it means so much to him. It was part of his heritage growing up. I also go with Jim to Mass and through the years he has grown so much in his faith, especially here at Alabama."

During his years of coaching, Jim has come to recognize that Chapel, pre-game prayer, post-game and practice prayers are most important to his team members. "Some coaches may shy away from that and at one time in my coaching, that might have taken me back. But I want my players to get the whole experience. I have found that the spiritual aspect is the most important one. I want to at least let them experience it and have a choice of accepting it or not. Some of them are introduced to it for the first time in our Chapel services. It is always on Sunday. I want to incorporate more on Sunday than just a game. In fact, some days I just wish I went to Chapel and went home. I don't come just for the game only.

"Certainly, I've had a change in my coaching style because I used to be a guy who did a lot of hollering and screaming because that was the way I was coached. Now I don't do that anymore."

Alabama fans are amazed with the calmness that Jim demonstrates when the pitcher is in trouble, men are on base, the game is on the line and Jim takes that slow and calm stroll to the pitcher's mound to converse with the pitcher.

Jim explains what he's feeling inside. "Well, I wasn't always calm. Sometimes I'm not as calm as it appears. Playing 50-70 games now and having coached 20 years, I'm not as anxious because of my pursuit to develop a closer relationship with the Lord.

"My life has changed. I have a wife and three children and I have more responsibilities. Baseball isn't the most important thing in my life as it once was."

Many lovers of baseball consider collegiate baseball as the purist and most exciting baseball there is. To narrow it down, the Western Division of the Southeastern Conference is about as good as college baseball gets.

Alabama is blessed to have one of the nation's top coaches in Jim Wells. His dad might have had him pegged to be an attorney, but God's plan prevailed. His own life has found new meaning in the faith as a result of baseball and a godly soul mate like Lisa.

In it all, his humility is ever present and not just because he drives a 10-year-old black pickup truck!

CHAPTER TWENTY-TWO

ALABAMA FCA
36-YEAR HISTORY

T he Fellowship of Christian Athletes at Alabama began in September, 1964 with nine young men and a pastor.

FCA itself was just 10 years old. What a grand idea it was to use the powerful influence of athletes and coaches as role models to project the Christian faith.

When FCA was organized by an Oklahoma junior college coach named Don McClanen in 1954, he had worked to start FCA for seven years before the organization became officially chartered. The well-known Christians in sports, in that day, were athletes such as Carl Erskine, Otto Graham, Bob Feller, Robin Roberts, Doak Walker, Kyle Rote, Alvin Dark, Bob Richards, Bob Mathias, Branch Rickey, and Red Barber.

Many of these men advertised for shaving cream and razor blades, so McClanen felt that surely they could endorse the Lord, too. The youth of America would be greatly served and influenced if notable athletes and coaches spoke out about their faith. Up until this time, it was a rarity to hear a known sports figure speak or write about his Christian convictions.

As FCA was launched, high school and college huddle groups were beginning to be organized in the early 60's across America. Dr. Allan Watson, pastor of Tuscaloosa's Calvary Baptist Church, felt that the University of Alabama should have an FCA huddle. His church, which was located within a stone's throw of Denny Stadium, had a most active curriculum and ministry to college students. Therefore, FCA was a natural at Alabama.

"I saw some committed Christian athletes who had much to give other athletes who needed their influence," says Dr. Watson remembering the start of FCA. "I had read about FCA and I just decided to invite several young men together and discuss the idea. Interest was so high that it was a joy to see FCA take off immediately at Alabama."

The first meeting took place in the Fellowship Hall, just below the

269

sanctuary of Calvary Baptist Church. It took place one weekday evening early in September of 1964. Dr. Watson called the meeting for the intent purpose of organizing an FCA huddle on the Alabama campus.

Five of the nine young men present were Steve Sloan, Paul Crane and Richard Cole of the football team, Eddie King, a track team runner, and myself. I was a graduate assistant to Charley Thornton who was Coach Paul Bryant's new Sports Information Director. We gathered in a circle of chairs in the center of the hall.

Steve was active in FCA at Bradley County High School in Cleveland, TN near Chattanooga. FCA in the Chattanooga area was one of the south's earliest hotbeds for athletic ministry. Steve was familiar with FCA. I had graduated in May from Samford University. Charlie Boyd, Rex Keeling and myself attended the first FCA National Conference at Black Mountain, NC in June. We had little information and experience, but our enthusiasm for the new movement carried the day.

Steve and Paul were roommates in their junior year. They were two of Coach Bryant's top players on the football team and that certainly enhanced our FCA organization process. Both would become All-Americans as seniors, Steve at quarterback and Paul as a center-line-backer.

At the first meeting, we decided to meet on Wednesday nights at 9:00 p.m. The late start enabled those in study hall to attend the meetings. Also, football practices sometimes went long and then there was supper. Therefore, the 9 o'clock starting time made good sense especially in the fall months.

Dr. Charles Barnes, Director of the Baptist Student Union on campus and located on University Boulevard, agreed to be the huddle advisor. "Charlie," as we called him had many athletes in his ministry over the years. Plus, the BSU had a nice building where we could hold our meetings. It was one block from Paul Bryant Hall and at that time, that was important. Not all athletes drove automobiles and trucks. Walking and catching rides was the mode of transportation for many.

In the center lobby of the BSU building were nice lounge chairs and we had our meetings right there. We started out with attendance being from 15-25 athletes, mostly football players. Assistant Football Coach Gene Stallings was a regular attendee at our meetings.

We had various speakers and many of our own athletes shared their testimonies. We also had Bible studies. It was no time until everyone looked forward to the meetings each Wednesday at 9. It was a time of inspiration and encouragement in the middle of the week. New friendships were formed. It was good to have this kind of Christian fellowship available on a secular campus. We always had refreshments and BSU Resident Director Dennis Holt did a wonderful job of providing good things to eat and drink for fellowship time afterwards. FCA quickly became a highlight of everyone's week.

Eddie King showed great enthusiasm for the FCA and was selected President. Steve Sloan was selected Vice-President, Paul Crane was treasurer and I was the secretary. Some of the regulars at the beginning were Richard Cole, Gaylon McCollough, and Ron Durby of the football team; Ed Massey and Tommy Limbaugh of the baseball team; Mike Williams, an intramural standout; Ben Cook, a sports information student worker; and Bill McDonald, a student trainer.

We were blessed to have Bill Glass, All-Pro defensive end for the Cleveland Browns and an evangelist, come to Tuscaloosa to speak for us. It was one of our largest crowds and it was a treat to have such a popular and current pro athlete.

BILLY GRAHAM COMES TO TUSCALOOSA

The huddle group received a huge boost the following spring when Billy Graham came to the campus for a one-night service in Denny Stadium. Tuscaloosa was chosen among four Alabama towns for Mr. Graham to preach in preparation for a 10-day Crusade the following June in Montgomery.

Tuscaloosa was still elated over winning the national championship during the 1964 season. The Graham service was scheduled for April 26, 1965. Dr. Frank Rose, Alabama's distinguished president and an ordained minister, and Coach Bryant hosted Mr. Graham. Joining Mr. Graham were team members Cliff Barrows, George Beverly Shea, T.W. Wilson and Grady Wilson.

Mr. Graham and his team used the plush guest rooms in the Paul Bryant Hall athletic dormitory and had supper there. A couple of hours before the service, our FCA officers and Richard Cole got to meet Mr. Graham and had our picture taken with him in the lobby of the dormitory. It was a thrill and an honor to meet Mr. Graham. We have always treasured the photograph we have of that occasion, and the picture appeared in *The Tuscaloosa News*. His coming gave our group broader identity.

We were so excited about the service that evening in the stadium.

As 15,000 gathered, the weather was threatening terribly as it can in Tuscaloosa in the spring. Cliff Barrows, Mr. Graham's song leader, rushed the service with a welcome and a song. Steve Sloan was selected to read the scripture and George Beverly Shea sang *How Great Thou Art*. Just 15 minutes after the service started, Mr. Graham came to the platform after a quick introduction by Dr. Rose. The rain had already started and Mr. Graham had on a raincoat. Dr. Rose and Coach Bryant were sitting on the platform.

Following the rain came thunder and lightening. How disappointing because everyone was so eager to hear Mr. Graham preach. His sermon was directed to the college age students. The lightening became so fierce that Mr. Graham had to stop his message after only five minutes. Then the rain poured down as never before in Tuscaloosa. The crowd began to rush to their cars. The water was ankle deep by the time people got to the streets. Still, it was a blessed experience and no one who attended that service will ever forget it.

The Graham team made it back to the President's Mansion for a reception. Dr. Rose offered Mr. Graham a dry suit. During the reception, Coach Bryant told a story about Dr. Rose to Mr. Graham that became one of his favorites. Alabama had just lost the Orange Bowl game to Texas in a controversial quarterback sneak call at the goal line by Joe Namath. Joe believed he had scored but the touchdown was denied. Alabama lost 21-17, but the national championship voting was done before the bowl games that season.

In relating the story to Mr. Graham, Coach Bryant said to him, "A few days after we returned from the bowl game, I got a call from Dr. Rose. We were talking about the game and he questioned one of the plays we ran. He said, 'Bear, I don't think I would have run that play!' I told Dr. Rose, 'I wouldn't have either if I had a week to think about it!' Close associates of Mr. Graham say that he has told friends that story many times with delight.

As word spread about our FCA huddle, many of our athletes began receiving invitations from churches, youth groups and schools to speak. Steve and Paul were in high demand and enjoyed sharing their faith around the state. The night after Mr. Graham spoke, Steve joined Miss America, Vonda Kay Van Dyke, for a Youth For Christ Rally at the Fairgrounds in Birmingham. *The Birmingham News* ran a front page advanced story with their pictures and the headline read, 'The devil hasn't got a chance.'

The first FCA year had been a total success. God had provided so much encouragement and unexpected blessings. The group was seemingly destined for ministry opportunities for athletes on Wednesday nights as well. "For me it was a true blessing to see FCA take off like it did and impact so many lives," says Dr. Watson. "Watching FCA grow turned out to be one of the real joys of my ministry at Calvary."

In June of 1965, Steve Sloan, Eddie King, Richard Cole, Dickie Bean and I attended the FCA conference at Black Mountain with 550 athletes and coaches from the southeast. We came back even more fired up about our second year. Steve inherited the quarterback job from Joe Namath and Paul Crane was one of the nation's best at center and linebacker. Such leadership not only gave FCA a strong identity, but both men were captains of the 1965 national championship team.

FCA meetings remained strong and well attended. FCA began to have such an impact that athletes other than football players were asked to give invocations at the Alabama home football games. Football players gave invocations for basketball games. Their witnesses though the prayers were meaningful, well received and appreciated by the fans.

Steve and Paul received more invitations to speak than they could possibly handle after the season. Invitations came by mail since athletes had no telephones in their rooms. Steve would hand write 30 letters on a weekly basis to send his regrets that he was committed, usually every Friday night, Saturday and Sunday. He took many engagements on weeknights in the spring, as did Paul and other athletes.

As the Christian athletes signed autographs, they would add a scripture reference below their name. On one such occasion, Paul signed his name and "Rom. 1:16" which says, 'For I am not ashamed of the gospel of Christ. For it is the power of God to salvation for everyone who believes, for the Jew first and also for the Greek.' A few days later, Paul got a letter that was addressed to 'Mr. Paul Crane, Paul Bryant Hall, Room 116, University, AL.' The young man thought Paul had given him his room number. We had a lot of laughs over that one.

In the spring of 1966, Billy Graham requested that Steve give his testimony at a Crusade service in Greenville, SC. Coach Bryant arranged the University plane for the trip to Greenville. Woody Hachett, a friend of all the athletes, was the school pilot and took Steve and several of us with him. We all got to sit on the platform. Steve did a great job, as usual, and we were thrilled to hear Mr. Graham preach an entire sermon this time. We flew back that night for class the next morning.

After the initial leadership moved on after the first two years, Richard Cole became the FCA leader. Richard, a minister's son, was totally committed to Christ and was an All-American defensive tackle on the 1966 team. Alabama finished 12-0 and Coach Bryant stated that this team "might have been his best team," but finished third in the final polls. Other leadership came from Tom Somerville, Mike Ford, Billy Scroggins, Mike Dean and trainer Gary Bannister.

Mike Dean was a coach's son from Atlanta. He had a little 5-year-old brother named David, who was so athletic and a real favorite of the players and coaches. At an FCA conference at Black Mountain, a photo was made of David wearing a No. 18 jersey with a football under his arm looking on at Mike's huddle group. The photo, made by *The Christian Athlete* editor, Gary Warner, became the 'trademark photo' depicting 'Influence' as the main theme of the national FCA. It is still used as thousands of prints have been distributed throughout America over the years. David is a football coach at Valdosta State University today.

In the early 70's, the Alabama FCA was blessed by the presence of a tall and lanky 6-foot-6 defensive end from Gadsden named John Croyle. His Christian faith meant everything to him and he was a dynamic witness as a student-athlete through the FCA. "Here's a guy who said exactly what he was going to do and we all laughed at him," says Mike DuBose of his former teammate. "We would say, 'You are crazy, John. There is no way you are going to pull that off, get all that land and put together an orphan's home.' We would be sitting around Bryant Hall and he would tell us what he was going to do, what his dream and vision was. He's done everything he said he was going to do with God's help. I am so proud of John."

With the help and encouragement of Coach and Mrs. Bryant, his teammate, John Hannah, and a few other people, John did start a home for boys right after he graduated. He started with five boys before he was married and today the Big Oak Boys and Girls Ranches have taken in over 1,300 homeless, abused, orphaned and abandoned children for 26 years. Near the end of his life, Coach Bryant was asked by a sportswriter, 'Who among all the players you have coached will have made the greatest contribution to society a 100 years from now?' Coach Bryant gave an immediate reply, "John Croyle."

Neb Hayden, who could pick a banjo like Richard Cole, led the group with Jeff Beard and Steve Wade at that time also.

In the spring of 1973, Dr. Barnes decided to pass the advisory reins to Gary White, who was an administrative assistant with numerous duties within the athletic department. Dr. Barnes had given much time and leadership to the group and had been God's man in that capacity for nine years.

"I became a Christian in the spring of 1972 in revival services at the Calvary Baptist Church," says Gary. "My decision came after years of watching the commitment of some strong Christian young men in the FCA. When I got saved, I made a total commitment and I started going to all the FCA meetings as well. When Charlie stepped down, John Croyle asked me if I would be interested in being the huddle advisor. I accepted." Gary continued to serve until 1985.

"Our numbers were not as great as they are today, but our guys were committed. We had a great run in the 70's with the football team and many of those players were so involved. Robert Fraley, who was golfer Payne Stewart's agent when they were killed last year, came to Alabama from Winchester, TN largely because he loved Steve Sloan so much. Steve was an assistant coach one year. Robert was most active in FCA.

"Others included Gary Rutledge, Sid Smith, Pete Cavan, Phil Murphy, Gary Hollingsworth, Randy Moore, Jay Vines, Ricky Davis, Bubba Sawyer, Bill Martin, Randy Hayes, a manager, and so many more.

"As women's athletics came on the scene in the mid-70's, Jean Mills, our tennis coach for women, held a Bible study for many of the women athletes. So I invited her group to join our FCA huddle and that is when we became a mixed group. Jerry Pate's sister, Nancy, was one of our first active women athletes."

Nationally, FCA held its first Girls Conferences in 1974. Some schools would have a separate girls and boys huddle, but others had meetings together. FCA has had a powerful influence with the strong emergence of women athletics across America over the past 25 years. Alabama's FCA huddle has been stronger because of the female participation.

When Gary became advisor, the huddle moved from the Baptist Student Union and met in other centers of Christian ministry on campus. They included the Wesley Foundation, the St. Francis Catholic Student Center, the Christian Student Center and the Episcopal Student Center. Near the end of his advisorship, the huddle moved to the team meeting room in Bryant Hall.

"For three or four years, our group had a retreat usually in February at the Bell's Wa-Floy Retreat in Gatlinburg, TN. We had some great times skiing and getting away for spiritual renewal," says Gary. "Also, during the time I served, my wife, Susanna, counseled girls on a regular basis. She was a godly woman who loved the Lord and counted it a blessing to guide and counsel so many young women." Gary's beloved wife, Susanna, a devoted teacher of the Bible, died of cancer in September of 1990.

"Coach Bryant was always supportive and appreciative of the FCA huddle," remembers Gary. "Each Christmas, he would give us a check that would take care of our needs financially for a year."

The 1978 and 1979 national championship football teams were led largely by men who were leaders in FCA. They included Jeff Rutledge, Steadman Shealy, Keith Pugh and Major Ogilvie. All were in demand for speaking engagements and their ministry was deeply felt throughout the state. Steadman also wrote a book entitled *Never Say Quit*. A few years later, Keith became the State Director of FCA for ten years before becoming a pastor.

When Coach Bryant passed away on January 26, 1983, the state mourned his sudden loss immensely as did the nation. Mrs. Bryant chose his pallbearers from among Christian players who were also the nucleus of the FCA huddle at that time. They were Walter Lewis, Jeremiah Castille, Darryl White, Mike McQueen, Tommy Wilcox, Paul Carruth, Paul Fields and Jerrill Sprinkle.

Moments before Coach Bryant died in the Druid City Hospital of a massive heart attack, it was almost prophetic that Dr. Allan Watson visited the legendary coach. "I went by to see Coach Bryant and he was cordial as usual to me. As we began talking, a doctor came in and Coach Bryant asked him if he would allow us a few minutes. 'I want to talk to the preacher,' he said. So we talked for a few minutes. He had coached his last game a month earlier. He even expressed how much FCA had blessed the program through the years and how much he appreciated it. I had prayer with him and five minutes after I left his room, he had the heart attack and died." What a timely visit by Dr. Watson and no doubt one that was foreordained by the Lord.

Near the end of Gary's advisorship, Rob Cain, a student worker for Gary, came with great enthusiasm for the Lord and led many Bible studies with the athletes in Bryant Hall. Jay Mathews, a member of the football team, was an outstanding leader in 1983-84.

Another member of the athletic staff, golf coach Conrad Rehling, had a profound influence in the FCA golf ministry nationally. Coach

Rehling gave a week or two each summer to FCA golf camps and still does.

After the 1985 school year, Gary asked me if I would take over as advisor of the FCA huddle. In May of 1983, I had returned to Alabama as Sports Information Director for Ray Perkins, who was Athletic Director and Head Football Coach. From 1967 to 1979, I had served on the FCA national staff from the Kansas City national headquarters. It was a blessing to serve in the national office in many capacities, traveling the nation for FCA. One of my duties was administrating the 2,000 high school and college groups across America. After six years in Kansas City, I served for six years as Regional Director of six states from Indianapolis. My area was the Big Ten states, plus Kentucky. Northern athletes and coaches quickly recognized my southern accent.

So when Gary asked me to serve as FCA advisor, I was excited. The beginning years of FCA at Alabama still remained treasured memories in my heart. After serving the nation and then six states, it was a joy to think about serving one college huddle group. Plus, it was my favorite one of all, of course.

Our meetings were still on Wednesday nights at 9 p.m. The meeting time had never changed over the past 21 years. We were now meeting in the football team meeting room in the academic wing of Bryant Hall. Hardy Walker, Ricky Thomas, Hoss Johnson and Mark Gottfried were the top leadership team.

Tragedy struck twice in the 1986-87 school year, and FCA's influence helped overcome the shock of two players who died within eight months of each other. In pre-season drills, interior lineman Willie Ryles collapsed on the practice field and died three days later, just as the Crimson Tide was about to fly to New York for the Kickoff Classic game against Ohio State. Then one week after the A-Day game in April, running back George Scruggs died in an automobile accident. George had been the game's MVP.

Ricky Thomas, a fine defensive back on the team, was a most sincere and mature Christian young man. God used Ricky with team members in an unusual way. After both tragedies, as many as 25 players went straight to Ricky's room for support. There Ricky opened the scriptures, talked to the stunned group of guys and prayed with them. Ricky was totally committed to Christ. He didn't waver. He was spiritually mature beyond his years. He was God's man for so many players in two tragic situations. Today, Ricky is an assistant coach for the Tampa Bay Buccaneers.

Through the years, Rev. Sylvester Croom Sr., a highly respected pastor in the community, ministered to athletes in meaningful ways. Ozzie Newsome, Johnny Davis and Rev. Croom's own sons, Sylvester and Kelvin, formed a strong spiritual connection with the team, as did many other players. When Coach Bill Curry came in 1987, he made Rev. Croom the team chaplain.

ONE FCA MEETING WITH ETERNAL VALUE

In the fall of 1987, Rev. Croom spoke one night at FCA. There were about 50 athletes present. His message that evening focused in on salvation, making sure you were ready to meet the Lord when you died. Normally, no altar calls were made at FCA meetings but on this particular night, Rev. Croom made a strong challenge in conclusion.

He made an appeal for anyone who wanted to receive salvation in Jesus Christ to just get up out of their desk chair, come forward and take his hand. We had no music. It was a tough appeal and a difficult one for a person to come forward in that setting before their peers.

Rev. Croom waited. There was dead silence in the room. After seemingly two or three minutes, a linebacker named George Bethune from Ft. Walton Beach, FL got up out of his seat. He was sitting in the back right corner of the room. George, unashamedly, walked through desk chairs and students to the front and took Rev. Croom's hand. He was the only one who came forward.

Sitting next to George in the back of the room was his roommate, Derrick Thomas. Derrick said later that he came within a half step of going forward himself. The following Sunday at the Rev. Croom's College Hill Baptist Church, George and Derrick went forward to be received in the church. The next Sunday night, Rev. Croom and his associate pastor son, Kelvin, led a baptismal service for George and Derrick. They were dressed in white robes and were the only two baptized that evening. My wife, Barbara, and daughters Elizabeth and Amy and I attended the thrilling service.

When Derrick, a Kansas City Chief and NFL all-pro, died tragically in January 2000, that event at FCA and at College Hill has obviously taken on much greater meaning now.

In the late 80's, tight end Howard Cross was an outstanding leader. Howard, with the huge hands and ready smile, was also an excellent speaker. Howard never spoke with notes, but he always did a superb job whether it was talking to a group of third graders or in a church service.

Our FCA huddle was recognized for its twenty-fifth year of ministry in pre-game ceremonies at the Alabama-LSU game in 1988. Steve Sloan was Athletic Director and General Dick Abel, FCA National President, came to celebrate this significant milestone. Gathered on the field for the announcement were Howard, Steve, General Abel, Dr. Charlie Barnes, Dr. Gary White and myself. Jon Gibbons, State FCA Director, and General Abel made special plaque presentations to Charlie, Gary and me, the three huddle advisors. It had truly been 25 years of meaningful service involving hundreds of athletes who had touched untold numbers of people.

The early 90's had solid leadership in placekicker Alan Ward and fullback Martin Houston. That leadership would be firmly evidenced later as Alan has served as the Greater Birmingham and North Alabama FCA Director for the past 10 years. Martin became an ordained minister and today pastors the University Worship Center Church on "The Strip" just off the campus on University Boulevard.

ROLE MODEL JAY BARKER TAPPED ON THE SHOULDER BY GOD

In 1990, a freshman named Jay Barker came on the scene. Jay was already known for his Christian commitment when he arrived. He was redshirted his first year. As we sat in Bryant Hall for lunch one day, I told Jay that if he became the starting quarterback at Alabama some day, he could not imagine the opportunities he would receive to speak and minister to people all over the state. I knew firsthand the barrage of requests Steve Sloan had received.

Never in our wildest dreams did we know that Jay would become the winningest quarterback in Alabama history. Jay took over at quarterback against LSU at Baton Rouge as a redshirt freshman in 1991. He went on to compile an amazing 35-2-1 record as the starting Crimson Tide quarterback. He made All-American and was fifth in the Heisman Trophy voting his senior year.

Still, with all of his success on the football field, Jay made a statement to 3,000 young people at Shades Mountain Baptist Church just before his sophomore year that people remember Jay for as much as his football prowess. Jay said, "I'm Jay Barker, 6-4, 215-pound quarterback for the University of Alabama. I've never had a drink of alcohol, I've never taken any drugs and I'm a virgin."

Jay had a powerful impact for Christ at Alabama. He epitomized the words, 'role model.' In his five years on campus, Jay probably only missed five FCA meetings. To Jay, he was just another one of the guys and loved leading the FCA meetings for three years with support from Matt Wethington.

About those invitations to speak? They were unbelievable. Jay received approximately 1,000 speaking requests his last year at Alabama. It seemed that every church in Alabama and some outside the state wanted their youth to hear Jay Barker. Jay accepted all he could possibly make and every one was an awesome time. In all of his appearances, he was quite an ambassador for the University of Alabama as well.

In his senior year against Georgia in Tuscaloosa in 1994, Jay passed for a school record 396 yards and miraculously led Alabama to a 29-28 come from behind victory on national television. In the ESPN post-game interview on the field, Jay gave a brief but strong statement of his faith. The following Tuesday, I received a call from Tom Bailey of *The Birmingham News* asking if I would consider writing a book about Jay's role model story. I was flattered and during Jay's Senior Bowl week in Mobile the following January, the paperback book was released. It was titled *In Due Time*. Over the next several months, over 50,000 copies were printed.

After Alabama, Jay spent the 1995 season with the New England Patriots and the next year with the Carolina Panthers. He sat out the 1997 season and is now with the Toronto Argonauts of the Canadian Football League for his third season. Jay is the starting quarterback for the second year in a row. He and his high school sweetheart, Amy DiGiovanna, married right after college and they have two sons. They make their off season home in Birmingham.

Beginning in 1995 with the help of Jim Smith, a Tuscaloosa pro golf shop owner, the Jay Barker Golf Tournament was established. It has been held at the North River Yacht Club each year and has been a huge success venture for FCA and other charitable causes.

With Jay's leadership, the FCA doubled in attendance to an average of 125 at each meeting. FCA outgrew its meeting place in Bryant Hall and moved back to the Baptist Student Center in 1992. Jay brought in Chad Sommers, one of his high school receivers at Trussville and an Alabama student, to lead the music.

The national FCA office singled out our group in 1993 when President Dick Abel asked me to write the 40-year history (1954-1994) of the national Fellowship of Christian Athletes organization. In 1993, I spent most all of my spare time writing the exciting history of the FCA movement. At the fortieth anniversary banquet held in Kansas City in February of 1994, the book was presented to the 350 national staff members present. The book was titled *Impact For Christ: How FCA Has Influenced the Sports World.* Coach Tom Landry wrote the foreword. At the occasion, Coach Grant Teaff, Executive Director of the American Football Coaches Association, and Anne Graham Lotz, evangelist and daughter of Billy Graham, were the speakers. It was a true honor to be selected to write the book. It was published by Cross Training Publishing of Grand Island, NE.

Through the years, FCA meetings have followed virtually the same format. Sometimes they start with a skit to loosen everyone up. An athlete reads the scripture and expresses what it means to him or her. Another would then pray. The singing of contemporary choruses and praise songs would follow, especially in the last decade. Various athletes would give a personal testimony. Sometimes, an athlete or student would sing a solo. Our meetings have always had a variety of programs on different faith and moral topics for college age students. Guest speakers comprise many of the programs.

In the fall months, many speakers were former football players who were involved in FCA while at Alabama. One or two programs each year dealt with love, courtship and marriage. Some speakers gave evangelistic messages. Bible studies would be led on prayer, temptation and handling trials in life. Videos and some speakers would deal with the perils of sexual promiscuity, alcohol, drugs and gambling. Two or three musical concerts are included each year. Many speakers, including our own coaches and staff, gave their testimonies. Some of our best meetings occurred when athletes shared experiences they were undergoing in their own personal walk with Christ.

In the mid-90s, the group started a Christmas Candlelight Service. This meeting involves students singing solos and duets, reading poems, and some expressing what Christmas means to them. At the end, each student holds a candle and the group sings "Silent Night" and "Joy to the World." The program has become a real hit. Easter programs reflect on the crucifixion of Christ. On a couple of occasions in recent years, students have washed each others' feet and affirmed their spiritual character to each other.

All programs end with prayer requests from the audience and then everyone rises, joins hands and someone will close in prayer. Refreshments are always served for a good fellowship time. Missy

Homan, daughter of former All-American Dennis Homan, shopped for refreshments for several years as has Sherry Craig, a local teacher with a great heart for FCA. Meetings always begin the first week of school and end the week before final exams in the spring. Generally, we have 28-30 meetings during the school months.

Chad Goss, a walk-on receiver with much enthusiasm for the Lord, followed Jay as leader along with Mickey Conn and Roman Colburn. God sent John David Phillips and Shaun Alexander in the mid-90s, plus baseball player Andy Phillips who provided strong leadership until their recent departures from the University. As they led, crowds soon averaged 175 in the fall and peaked to an average of 240 in the fall of 1999. Three crowds went over 300, the largest in the huddle's history.

The growth required another location. In January, 1998, FCA moved to the Allan Watson College Annex Building across the street from the Calvary Baptist Church and one block from Bryant-Denny Stadium. The College Annex room was newly built and perfectly served the FCA needs for parking, videos, PA system and kitchen requirements.

So after 36 years of ministry, FCA has come full circle back to where it started, but more importantly, the ministry is stronger now than at any other time in its history. While most of the leadership has come from the football team, all other sports have been most active. Women athletes have contributed so much to the fellowship. In recent years, Amy Lannom, Tonya Tice, Leah Monteith Goss and Reagan Croyle of the basketball team; and Sheryl Dundas, Danielle McAdams and Merritt Booth of the gymnastics team have given outstanding leadership to the huddle.

SQUAD SUNDAY - A SPECIAL DAY FOR ATHLETES

Over the years, several landmark events have occurred through the FCA that has broadened the base of outreach and ministry in immeasurable ways. One such event began at the very beginning of the huddle group itself. Dr. Watson inaugurated "Squad Sunday" at Calvary Baptist Church in 1964. The football team and coaches were invited as special guests to attend the Sunday morning worship service one week prior to the start of each football season.

"It was an idea that seemed most appropriate as FCA was organized," remembers Dr. Watson. "We decided to honor a player each year who had exemplified the most outstanding Christian leadership on the team. Then in 1972, when one of our former football players,

Charlie Compton, died as a missionary in an automobile accident while serving in Brazil, we named the award after him. He was from Sylacauga and was an outstanding tackle for Alabama in 1942 and 1946-47. He was also a World War II hero. Charlie played on Saturday and preached on Sunday while at the University. He and Dr. and Mrs. Barnes were close in ministry through the Baptist Student Union.

"We also invited outstanding Christian men in FCA to come and speak in our Squad Sunday services. It didn't take long for Squad Sunday to become larger in attendance than Easter Sunday. Coach Bryant always came when he was the coach. He was most supportive."

Speakers over the years have included Steve Sloan, Paul Crane, Bubba Scott, Bobby Richardson, Tony Romeo, James Jeffrey, Loren Young, Paul Dietzel, Steve Davis, Bill Battle, Hootie Ingram, Mike Kolen, Governor Fob James, Clebe McClary, J.C. Watts, John Erickson, John Hannah, Walter Draughon, John Croyle, Jerry Clower, Grant Teaff, Raymond Berry, Johnny Musso, Jeremiah Castille, John David Phillips, Shaun Alexander and Andy Phillips. The speaker in 1999 was Dr. Ross Rhodes, Chaplain of the Billy Graham Evangelistic Association. All former pastors have spoken including Dr. Watson, Dr. Tim Owings, Dr. Edgar Arendall (interim pastor) and Dr. Bruce Chesser spoke at the 2000 service.

For several years, all athletic teams and coaches at the University have been invited for the service, including cheerleaders and Million Dollar Band members.

Charlie Compton Award recipients have been chosen by Calvary pastors, head coaches, FCA advisors and since 1990 by the team.

The Charlie Compton Award recipients through the years were:

1964 – Gaylon McCollough	1982 – Darryl White
1965 – Steve Sloan	1983 – Walter Lewis
1966 – Richard Cole	Mike McQueen
1967 – Wayne Atcheson	1984 – Paul Fields
1968 – Mike Ford	1985 – Hardy Walker
1969 – Mike Dean	1986 – Ricky Thomas
1970 – Neb Hayden	Hoss Johnson
1971 – Jeff Beard	1987 – Kerry Goode
1972 – Steve Wade	1988 – Howard Cross
1973 – John Croyle	1989 – Willie Wyatt
1974 – Gary Rutledge	1990 – Alan Ward
1975 – Robert Fraley	1991 – Martin Houston

1976 – Sid Smith	1992 – Willis Bevelle
1977 – Pete Cavan	1993 – Jay Barker
1978 – Jeff Rutledge	1994 – Tommy Johnson
1979 – Steadman Shealy	1995 – Tony Johnson
Keith Pugh	1996 – Chad Goss
1980 – Major Ogilvie	1997 – Curtis Alexander
1981 – Mark Nix	1998 – John David Phillips
	1999 – Shaun Alexander

THE 50-YARD LINE PRAYER

Another landmark event that began through FCA came in 1987. Some Alabama baseball players attended an Athletes In Action conference in Colorado and met some Penn State football players. Since Alabama and Penn State were playing early in the season, the Penn State players asked the Alabama players that they gather after the game for prayer. The game was played in State College on national television. The word was passed on to Howard Cross, our FCA leader. Players from Penn State and Alabama met after the game at the 50-yard line and had a prayer.

The idea was well received by our players and Howard, being such a dynamic leader, had a prayer the next week with Florida players in Birmingham. Players would sometimes contact a friend on the opposing team and set up the prayer. Through the years, contacts have been made through FCA staff members to FCA team leaders and advisors for the prayer.

Much could be written about the impact the post-game prayers have had upon our own athletes and the opponents as well. Players would simply gather and decide who would say the prayer in a second's notice. The moment of fellowship is quickly drawn between the opponents, win or lose. At the FCA Sun Bowl Breakfast with Army in 1988, Howard announced to several Army players present that our FCA guys would like to meet them after the game for a prayer. When the game ended, it was startling to see that the entire Army team stayed to kneel in prayer with our guys.

The witness of the post-game prayers has had a far reaching effect. When Howard joined the New York Giants in 1989, he assembled three or four of his teammates, with some opponents, for a prayer and was sharply criticized by a *Sports Illustrated* writer. Howard continued when few or no post-game prayers were taking place in the NFL. Today, a post-game prayer among players in the NFL is a common practice.

In the last several years, numerous college teams gather for prayer with opponents after games including many high schools. The prayers bring a spiritual bond among opponents that the players will remember for a lifetime. Numerous reports from fans, especially from dads who express how much that moment is worth to their sons watching from the stands, has been most inspiring through the years.

It all began with Howard, and our other football FCA leaders have carried on through the 1999 season with Shaun Alexander and Ryan Pflugner. More athletes gathered last season from both teams for prayer than at any other time since the idea began in 1987. With common opponents like Auburn, Tennessee, LSU, Mississippi State, Vanderbilt and Ole Miss, no contact has become necessary prior to the games. Today, players gravitate to midfield on their own for prayer.

The Fellowship of Christian Athletes has been meeting for the past 36 years each Wednesday night at 9 o'clock from August through April. It is an incredible record. For years, the national FCA headquarters in Kansas City has recognized the Alabama FCA huddle as the longest running college huddle group in America for continuous service. The spectrum of service on campus, across the state to hundreds of churches and communities, and ministry by FCA participants across the nation in their vocations can be measured only by Almighty God.

Untold numbers of athletes came to Christ during their college years through FCA. Today many of the former athletes are pastors, preachers and teachers of God's word. Others are in full time ministry in parachurch groups. Hundreds are leaders in their churches and in Christian organizations that proclaim the message of Jesus Christ.

The Alabama FCA has a rich heritage of Christian service. Yet the work is stronger today than ever before and the future presents even greater opportunities. With the departure of Shaun Alexander and Ryan Pflugner, God has sent Jarret Johnson, Brandon Miree, Tyler Harris, Joni Crenshaw and others to raise the banner with new leadership beginning in the year 2000. For the third year, the core leadership group will meet each Monday morning at 7 a.m. for breakfast and will discuss meetings, plans and evaluate the ministry. It has been an exciting time and a very productive hour to build the ministry.

During my 15-year tenure as advisor, I have written a weekly FCA newsletter which is distributed to some 500 athletes, coaches and staff. It announces the FCA program that evening and I include quotes of inspiration and motivation, plus scripture verses.

Over the past 36 years, the Alabama FCA has had only three advisors, which speaks well of the solidarity of the group. Dr. Charlie Barnes and Dr. Gary White served from 1964-85. Since that time, I have appreciated two special men who support the athletes and me by attending almost every week. John Merrill, a community leader in Tuscaloosa, was SGA president in 1985 and has been attending FCA meetings since that time. Rev. Dan Kilgore became pastor of the Trinity United Methodist Church in 1993 and has been a fixture in FCA each Wednesday night. Their support and friendship with the students has been a valuable strength to the group and their lives have been enriched as well.

COACH BRYANT'S PHONE CALL TO COACH STALLINGS

In 1990, when Coach Gene Stallings became head football coach, he invited me to share with the football team the ministry of FCA on campus. I shared on the first day of classes. He allowed me to tell about the meetings, where we met, the history of the program and encourage the players to attend. Then he would give his strong endorsement of FCA and why his players should participate. We did that every year and Coach DuBose continued to make time for the FCA pitch, since he became head football coach as well.

Every year, Coach Stallings would tell the same story in his remarks to the team. "When I left Alabama and became head coach at Texas A&M, I received a phone call from Coach Bryant one day. He said, 'Bebes, do you know what is the worst thing that has happened to our football team? It's the FCA. Those players are doing nothing but hugging on one another, loving on one another and they won't hit anybody.'

"After the season that was another banner year for Coach Bryant, I got another call from Coach Bryant. He said, 'Bebes, you know what is the best thing that has happened to our football team? It's the FCA. It has brought such a oneness and closeness to our team. We were unified because of the influence FCA had on our team.'" Coach Stallings also adds, "That is one of the reasons why I have always believed in the FCA and have always encouraged my players to be involved in it."

FCA's strong influence has paved the way for other coaches on all teams to have chapel, Bible studies and so many opportunities for spiritual growth and emphasis with their players. The spiritual base has influenced many young men and women to choose Alabama over the years, and even coaches and staff.

When Coach DuBose became head coach in 1997, he was approached by athletic trainer Bill McDonald, and some of the Christian leadership among the team about having a Chapel service on football weekends. He gave immediate approval and that year he and I selected former players mainly to give 15-20 minute messages on Friday night or Saturday morning of the game.

In 1998, Coach Ronnie Cottrell joined his staff from Florida State and suggested that a team chaplain be selected. Coach DuBose chose Dr. Bruce Chesser, pastor of the Calvary Baptist Church, and he began to give the chapel messages for all games except the Birmingham games, which former Crimson Tide receiver Keith Pugh continued to give. Keith is pastor of the First Baptist Church in Sylacauga. Chapel services are voluntary but are well attended, and add to the spiritual preparation before the team boards the busses for the stadium on Saturday.

Also added in 1998 was a 30 minute Prayer Time before curfew on Friday nights. Players gathered in John David Phillips room the first year and Ryan Pflugner's room in 1999. As many as 30 players would assemble as one player would have a scripture passage prepared, then prayer requests followed, two players would pray and I would close in prayer as everyone joined hands. It is always a very special time to reflect on matters of the spirit and faith.

MAKING THE "DRESS LIST"

Chris Samuels, our great All-American tackle and third player to be chosen in the 2000 NFL draft by the Washington Redskins, gave the scripture for the first game in 1999 as we played Vanderbilt in Nashville.

Chris read his scripture and then gave the following remarks. "You know guys, every Thursday they post a 'Dress List' on the locker room door as to who gets to dress out on Saturday. There are some of us who know that we are on the list. We don't even have to check and see if our name is on the list. But there are some guys who don't know for sure if their name is on the list. They have to check and see. Some make it and some don't.

"The point is this. When we know God, and his son Jesus Christ and have him in our heart, we know that when we die, we are on God's 'Dress List.' We know we are going to Heaven. What we have to be concerned about is that we make sure that our teammates are on God's 'Dress List.' If they are not, we need to help them know how to get on the list. That's all I have to say."

My heart leaped when I had heard one of the most profound spiritual illustrations in my life. It came from an athlete so innocently expressing to his buddies his thoughts about the scripture he had read. I thought of preachers who could preach that illustration all day long.

The FCA movement has always existed "to present to athletes and coaches, and all whom they influence, the challenge and adventure of receiving Jesus Christ as Savior and Lord, serving Him in their relationships and in the fellowship of the church."

The Alabama FCA movement has been faithful to that purpose over the past 36 years. It has been a grand journey and the impact will last for eternity. That is the best part.

Through it all, the most appropriate conclusion is this….**TO GOD BE THE GLORY. GREAT THINGS HE HAS DONE!**